GOOD JOBS, BAD JOBS

GOOD JOBS, BAD JOBS

THE RISE OF POLARIZED AND PRECARIOUS EMPLOYMENT SYSTEMS IN THE UNITED STATES, 1970s TO 2000s

ARNE L. KALLEBERG

A Volume in the American Sociological Association's
Rose Series in Sociology

Russell Sage Foundation • New York

Library of Congress Cataloging-in-Publication Data

Kalleberg, Arne L.
    Good jobs, bad jobs : the rise of polarized and precarious employment systems in the United States, 1970s–2000s / Arne L. Kalleberg.
        p. cm.
    Includes bibliographical references and index.
    ISBN 978-0-87154-431-5 (alk. paper)
  1. Manpower policy—United States. 2. Quality of work life—OECD countries. 3. Labor market—United States. 4. Labor supply—United States. 5. Industrial management—United States. I. Title.
    HD5724.K35 2011
    331.10973—dc22

                                                                                    2011002139

The paper used in this publication meets the minimum requirements of American National Standard for Information Sciences—Permanence of Paper for Printed Library Materials. ANSI Z39.48-1992.

Text design by Suzanne Nichols.

RUSSELL SAGE FOUNDATION
112 East 64th Street, New York, New York 10065
10 9 8 7 6 5 4 3 2 1

The Russell Sage Foundation

The Russell Sage Foundation, one of the oldest of America's general purpose foundations, was established in 1907 by Mrs. Margaret Olivia Sage for "the improvement of social and living conditions in the United States." The Foundation seeks to fulfill this mandate by fostering the development and dissemination of knowledge about the country's political, social, and economic problems. While the Foundation endeavors to assure the accuracy and objectivity of each book it publishes, the conclusions and interpretations in Russell Sage Foundation publications are those of the authors and not of the Foundation, its Trustees, or its staff. Publication by Russell Sage, therefore, does not imply Foundation endorsement.

Previous Volumes
in the Series

Forthcoming Titles

The Rose Series in Sociology

THE AMERICAN Sociological Association's Rose Series in Sociology publishes books that integrate knowledge and address controversies from a sociological perspective. Books in the Rose Series are at the forefront of sociological knowledge. They are lively and often involve timely and fundamental issues on significant social concerns. The series is intended for broad dissemination throughout sociology, across social science and other professional communities, and to policy audiences. The series was established in 1967 by a bequest to ASA from Arnold and Caroline Rose to support innovations in scholarly publishing.

DIANE BARTHEL-BOUCHIER
CYNTHIA J. BOGARD
MICHAEL KIMMEL
DANIEL LEVY
TIMOTHY P. MORAN
NAOMI ROSENTHAL
MICHAEL SCHWARTZ
GILDA ZWERMAN

EDITORS

Contents

About the Author

Arne L. Kalleberg is Kenan Distinguished Professor of Sociology at the
University of North Carolina at Chapel Hill.

Acknowledgments

THE CENTRALITY of work to individuals, organizations, and societies makes the topic of job quality fundamental to an understanding of individual well-being and social welfare. The growing polarization between good jobs and bad jobs since the 1970s has preoccupied me for much of my professional career. The American Sociological Association's Rose Series in Sociology offered me the opportunity to write a book that provides an overview of the polarization in job quality and the rise of precarious work for a broad audience of social scientists, policymakers, and other interested parties. I have striven to document and explain the structural transformation in employment systems over the past four decades and not be distracted by the shifting tides of economic expansions and contractions and the immediate impacts of cyclical changes during this period.

In the course of writing this book, I have accumulated a number of intellectual debts. I am grateful to Dan Clawson, who was the Rose series editor who originally encouraged me (nearly ten years ago now) to write this book and bugged me until I managed to get it well under way. I also thank his Rose series coeditors from the University of Massachusetts–Amherst for their advice and feedback: Douglas Anderton, Naomi Gerstel, Joya Misra, Randall Stokes, and Robert Zussman. Subsequent Rose series editor Michael Schwartz and his fellow coeditors at the State University of New York at Stony Brook picked up where the UMass group left off, and I thank them as well for their continued encouragement.

Writing a book for the ASA's Rose Series in Sociology enabled me to continue my pleasant association with the Russell Sage Foundation, which is the publisher of this series. I am especially grateful to its president, Eric Wanner, for his continued support and to its director of publications, Suzanne Nichols, who has been steadfast in her enthusiasm for the book. My seminar at the Russell Sage Foundation in 2004 at which I presented my preliminary ideas to the Rose coeditors and other participants raised new questions and ideas for me to consider in explaining changes in job quality. I am especially appreciative of the suggestions at that seminar made by Nancy DiTomaso, Cynthia Fuchs Epstein, Kathleen Gerson, Leslie McCall, Joanne Miller, Michael Schwartz, Ed Wolff, and Julia Wrigley. The Russell Sage Foundation also provided me with the opportunity to spend the summer of 2009 in New York City to make the final push on finishing the book.

I also received terrific feedback and suggestions from the participants at numerous presentations I gave during the course of writing the book. I am particularly obliged for the suggestions on the two concluding policy chapters provided at seminars at the University of Pennsylvania's Wharton School in 2009, the Department of Public Policy at the University of North Carolina at Chapel Hill in January 2010, and MIT's Sloan School of Management in March 2010. I am especially thankful for the ideas and clarifications advanced at these seminars by Ivar Berg, Charles Heckscher, Tom Kochan, Frank Levy, and Michael Piore.

I have also benefited from the generosity of friends and colleagues who read one or more earlier versions of the book and gave me a wealth of critical and constructive comments: Eileen Appelbaum, Steve Barley, Peter Cappelli, Duncan Gallie, Francis Green, Paul Osterman, Becky Pettit, and Don Tomaskovic-Devey. A number of graduate students in sociology and public policy at the University of North Carolina at Chapel Hill also made incisive critiques of earlier drafts, especially Joe Bongiovi, Colin Campbell, Shelley Golden, Rafael Gallegos Lerma, Jennifer Miller, Jessica Pearlman, Jordan Radke, and TiantianYang. I am especially indebted to the two anonymous reviewers of the manuscript (Ruth Milkman and Chris Tilly), whose insightful, thorough, challenging, and candid comments made me rethink and refine key aspects of the argument and presentation.

I owe special thanks to two of my collaborators on topics covered in this book. My work with Peter Marsden over the years helped considerably in shaping the ideas in chapters 5 and 9. My joint work with Ted Mouw was central in writing parts of chapter 6 and his help was essential for estimating many of the models reported in chapters 7 to 9. I also gratefully acknowledge the statistical help provided by two UNC sociology graduate students, Stefanie Knauer and Jeffrey Rosenthal.

Finally, I dedicate this book to my wife, Judith; my children, Kathryn, Jonathan, and Kari; and my grandchildren, Elise and Margit. You all make me very happy.

Arne L. Kalleberg
University of North Carolina at Chapel Hill

═ Chapter 1 ═

Job Quality in the United States

W ORK IN America has undergone marked transformations in the past four decades. Globalization and deregulation have increased the amount of competition faced by American companies, provided greater opportunities for them to outsource work to lower-wage countries, and opened up new sources of workers through immigration. The growth of a "new economy" characterized by more knowledge-intensive work has been accompanied by the accelerated pace of technological innovation and the continued expansion of service industries as the principal sources of jobs. Political policies such as the replacement of welfare by workfare programs in the 1990s have made it essential for people to participate in paid employment at the same time that jobs have become more precarious. The labor force has become more diverse, with marked increases in the number of women, non-white, older, and immigrant workers, and growing divides between people with different amounts of education. Ideological changes have supported these structural changes, with shifts toward greater individualism and personal accountability for work and life replacing notions of collective responsibility.

These social, political, and economic forces have radically transformed the nature of employment relations and work in America.[1] They have led to pervasive job insecurity, the growth of dual-earner families, and 24/7 work schedules for many workers. More opportunities for entrepreneurship and good jobs have arisen for some, while others still only have access to low-wage and often dead-end jobs. These changes in work have, in turn, magnified social problems such as poverty, work-family conflicts, political polarization, and disparities by race, ethnicity, and gender. The growing gap between "good" and "bad" jobs represents a dark side to the booming American economy of the 1980s and 1990s; it has contributed to a crisis for the middle class in the United States in the past decade.

Changes in work and the workforce in the United States since the 1970s have made the quality of employment problematic. The notion of job quality communicates that it is the nature of work that is important to

1

workers, not just whether they have any job at all. Creating good jobs and avoiding bad jobs are major priorities because work is central to human welfare and the functioning of organizations and societies. Jobs are the main way by which individuals are linked to the economy and are slotted into places within the system of social stratification. In the United States, a job is the primary source of one's ability to obtain essential things such as food, housing, and education; a job also has profound consequences for one's social, psychological, and economic well-being. Good jobs provide a foundation for a high quality of life, healthier workers, and stronger families and communities. Workers who have job security and who have reasonable expectations regarding future job opportunities are more likely to be able to put down roots in a community, conceive and raise children, buy a house, and invest in family lives and futures. The amount of control that a person is able to exercise in the workplace has far-reaching effects on one's psychological functioning and non-work life.

This book examines changes in job quality in the United States since the mid-1970s, a period when there were broad transformations in work organization and employment relations in the United States. Beginning in the late 1970s, changes in the contexts of work—the work structures, the institutions, and the rules and norms governing the employment relationship—led to changes in work and job quality. Changes in the demographics of the labor force, such as gender, education, immigration status, race, and age, affected the types of jobs that people valued as well as the kinds of jobs they were able to obtain. The result of these changes has been a polarization of jobs and employment relations with regard to aspects of job quality, such as security and stability, economic compensation, control over work activities, and time spent on the job. Studying changes in job quality provides insights into theories of work organization and social stratification, and how economic and social changes affect the working lives of individuals, their life chances, and their families.

There is an enormous literature written by social scientists about changes in work and employment relations and how they have affected the quality of jobs. However, there have been relatively few attempts to examine the diverse components of job quality in the United States.[2] Social scientists have tended to focus on discrete dimensions of job quality. Economists have studied primarily wages and fringe benefits; psychologists evaluate jobs in relation to a wider array of individual needs and values, focusing on job satisfaction; and sociologists and institutional economists have emphasized changes that have occurred in the organization of work. These piecemeal approaches have hampered a comprehensive understanding of how the transformation of work and the labor force have affected job quality overall.

This book adopts an integrated perspective on job quality that combines insights from economics and psychology, as well as from the sociological study of social stratification, organizations, occupations, industries, and work, to describe how variations in macro-level institutional, organizational, and cultural contexts of work in the United States have generated differences in jobs and workers' responses to these differences during the latter part of the twentieth century. I draw upon the results of others' research as well as primary analyses of survey data to evaluate the evidence that social scientists have accumulated on the topic of job quality in the United States since the 1970s, and I point to some of the main implications of this research for policies to improve the quality of jobs.

In this chapter, I first discuss the often problematic nature of job quality. I then identify some basic dimensions of job quality and indicate what differentiates "good" and "bad" jobs. Next, I provide an overview of my argument that there has been a growing polarization in both economic and noneconomic dimensions of job quality in the United States. This polarization is structural, not cyclical, and is due primarily to a growing mismatch between social and economic institutions and the changing nature of work and the labor force.

The Problem of Job Quality

Concerns about the quality of jobs are nothing new. The prevalence of bad jobs, in particular, has long been a major problem in the United States and in many industrial societies. Marginal and irregular work was common among the laboring classes in industrial countries in the nineteenth century. Until the end of the Great Depression, most jobs were insecure, and most wages were unstable.[3] Pensions and health insurance for workers were almost unheard of in the United States before the 1930s, and benefits were contingent on workers' docility rather than given as entitlements.[4]

Laws enacted during the 1930s dramatically increased the number of workers whose jobs provided a living wage, employment security, and fringe benefits.[5] Workers' rights to bargain collectively, along with increased government control over working conditions and employment practices, restricted employers' power over the terms of employment. By the 1940s, the ratio of good jobs to bad jobs had increased sharply.[6]

During the postwar boom period in the United States, economic compensation generally increased for most people, leading to a growth in equality that has been described as the "Great Compression."[7] Opportunities for advancement were generally plentiful, enabling many workers to construct orderly and satisfying career narratives. The attainment of a basic level of material satisfaction freed workers to emphasize other concerns in evaluating whether their jobs were good, such as opportunities for challenge, meaning, and other intrinsic rewards.

Although regular full-time jobs were the norm by the 1950s, employers continued to rely on a peripheral workforce to contain labor costs and to act as a buffer to protect the jobs of their "permanent" employees.[8] In fact, the growth of "good" jobs that were covered by collective bargaining and federal labor-protection laws made the "badness" of peripheral jobs even more striking. In the 1950s, concerns about work were symbolized by the conformity represented by the "organization man,"[9] while the 1960s raised fears about the disappearance of work through automation and the challenges of the "leisure society."

The late 1960s and early 1970s brought widespread anxiety concerning the quality of noneconomic aspects of jobs. This fueled debates about the human purpose and the meaning of work and the work environment. It was widely feared that job dissatisfaction was on the rise as workers, particularly young ones, developed high expectations for control over work and intrinsic rewards, which clashed with the reality of the routine, Taylorized, and Fordist jobs within mass production industries.[10] In 1973, the Special Task Force to the Secretary of Health, Education, and Welfare issued a report in response to perceived widespread dissatisfaction, and terms such as "blue-collar blues," "white-collar woes," and "managerial discontent" filled the pages of academic writings and the popular media. This apprehension was exemplified by the large-scale worker unrest among the mostly younger workers at the General Motors plant in Lordstown, Ohio, in the late 1960s.

Nevertheless, there was considerable optimism in the early 1970s that the engine of economic growth in the United States would create a "tide that would raise all boats," as President John F. Kennedy famously predicted in the early 1960s. In this optimistic scenario, it was believed that low-paid, unstable, dead-end jobs would be swept away by economic progress and replaced by well-paid, secure jobs that were connected to pathways of upward mobility.[11]

Unfortunately, this optimism was misplaced. In the 1980s and 1990s, wages were stagnant for many people, and jobs became more pressured and demanding. Concerns about work were widespread, encompassing a large range of issues, including greater insecurity, work-family tensions, unemployment, stresses produced by too much or too little work, declining standards of living, inequalities in economic and noneconomic job rewards, and lack of health insurance and pension benefits, among many others. Low wages and job insecurity left many Americans at or below the poverty line, even in periods of high employment, such as the latter part of the 1990s.

The 2000s thus far have combined high uncertainty and insecurity with relatively low economic growth. The end of the twentieth century and the first decade of the twenty-first century saw a reawakening of fears, especially those about the economic aspects of job quality. Academic and media attention focused on peoples' anxieties about their inability to obtain jobs that paid a living wage, were relatively secure, and could provide opportunities for advancement. Political debates about the state of the economy paralleled discussions among social scientists about whether recent changes in the world of work resulted in gains or losses for different groups of workers.

While many of these concerns are not new, they created especially great disruptions in peoples' established patterns and expectations about their work lives since they came after three decades marked by sustained growth and prosperity following World War II. As a consequence, these changes present new and pressing challenges for individuals and their families, businesses, labor, governments, and society.

Dimensions of Job Quality

A job refers to the specific set of tasks that people do for a living. Jobs are embedded in broader aspects of working conditions that characterize the employment relationship, such as those classified as occupations and workplaces. Jobs are complex and can provide workers with many potential job rewards—benefits and utilities that individuals may potentially obtain from their work activities.[12] Jobs are made up of bundles of rewards, and the multidimensionality of job quality is reflected in definitions that recognize the diverse aspects of what constitutes a "good" job.[13]

While there are many aspects of work that might constitute potential rewards, most people would agree that job quality depends heavily on economic compensation such as earnings and fringe benefits like health insurance and pensions; the degree of job security and opportunities for advancement to better jobs; the degree to which people are able to exercise control over their work activities and to experience their jobs as interesting and meaningful; and the extent to which peoples' time at work and control over their work schedules permit them to spend time with their families and in other, non-work activities that they enjoy.

Some of these aspects of job quality are easier to evaluate and measure than others. There are relatively good data on the distribution of (and changes in) earnings and fringe benefits, for example. Others— such as job security and statistical probabilities of opportunities for advancement—are measurable in principle, but the data on them are not readily available. Still other dimensions of job quality are difficult to measure even in principle—cooperation among coworkers, degree of personal autonomy, and intrinsic rewards—although a number of alternative measures of the latter two concepts have been proposed (see chapter 7, this volume).

In view of the complexity underlying job quality, I use a relatively simple classification that distinguishes between economic compensation, such as pay and fringe benefits (especially health insurance and retirement benefits, but also flexible work time options such as family leave), and noneconomic benefits, such as the degree of control that workers have over their work tasks, intrinsic rewards, and the time that they spend at work.

Economic Dimensions of Work

Economists often assume that job rewards reflect a person's skill and effort; hence, there might be good and bad workers, but not good and bad jobs.[14] Others accept the idea that some jobs pay better than others, regardless of the skills of the incumbents of these jobs. Economists tend to equate job quality with the level and stability of economic compensation (especially wages), framing debates about good jobs versus bad jobs in terms of differences between jobs in their earnings: good jobs are high-wage jobs, while bad jobs are low-wage jobs.[15] This assumption is not unreasonable, as earnings are a fairly reliable indicator of the differences between good and bad jobs.[16]

A large literature (mainly in economics, but increasingly in sociology) seeks to document and explain the changes that have occurred in wages and earnings in the United States in the past several decades. These studies have examined changes in levels of earnings, as well as in earnings inequality and earnings instability (see chapter 6, this volume).

Economic compensation also includes fringe benefits such as health insurance and retirement benefits. Some researchers have included the rate of employer-provided health insurance as part of their measure of job quality.[17] Fringe benefits are an important form of job reward in the United States due to the employer-centered model in this country that underlies much of the distribution of health insurance, retirement pensions, and other economic benefits.

Control over Work

Some jobs may pay relatively modestly yet still be considered good jobs because they are challenging, meaningful, and allow people the flexibility to take care of their non-work activities. While economists often ignore nonwage attributes of jobs in the debate concerning good versus bad jobs, sociologists have long emphasized the importance of noneconomic aspects of jobs.[18] Marx underscored the desirability of workers' being able to conceptualize how to do their work as well as their ability to execute it.[19] When conception is not separated from execution, workers can exercise discretion over their work and have real input into decisions that affect them. A large literature in sociology has underscored the importance of workers' autonomy and control—self-direction over what they do and how they do it—for their well-being.[20] Psychologists have also stressed the centrality of noneconomic dimensions of jobs, such as autonomy and control, for the quality of one's work experience and the ability of workers to achieve self-actualization.[21]

Workers who are able to control how and what they do at work are also more likely to obtain intrinsic rewards from their jobs. Intrinsic rewards are benefits and utilities that people obtain *from* task performance, as opposed to extrinsic rewards such as money or fringe benefits, which people obtain *for* performing their work. Intrinsic rewards reflect people's ability to utilize their skills, knowledge, and abilities in their jobs. Some people obtain satisfaction from their jobs primarily because they have the opportunity to develop their abilities and to have interesting, meaningful, and challenging work over which they can exercise responsibility, as opposed to being mere cogs in a machine.

A second aspect of control is the capacity to decide the pace and scheduling of work. Not having control over one's work pace is a disutility of jobs that detracts from the quality of work experience. Workers who have little control over how much effort they expend or the number and timing of hours that they work are likely to suffer from stress and other negative consequences.

Skills are another important aspect of job quality. Some writers (for example, see Green 2006) regard skill as a separate dimension of job quality because skill utilization has intrinsic value and is an end in itself. My view is that skills are important for job quality mainly because the greater market power enjoyed by those with more skills results in certain job rewards such as greater earnings, fringe benefits, and control over one's work schedule. Moreover, skills are intimately related to the amount of autonomy and control that workers have over their tasks as well as to the intrinsic rewards they derive from their jobs. Thus, while I discuss skills in various places throughout the book, I do not consider skills to be a distinct aspect of job quality.

Good Jobs and Bad Jobs

People have differing opinions about what constitutes a "good" job since they seek to achieve a variety of goals from work.[22] Some will define a good job as one that pays well or provides health insurance, is secure, or leads to higher paying jobs in the future. Others will maintain that a good job is one that a person enjoys or finds interesting, challenging, and fulfilling. Still others believe that a good job is one that, alternatively, provides them with a convenient and easy commute; allows them to leave "work at work" and does not interfere with life on weekends or in the evenings; permits them to work in pleasant surroundings; does not (or does) require moving around from one place to another; is low (or moderate) on stress; is stable or provides opportunities for change; is flexible; provides access to friendly coworkers or supervisors; gives them the opportunity to "make a difference" by helping other people; and so on.

To some extent, then, the quality of jobs should be evaluated in terms of personal choice. Whether particular job characteristics constitute potential job rewards thus depends on individual differences and the importance that people place on various aspects of jobs, or their "conceptions of the desirable" with regard to their work activity.[23] Some people like to work with their hands as opposed to dealing with people or ideas. Some prefer to work full-time, while others would rather work part-time. Some people see work as a source of self-actualization, while others regard their job as simply a means to earn a living so that gratification can be sought in other ways.

Within a society, a person's work values and expectations are related to his or her gender, race, and age, as well as education and work experience.[24] In the 1970s, younger workers appeared to emphasize the importance of intrinsic rewards—raising fears among the media, social scientists, and managers about possible widespread "alienation" from work—while older cohorts of workers remained concerned with obtaining extrinsic benefits like earnings and job security. Workers have economic and psychological needs that they try to satisfy via work, but not all of them can be fulfilled through employment relationships at any particular time.[25]

There are also modal, cultural, and institutional understandings of what constitutes good and bad job characteristics in a particular society and time period.[26] Understandings of job quality differ in part according to the opportunities that are available for the attainment of various kinds of job rewards. Workers are likely to calibrate their standards of what constitutes a good or bad job based on economic conditions. During economic downturns, for example, workers are likely to be happy to have a job at all (even a "survival" job) as opposed to suffering through long-term spells of unemployment. During the Great Depression, for example, a good job was one that provided enough money to live on. Moreover, during the Great Recession of 2007 to 2009, standards for evaluating a job as good were also likely based on whether the job provided decent wages and health insurance.[27] According to Jean Eisen, a person in Southern California who lost her job selling beauty salon equipment two years prior to being interviewed in 2010, "There are no bad jobs now. Any job is a good job."[28] By contrast, in the relatively affluent decades of the 1960s and early 1970s, the standards for evaluating a job as good might have been raised to one that provided meaningful and interesting work that enabled persons to "self-actualize" or to "be all that they could be."

Despite these individual and subjective differences, there are certain objective characteristics that most people would agree are necessary for a job to be considered a good job (or, at least, not a bad job). A basic requirement is that the job should pay a wage that is high enough to satisfy a person's basic needs. Another requirement is fringe benefits to also accommodate those needs. In the United States, these benefits would include health insurance and, to some extent, retirement benefits, since these kinds of social supports are generally distributed (if at all) through the workplace and not through the societal welfare system. Of course, the relative value of wages and fringe benefits varies from person to person; if a person has an employed spouse or parent whose job provides health insurance coverage for the family, then the worker might place greater emphasis on wages and less on fringe benefits.

In general, then, a good job is one that

1. Pays relatively high earnings and—perhaps more importantly— provides opportunities for increases in earnings over time

2. Provides adequate fringe benefits, such as health insurance and retirement benefits

3. Enables the worker to have opportunities for autonomy and control over work activities

4. Gives the worker some flexibility and control over scheduling and terms of employment

5. Provides the worker with some control over the termination of the job

Some of these components may be positively related, at least for some people at certain times. Members of professional occupations in particular settings, for example, may have considerable control over their work and schedule while also being economically well compensated. On the other hand, the absence of a particular good job characteristic does not necessarily make a job bad. Conversely, not all of these components are necessary conditions for workers to consider a job to be good. Unionized manufacturing jobs, such as welding or other semiskilled work in the auto or steel industries, for example, were generally regarded as good jobs in the three decades following World War II since they paid relatively high wages and supplied good benefits despite not providing workers with much opportunity to exercise autonomy and control.

On the other hand, a job is generally regarded as bad if it

1.   Pays low wages and does not lead to higher wages over time

2.   Does not provide fringe benefits, such as health insurance and pension benefits, especially if one's family has no other source of such benefits

3.   Does not enable the worker to exert control over the work activities

4.   Does not provide the worker with flexibility to deal with non-work issues

5.   Does not give the worker some control over the termination of the job

Likewise, the absence of particular bad job characteristics does not necessarily make a job good; for example, a job that pays slightly above the minimum wage is not necessarily a good one, and some workers who are given a lot of autonomy (such as nursing assistants, who are often not closely supervised) may also receive low wages and no fringe benefits.[29]

Jobs also differ in their degree of security and opportunities for advancement to better jobs. All jobs have become increasingly precarious in the past four decades (see chapter 5, this volume), though some jobs and persons are more vulnerable than others to both the risk and consequences of job loss. Since both good jobs (for example, well-paid consultants) and bad jobs are generally insecure, it has become increasingly difficult to distinguish good and bad jobs on the basis of their degree of security.

Jobs that do not provide any real opportunities for advancement to better jobs (or to increased wages in the current job) might also be regarded as bad jobs. Such "dead-end" jobs do not offer the promise of more noneconomic and economic rewards in the future. Lack of advancement opportunities is especially problematic for people who have completed their formal education and have families to support.

Overall Job Quality?

There are good theoretical reasons to expect that the dimensions of job quality are, in general, positively interrelated, and so one can speak of the overall "goodness" or "badness" of jobs. Labor market segmentation theories, for example, assume that various aspects of job quality covary such that "only certain configurations of [governing] rules tend to fit together" (Tilly 1997, 269).

For example, the dual labor market theory proposed by institutional economists in the 1960s and 1970s posited that various dimensions of job rewards cohere together into clusters of good jobs and bad jobs. The primary labor market segment was made up of good jobs (that is, well-paying, relatively secure jobs that were associated with job ladders in large firms), and a secondary segment consisted of bad jobs (that is, relatively insecure jobs associated with low-wage employment and the absence of job ladders and opportunities for advancement to better jobs).[30]

Economic and noneconomic rewards may also be positively related due to their common dependence on skills. High-skilled workers are generally in high demand, which tends to bring them greater earnings. Workers with more skills usually have higher market power, especially due to the growing marketization of employment relations (see chapter 2, this volume), a trend that has led to employers' assessing an employee's value as being proportionate to his or her value to other employers. Therefore, more highly skilled workers are apt to have more autonomy and control over their work activities and schedule, as well as greater job security and earnings. Since high-skill jobs require more extensive training, employers are more likely to set up job ladders to facilitate the acquisition of skills, which leads to career advancement over time within occupational internal labor markets, if not firm internal labor markets (or FILMs).

An alternative view is that interrelations among job rewards are relatively weak. Workers who have jobs that are intrinsically interesting or convenient (in terms of flexibility) may not necessarily be well paid or have opportunities for advancement with an employer. In addition, some relatively low-skill jobs in the primary labor market (unlike those in the secondary market) were often unionized, so they still tended to be relatively secure, middle-class jobs that provided good fringe benefits in addition to relatively high wages. This is consistent with the "summative" view of job quality held by neoclassical economists, who assume that employers can vary job rewards at will (within certain limits); a job can be good on some dimensions but not on others. This leads to the possibility of compensating differentials, or employers' utilizing one kind of benefit to compensate for another;[31] workers can trade off the attainment of some types of job rewards to obtain other job rewards. Employers may have to pay workers more, for example, to get them to work in insecure conditions where there may not be much chance of advancement, as is the case in many consulting arrangements. Increases in job insecurity may also be somewhat compensated by greater autonomy, at least for some people, such as highly skilled independent contractors.

It is likely that interrelations among dimensions of job rewards have loosened over time. For example, all jobs have become more insecure, as I discuss in chapter 5. Thus, job security has become more weakly or even negatively related to income and other job rewards. Changes in the various kinds of job rewards over the past three decades may also have offset one another to some extent: organizational restructuring may have had negative consequences for security and earnings while increasing opportunities for control over work tasks and intrinsic rewards.

In any event, the current state of data collection in the United States and elsewhere is such that there is no single measure or index of job quality that enables us to examine changes in job quality over time and includes both economic and noneconomic factors.[32] Hence, I concur with the following conclusion reached by the European Commission:

> Given its relative and multidimensional nature, there can be no one single measure or index of employment quality . . . There is no standard or agreed definition of quality in work in the academic and expert literature. Given the lack of a single composite measure, most studies adopt and suggest various key dimensions of job quality. (Commission of the European Communities 2001, 7)

Therefore, I examine economic and noneconomic job rewards separately.

Explaining Changes in Job Quality

Changes in job quality result from the interplay between two main sets of factors. First, economic, political, and sociological forces shape the structural and institutional contexts of work[33] and help to explain how and why employers make various decisions, how industries grow and decline, how occupations expand and contract, and how workers are able to exercise, in varying degrees, individual and collective power in relation to their employers.[34] Second, changes in the composition of the labor force and in the needs and preferences of workers affect the fit between job characteristics and workers' values, needs, and expectations, thus influencing what features of work are salient for defining a good (or bad) job.

This book elaborates on the interplay between institutional structures and the composition of the labor force in generating polarization in job quality in the United States since the mid-1970s. Chapter 2 provides an overview of the transformations in social and economic institutions that have led to changes in the economic and noneconomic dimensions of job quality since the mid-1970s, the time period when it is generally agreed that the most recent era of polarization and precarious work in the United States began. The increasingly market-driven approach that came to be known as neoliberalism intensified economic integration and price competition. Technological advances both forced companies to become more competitive globally and made it possible for them to do so. Changes in capital markets that rewarded managers for short-term profits encouraged them to treat labor as a variable rather than a fixed cost, leading to outsourcing and the growth of temporary and other forms of nonstandard work.

The neoliberal revolution spread globally, emphasizing the centrality of markets and market-driven solutions, privatization of government resources, and removal of government protections. Changes in legal and other institutions mediated the effects of globalization and technology on work and employment relations.[35] Government regulations that set minimum acceptable standards in labor, product, and capital markets eroded. Ideological changes toward greater individualism and personal responsibility for work and family life supported these structural changes; the slogan "you're on your own" replaced the notion of "we're all in this together."[36] Beginning in the era of the Reagan administration, the lack of enforcement of labor standards, along with coordinated anti-union business strategies, contributed to a continuing decline of unions, thereby weakening a traditional source of institutional protections for workers and severing the postwar business-labor social contract in the United States. Union decline and labor market deregulation reduced the countervailing forces that had previously enabled workers to share in the productivity gains that were made. The balance of power shifted heavily away from workers and toward employers.

Neoliberalism at the societal level was mirrored within the workplace as employers sought greater flexibility in their relations with workers. The standard employment relationship, in which workers were assumed to work full-time for a particular employer at the employer's place of work, began to erode. Managements' attempts to achieve flexibility led to various types of corporate restructuring and transformations in the nature of the employment relationship. The work process also changed during this period as increases in knowledge-intensive work accompanied the accelerated pace of technological innovation. Service industries increasingly became the principal source of work as the economy shifted from manufacturing-based mass production to an information-based economy organized around flexible production.

These institutional transformations were accompanied by important changes in the composition of the labor force that played a central part in the story about changes in job quality, as discussed in chapter 3. The labor force became more diverse, with marked increases in the number of women, nonwhite and immigrant workers, and older workers. The growth of dual-earner families made it more important for workers to have control over their work schedules and the flexibility to attend to non-work, familial activities. The growth in immigration due to globalization and the reduction of barriers to the movement of people across national borders produced a greater surplus of low-skilled labor, encouraging employers to create more low-wage jobs. The expansion of educational attainment within the labor force enhanced the importance that workers placed on challenging work and led to growing gaps in earnings and other indicators of labor market success between people with different amounts of education.

Polarization in Job Quality

These macro-level transformations in economic and work structures that began taking place in the middle of the 1970s—along with changes in the composition of the labor force—led to a polarization in specific dimensions of job quality and the spread of precarious work. There has been an expansion in both good and bad jobs, reflected in an increase in high-skill, good jobs and low-skill, bad jobs, along with a decline in semiskilled, well-paying jobs that has shrunk the size of the middle class. Moreover, education has become a key factor for differentiating those who have good jobs from those with bad jobs (see chapter 3, this volume). The growth of polarized work during the past four decades, which I will discuss in chapter 4, represents a departure from the three decades following World War II marked by sustained growth and relatively shared prosperity.

This polarization is not new, but the duality between the primary and secondary labor markets has increased along with the disappearance of relatively low-skill, traditional, middle-class jobs with good pay and benefits, job stability, and steady promotions. The decline of the middle class has reversed the predictions of the theory of embourgeoisement, which predicted that the working class would be integrated into the middle class. Due to their greater reliance on increasingly uncertain jobs, the American middle class has come to resemble the classic proletariat.[37] In particular, "subordinate primary labor market" jobs are among those most threatened by corporate restructuring and downsizing, and no longer enjoy the institutional protections once provided by unions.

Along with the growth of polarization was the general increase in precarious work and job insecurity for all workers, as I discuss in chapter 5. All jobs—blue-collar occupations as well as previously privileged white-collar occupations—are now more insecure and associated with higher levels of risk for workers.[38] The ties between employers and employees have become more tenuous, layoffs have increased and have become relatively permanent, and nonstandard work arrangements have proliferated. Job insecurity has led to economic insecurity, which "isn't just a problem of the poor and uneducated . . . Increasingly, it affects . . . educated, upper-middle-class Americans" (Hacker 2006, 6). While all jobs have become more precarious, some workers have been less vulnerable than others, and the labor force has become increasingly polarized into those with more education and marketable skills and those without these human capital attributes.

The growing gap between good- and bad-quality jobs is a long-term structural feature of the changing labor market. Polarized and precarious employment systems result from the economic restructuring and removal of institutional protections that have been occurring since the 1970s; they are not merely temporary features of the business cycle that will self-correct once economic conditions improve. In particular, bad jobs are no longer vestigial but, rather, are a central—and in some cases growing—portion of employment in the United States.

At the same time, economic fluctuations in business cycles need to be taken into account when examining the evidence regarding changes in job quality during various periods since the 1970s. Ceteris paribus, we would expect good economic times to be associated with better jobs. High economic growth (characterized by tight labor markets and falling unemployment) generally provides workers with greater employment security and gives them more power in relation to their employers. In economic conditions that are favorable for workers, employers tend to try to do what they can to retain valued workers; thus job quality is likely to improve. By contrast, when unemployment is high, companies have fewer incentives to provide high earnings and benefits to their employees, who now generally have fewer alternative job opportunities. Downturns in the economy may also lead employers to require some employees to work longer hours and work more intensely and also to cuts in hours for other employees. Figure 1.1 summarizes the changes in business conditions that have occurred from the 1970s to 2010, as represented by the unemployment rate[39] and by recessionary periods.[40]

Polarization in work is but one aspect of large-scale changes in American society. The decline in the middle class and expansion of the very rich and very poor has resulted in the creation and maintenance of

Figure 1.1   Unemployment Rates and Recessions, 1970 to 2010

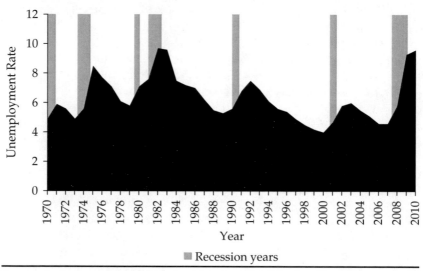

■ Recession years

Sources: Author's compilation based on data from the following: Unemployment rates from U.S. Department of Labor (2011); recessions from National Bureau of Economic Research (2010).

"two Americas" that differ widely in their life chances and political attitudes and preferences. The economist Richard Freeman (1997, 3) warned of an emerging apartheid economy in the late 1990s:

> Left unattended, the new inequality threatens us with a two-tiered society . . . in which the successful upper and upper-middle classes live fundamentally different from the working classes and the poor. Such an economy will function well for substantial numbers, but will not meet our nation's democratic idea of advancing the well-being of the average citizen. For many it promises the loss of the "American dream."

Chapters 6 through 8 summarize the consequences of polarized employment systems on several key components of job quality: economic aspects of jobs, such as wages and fringe benefits (chapter 6); noneconomic benefits, such as the control people have over their work activities and the extent to which they are able to obtain intrinsic rewards (chapter 7); and how hard people work and their control over work schedules (chapter 8). Chapter 9 summarizes some of the evidence on changes in overall job quality as represented by the concept of job satisfaction, the most commonly studied indicator of the overall quality of jobs.

American Exceptionalism?

All high-income industrial countries face similar pressures due to the social and economic forces associated with more intense globalization, technological advances (especially in information and communication technologies), greater mobility of capital and labor, new forms of organizational interdependence, and weakened unions. In important ways, these pressures affect the institutional frameworks governing employment relations in all high-income countries.[41]

The adoption of particular work practices are conditioned by institutional structures, however, and changes in the distribution of job quality are not an inevitable outcome of market forces. The emergence of polarized and precarious employment systems in the United States was shaped primarily by the responses of employers to pressures for more flexibility. Employers' actions were facilitated by an institutional environment that was characterized by a weak labor movement and relative lack of government regulation and interference. The absence of strong labor market institutions encouraged the growth of polarized and precarious employment systems, as employers in the United States had relatively free rein to create bad jobs as well as good jobs.

Focusing on one country makes it difficult to assess the role of institutions in transforming employment systems since there is relatively little variation in labor market institutions in the United States. While there may be regional or local differences in union power or labor market regulations, these variations are relatively minor compared with the range of possibilities. Thus, while this book is about the changing nature of labor market institutions and employment practices in the United States, it will be useful to compare the responses of American employers, governments, and workers with the responses of other countries facing similar macrostructural forces, such as globalization, technological change, and so on. Throughout the book, I attempt to briefly highlight the responses of several Western European countries that share some similarities with the United States with regard to political, economic, and social institutions.

The response by employers in the United States represents an Anglo-Saxon model that is characteristic of liberal market economies (such as the ones in this country, Britain, and Australia) that do not have very "inclusive" labor market institutions, like centralized and solidaristic collective bargaining and strong minimum wage laws. I further develop this argument later in the book. Inclusive labor market institutions extend the gains made by workers with relatively high power to those with relatively little power, as is the case in countries like Denmark and

France.[42] On the other hand, in non-inclusive countries such as the United States,

> labor market institutions have been inadequate to protect workers' interests. . . . The result has been a deterioration in the quality of jobs that do not require a university degree, an increase in the incidence of low-wage work, and a widening of the earnings gap between high- and low-paid workers. (Appelbaum 2010, 186)

In liberal-market, non-inclusive countries, there has also been a growing polarization in noneconomic aspects of job quality, such as work intensity and control over work, as will be seen in chapters 7 and 8.

Toward a New Social Contract

The arguments and evidence presented in this book about the polarization of job quality and the growth of precarious jobs point to the need for a new social contract to address a range of problems created by the changes in employment relations and the growth of bad jobs. Chapter 10 sketches the components of such a new social contract, drawing inspiration from the experiences of other countries with policies related to "flexicurity" as well as from the lessons learned from the New Deal. These historical and comparative models underscore the necessity of integrating employment and social policies in order to protect people from the negative consequences of market forces and to provide them with opportunities to succeed in unstable and uncertain labor market environments.

The final chapter discusses some of the issues related to the realization of this new social contract. Implementing the needed strategies requires the coordinated efforts of government (at federal, state, and local levels), business, and labor. This constitutes major challenges for social and economic policies in the United States in light of this country's relatively passive labor market policies, comparatively small public sector employment (achieved in part through privatizing government jobs), and history of only moderate support for the disadvantaged. The final chapter discusses some of the obstacles we face in achieving the new social contract and concludes by suggesting some strategies that may overcome these obstacles.

= Part I =

Changing Work Structures and Workers

Chapter 2

Economic Transformation and the Decline of Institutional Protections

MACROSTRUCTURAL CHANGES in political, social, and economic institutions and structures constitute the basic drivers that have shaped the organization of work in the United States since the mid-1970s. These changes thereby largely account for the growth of polarized and precarious employment systems during this period. Forces such as the globalization of production, technological change, and the continued rise of the service sector—combined with political decisions to deregulate markets and to reduce enforcement of market standards—weakened unions and the collective power of workers while strengthening the control of employers, who consequently had relatively free rein to restructure employment relations.

In this chapter, I outline the structural forces that contributed to the growth of polarized and precarious employment systems that has occurred in the United States since the mid-1970s. I first provide an overview of the post–World War II employment systems, which were characterized by relative growth and security as well as the existence of a social contract among business, labor, and the government. This interregnum period was unusual for its sustained growth and stability and represents a departure from the periods of precarious work that preceded and followed it. I then summarize the macrostructural forces that led to the demise of this social contract as employers sought to achieve greater flexibility in response to changes that began occurring in the mid-1970s in the competitive and cultural landscape. As I argued in the last chapter, these changes represent long-term structural transformations in employment relations rather than being simply reflections of short-term business cycles. Social and economic forces, such as those associated with increased globalization, technological and organizational change, and greater mobility, have affected all high-income countries, but their impact on employment systems in the United

States was mediated by the institutional structures characteristic of this country.

Employment Systems in the Postwar Period, 1945 to the Mid-1970s

The events of the past four decades follow a thirty-year period of exceptional sustained growth and prosperity in the United States after the end of World War II, from 1945 until the mid-1970s. During this period, the American economy experienced an economic boom, described by some as the Pax Americana.[1] Unlike Japan and most countries in Europe, which were economically ravaged by the war, the United States was able to maintain its productive capacity and thus had a major comparative advantage in international competition. Facing minimal foreign competition, American companies prospered greatly and dominated world markets in many mass production industries. They searched for new markets abroad, in part because Americans had all the consumer goods they could purchase. While there was competition in some sectors of the domestic economy, government regulations in the United States limited competition in many others, such as in the finance and transportation industries.

The 1950s and 1960s were an "age of security" during which economic growth was linked to security.[2] Managers generally controlled American companies during this period and, as critics of managerial capitalism (such as Berle and Means [1932]) argued decades earlier, companies served the needs of managers rather than stockholders. This form of corporate governance created incentives for organizations to grow; for example, the strongest correlate of executive pay during this period was the size of the firm.[3] The growth in firm size was also associated with an increase in white-collar occupations, such as managers and their staffs of administrative and clerical workers.

The manufacturing, construction, and transportation industries all expanded during this period. These industries offered blue-collar jobs that required relatively few skills, but paid well and provided job security—largely because these industries were unionized. Unions negotiated benefits for their members, while union threat effects led nonunion employers to provide similar benefits to their workers in order to forestall further unionization.

A social contract between labor and capital existed from the end of World War II until the 1970s. This social contract, or capital-labor accord, institutionalized the mutual expectations and obligations for work and employment relationships held by workers, employers, and their communities.[4] Workers received fairly secure and well-paid jobs in exchange for labor peace and productivity.[5] Large companies in mass manufacturing industries enjoyed considerable market power, and so were able to maintain high profits and still treat labor as a fixed cost of production by passing on their high labor costs to consumers. Unions, which at their peak represented about a third of the private sector workforce, played a key role in maintaining the social contract by serving as a countervailing force to keep corporations in check.[6]

Not all companies were large and profitable during this period, however. Smaller businesses were less able to rely on these strategies for maintaining industrial peace. The concept of a dual economy put forth by Robert Averitt (1968) described the situation whereby a relatively small but powerful group of large, unionized, core firms in concentrated product markets that enjoyed high profits coexisted with a much larger but less powerful group of small, nonunionized periphery firms that operated in competitive product markets where profits were problematic.

The postwar period was also characterized by an interventionist political environment that was generally favorable to all employees and provided a relatively strong safety net—at least by American standards—beneath the labor market. Governmental efforts to address social and economic problems, such as the War on Poverty and the civil rights laws of the 1960s, expanded the size of the United States government and reinforced the belief that the government had remedies for social and economic ills as well as the resources available to put them into action.[7] A variety of labor laws designed to provide workers with protections was also enacted, such as the Equal Pay Act of 1963 and Title VII of the Civil Rights Act of 1964.[8]

These structural features of business, labor, and the government jointly created the postwar institutional labor market framework in the United States. This framework was associated with economic optimism and growth, which was reflected in rising wages and job security, at least in the employment systems of large firms. In the post–World War II period, most large corporations had put in place a system of internalized employee management, characterized by firm internal labor markets (FILMs), in which loyalty was exchanged for security.[9] In this FILM system, careers generally unfolded within the firm according to internal rules; relatively unskilled workers were hired into entry-level positions and then progressed upward on job ladders within firms that were associated with the acquisition of increasingly greater skills and knowledge.[10] White-collar workers and managers were also generally considered to be fixed factors of production and thus were mostly protected from layoffs. Fluctuations in business cycles were handled mainly by laying off blue-collar workers, though it was generally understood that such layoffs were acceptable only if the economic health of the firm was threatened and that workers would be hired back once business conditions improved.

There were two dominant models of employment systems in large corporations during this period: the industrial union model (for instance, employment practices in the auto industry) and the IBM model (that is, the aggressive nonunion model).[11] Both models, made possible because of the strong economic growth in the postwar period, emphasized the following values: long-term attachments between employers and employees; the notion that the workplace is a community (an idea grounded in the Human Relations movement); the development of internalized careers within the firm; the importance of internal equity in firms' wage structures; and the concept that managers and white-collar workers were fixed costs of production, with adjustments handled by laying off blue-collar workers, typically temporarily.[12] For larger firms, these principles were described as the optimal practices for managing employees and represented "a central set of norms, behaviors, and institutions that structured the core of the labor market."[13]

Macrostructural Forces for Change

This postwar institutional structure was challenged by a variety of macroeconomic and sociological forces that marked the end of the post–World War II Pax Americana and eventually led to fundamental transformations within employment systems. The years 1974 and 1975 saw the start of macroeconomic changes (such as oil shocks or increases in price competition) that put pressure on the core sectors of the economy. These pressures were accompanied by a decline in protections for workers through labor market institutions, such as unions, minimum wage laws, and protective legislation. As union strength declined and government regulations on the labor market were reduced, the balance of power shifted to employers, who were able to restructure employment systems to achieve greater flexibility for themselves. Consequently, the postwar institutional structure of the labor market was fundamentally altered, and the traditional employment relations of the postwar period were transformed.

The Double Movement

This shift from the postwar "age of security" to the "age of flexibility" that began in the mid-1970s is illustrated by Karl Polanyi's notion of a "double movement." In *The Great Transformation* (1944), Polanyi described the organizing principles of industrial society in the nineteenth and twentieth centuries in terms of a struggle between unfettered markets and social protections. One side of this double movement was guided by the principles of economic liberalism and laissez-faire that supported the establishment and maintenance of free and flexible markets (that is, the first Great Transformation in the nineteenth century). The other side was dominated by moves toward social protections that were responses to the psychological, social, and ecological disruptions that unregulated markets imposed on people's lives. The long historical struggle over employment security that emerged as a reaction to the negative consequences of precarity in the United States in the early part of the twentieth century ended with the victories of the New Deal and other social and economic protections in the 1930s that were solidified in the postwar Pax Americana employment systems.[14]

Figure 2.1 illustrates this pendulum-like "double movement" between flexibility and security over the past two centuries: the spread of free, flexible markets in the nineteenth and early twentieth centuries led to demands for greater social protections and security in the 1930s (and

Figure 2.1   The "Double Movement"

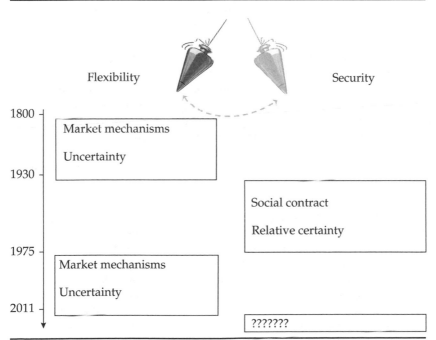

Source: Kalleberg (2009), printed with permission of the American Sociological Association.

now in the 2000s); consequently, in the mid-1970s, regulated markets and concerns about the ability to compete in price-competitive markets led businesses and governments to demand more flexibility.

The story of how and why the American labor market changed can be summarized in terms of a few main institutional changes that have altered the landscape of work in the United States since the 1970s. There is a fair amount of agreement as to the nature of the economic, political, and social forces that contributed to these changes, as reflected in the recent writings upon which my discussion draws.[15]

Globalization and Spatialization

> Each generation considers its own time to be unique. Today's popular demon is foreign competition. Forty years ago, it was automation.[16]

Beginning around the mid-1970s, American businesses began to face a growing increase in international competition. Foreign producers were able to manufacture goods cheaper and often better than before, thus challenging U.S. companies in many domestic product markets. The impact of foreign competition became noticeable especially after the Organization of the Petroleum Exporting Countries' (OPEC) price increases for oil in the mid-1970s, particularly the second round of increases in 1979. Gradually, Japanese automobile companies and South Korean steel companies began taking market share from American producers, a trend that came to characterize many manufacturing industries.

The increase in international competition for manufactured goods and foreign trade was part of a larger trend toward globalization in product, capital, and labor markets. Direct investment in the United States from foreign sources, for example, also increased.[17] Labor markets became more global as American companies were drawn to low-wage areas in other parts of the world to outsource production as well as financial and other services. This trend was facilitated by technological advances in information and communications technologies, such as the spread of computerization and the development of the Internet, which enhanced connectivity around the world. Moreover, the globalization of labor markets led to increased immigration to the United States, especially from Latin America, which brought large quantities of laborers who were willing to work at relatively low wages (see chapter 3, this volume). International trade in manufacturing proportionately eliminated more jobs for less-educated workers in relatively low-skill jobs in the United States, although there was a net decline in jobs for all workers.[18]

This internationalization of work and markets had profound impacts on the nature of business competition, the kinds of workers who were available through increased mobility and immigration, the availability of capital, and so on. It also led to a spatial restructuring of work on a global scale, as geography and space became increasingly important dimensions of labor markets, labor relations, and work.[19] Greater connectivity among people, organizations, and countries, made possible by advances in technology, made it relatively easy to move goods, capital, and people within and across borders at an ever-accelerating pace. "Spatialization" freed employers from conventional temporal and spatial constraints and enabled them to locate their business operations optimally to access cheap sources of labor.[20] Such geographical relocation of production has tended to weaken labor in the areas from which capital was relocated but to strengthen labor movements in the new geographical sites.[21] Advances in information and communication technologies allowed employers to exert control over decentralized and spatially dispersed labor processes. Moreover, China, India, and the former Soviet bloc countries' entry into the global economy in the 1990s doubled the size of the global labor pool, further shifting the balance of power from labor to employers.[22]

Increased Price Competition in Product Markets

The increase in the internationalization of production and the expansion of globalization were parts of a larger phenomenon: the growth in price competition among firms in product markets. Various forces contributed to increased competition in product markets, making it much tougher for American business to obtain profits (or "rents," as economists frequently call them). In contrast to the post–World War II period during which many large American firms held oligopolistic positions in many key industries, the late-1970s ushered in a period of price competition that put pressure on all organizations to become more efficient and to reduce costs.

Government deregulation also increased product market competition in a number of domestic industries, such as airlines (in 1978) and trucking and railroads (in 1980). At the same time, a gradual easing of regulations in financial services and telecommunications also occurred.[23] Deregulation of these industries was part of the U.S. government's general withdrawal of its activist stance of the postwar period and reflected neoliberalism's increasing emphasis on markets as the solution to economic problems.

Product market competition also grew due to shifts in consumer tastes and advances in technology that shortened product cycles and put greater premiums on flexibility in manufacturing processes. Production processes emphasizing flexible specialization began to replace mass production as the main way of manufacturing products, a development that Michael

Piore and Charles Sabel (1984) referred to as the "Second Industrial Divide." Flexible specialization was facilitated by technological changes, such as the rise of computerization and advances in communication, which allowed organizations to become more spatially decentralized and to export work activities to all parts of the world. These technological changes further fueled the trend toward global markets while making it less advantageous for companies to make fixed investments in their workers. The growth of price competition in product markets forced American companies to cut costs and improve their own production processes.[24]

The Changing Role of Capital Markets in Corporate Governance

The nature of capital markets and their impact on the organization of work also changed during this period. Stock ownership became increasingly concentrated in the hands of institutional investors such as public and private pension funds, other investment funds, and insurance companies.[25] These institutional investors increased their pressure on managers to create shareholder value, often at the expense of the rights of other stakeholders, such as workers.[26] This signaled a more active role played by capital markets in organizational functioning and led to changes in the patterns of corporate control and governance. Threats of hostile takeovers and leveraged buyouts illustrated companies' greater vulnerability to raiders, forcing managers to become more cost- and profit-conscious. This promoted a short-term, bottom-line mentality among managers.

These changes in the role of capital markets in corporate governance led to financial restructuring and contributed to the growing financialization of the economy.[27] The expanded role of institutional investors and capital markets also compelled managers to try to achieve higher profits more quickly. In turn, this tended to change the perspectives of senior management and created a bias among managers toward making fewer investments in their human resources.[28] These pressures from institutional investors and capital markets also led to an increase in mergers and acquisitions, which would be an important driver of the waves of downsizing that began in earnest in the 1980s.

The Weakening of Government Intervention in the Labor Market

The deregulation of key industries (such as airlines, trucking, financial services, and communications) reflected a broader trend toward a reduction in government intervention in the economy. The changing political environment that weakened the presence of government in the labor market represented a victory by those who felt that the old system placed unnatural constraints on market forces. They believed that the best way to deal with the new competitive environment was to release the forces of the market.[29] Robert Kuttner (1996) described the unfettering of the market as "everything being for sale," while Paul Osterman and his colleagues (2001) noted that the government withdrew its active role in the labor market in response to fiscal pressures as well as to political ideologies that emphasized market mechanisms as the most efficient solutions to social issues.

As government intervention in the labor market decreased, labor laws and standards were less rigorously enforced. The Reagan administration, for example, provided little support for federal agencies charged with monitoring Occupational Safety and Health Administration (OSHA) and Equal Employment Opportunity Commission (EEOC) regulations, which considerably diminished the impact and effectiveness of these laws.[30]

Employers were also able to get around the constraints imposed by labor laws such as The Employment Retirement Income Security Act (ERISA) by taking advantage of the growing opportunities to lease workers and otherwise utilize nonstandard work arrangements, such as independent contractors and temporary help agencies. Because many employers tried to avoid the rigidities associated with the standard employment relations that were protected by legislative requirements, many of the labor laws passed during the postwar period consequently and unintentionally encouraged subcontracting and other nonstandard work arrangements in an indirect way.[31]

The Continued Expansion of the Service Sector

The massive shift in employment from industries that produce goods to those that produce services is a trend that has continued throughout the postwar period. It is a reprise of the historical shift from agriculture to industry in the nineteenth and early twentieth centuries. The growth of the service sector is a key aspect of the expansion of the "new economy" and the knowledge society, in which information is the central source of power and productivity. More than 85 percent of people in the United States worked in service industries in 2009, up from nearly 70 percent in 1970.[32] Employment among the five hundred largest service companies grew from 9.3 million jobs in 1982 to 11.3 million in 1993, while employment among the top five hundred manufacturing companies dropped from 14.4 to 11.5 million over the same time period.[33]

Market forces have also extended into services through the privatization of activities that were previously done mainly in the household, such as child care, cleaning, and cooking. Women are more likely to work in the service sector; about 90 percent of women who currently work in the labor force are employed in the service sector, compared with about three-quarters of men.

The growth of the service sector has occurred in all industrial countries, though it takes different forms in different nations, depending largely on the role of the public sector in the provision of services.[34] In the United States, the trend toward increased employment in the service industry was fueled in part by the other macrostructural changes discussed in this chapter. The growth of foreign competition, for example, helped to reduce the size of the domestic manufacturing sector since a growing proportion of goods were now made outside of the United States. The financialization of the economy, the expansion of consumerism, and changes in family structure toward more dual-earner incomes all contributed to the growth of business and personal services. Technological changes have also enhanced the efficiency with which goods are manufactured, thereby reducing the number of jobs needed to make these goods.

The growth of services has figured prominently in the "good jobs versus bad jobs" debate for a long time. Over thirty years ago, Eli Ginzberg (1979, 37) pointed to the increase in service sector jobs during the earlier period of 1950 to 1979 as an indication of the growing number of bad jobs. He noted that jobs in these sectors were more often part-time and that the wages tended to be low relative to manufacturing jobs. More recently, the coining of the term "McJobs" points to the low-wage, often part-time, insecure jobs in the service sector as the exemplars of the kinds of jobs that have been increasingly created in the U.S. economy.[35] Many bad jobs are part-time jobs, and most of these part-time jobs are concentrated in a few service industries.

These bad service jobs are assumed to have replaced higher-paying manufacturing jobs, which were more likely to be unionized and higher-skill.[36] Many of the blue-collar, unionized, and relatively low-skill but high-paying jobs that fueled growth in the middle class throughout much of the post–World War II period disappeared during the 1980s and were replaced by low-wage, service jobs.[37] The growth of the service sector has also fueled the expansion of contingent and nonstandard work, since jobs in the service sector are often easier to schedule in a flexible way.

Not all service jobs are bad, of course. The service sector is very heterogeneous and includes highly skilled professional and business services, such as college professors, medical doctors, and architects, as well as low-paid positions, such as retail clerks and domestic workers. In chapter 4, I discuss this polarization of the service sector into good and bad jobs in greater detail.

Ideological Shifts: Toward Greater Individualism

Ideological changes toward greater individualism and personal responsibility for work and life supported these economic and political structural changes. Gradually, the idea that people were themselves responsible for coping with the consequences of economic transformation replaced the New Deal–era belief that the government would provide economic security for all. The notion of "we're all in this together" (WATT) was supplanted by the ideology, "you're on your own" (YOYO).[38] The individualism that accompanied this ideological shift provided the normative basis for the marketization and deregulation of labor markets set in motion by President Carter and later enhanced by President Reagan.[39]

The ideology of individualism buttressed the neoliberal revolution that spread throughout the world, emphasizing the centrality of markets and market-driven solutions, the privatization of government resources, and the removal of government protections in many countries. This "personal responsibility" crusade and the notion of "taking ownership" of one's own life were fueled by well-financed conservative think tanks (such as the Cato Institute and the Heritage Foundation) that worked during this period to reduce the safety net and to foster the role of markets.[40]

The Decline of Unions and Worker Power

Worker power refers to the ability of employees, collectively or individually, to obtain an advantaged position in the stratification system. In this respect, worker power represents the differential "market capacity" of workers, which, in turn, leads to better economic and noneconomic job rewards.[41] Since the employment relation is fundamentally a political and power relationship, employees must be able to exercise power—both individually and collectively—over their skills, jobs, and employment situations to some degree in order to gain higher benefits or wages and to exercise their voice with regard to working conditions, control over work tasks and schedules, and other noneconomic job attributes.

Worker power is a relative concept, and workers may obtain power relative to other workers as well as to their employers.[42] In this chapter, I focus on the collective power of workers with regard to employers; I discuss individual sources of worker power in chapters 3 and 4. Specifically, I concentrate on collective power that is exercised through unions, leaving a discussion of other forms of associational power, such as occupations, to chapter 4.[43]

Unions enable workers to realize their economic interests by exerting collective power in the form of bargaining and other institutionalized arrangements in relation to employers. There has been a fairly steady decline in the percentage of labor force members belonging to unions since the 1950s.[44] Figure 2.2 shows the trends in union membership since the early 1970s by public and private sectors. The decline in unionization has been concentrated in the private sector of the economy: the percentage of union members in the public sector first exceeded union density in the private sector in 1974; union membership in these two sectors has become increasingly polarized since then.[45]

The decline of union membership and power in the United States occurred concomitantly with the breakdown of the postwar institutional labor market structure (the capital-labor accord discussed earlier), which began to unravel in the late 1970s. By the mid-1980s, scholars began identifying a significant change in the U.S. system of collective bargaining and industrial relations that reflected "deep-seated environmental pressures that had been evolving quietly for a number of years" (Kochan, Katz, and McKersie 1986, 4). In place of the collective bargaining system of the postwar period, they pointed to the rise in the 1980s of an alternative, nonunion human resource management system.

The continued decrease of union density in the private sector is intimately related to the macrostructural forces described earlier in this

Figure 2.2   Trends in Unionization, Public and Private Sectors, 1973 to 2009

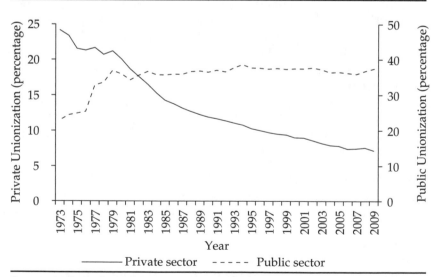

Sources: Author's figure based on Current Population Survey data from Hirsch and McPherson (2010) and Rosenfeld (2010).
Note: Rosenfeld provides 1982 estimates by averaging 1981 and 1983 rates.

chapter, which have accelerated the waning of unions and, in turn, have been facilitated by union decline. The growth of price competition encouraged employers to adopt strategies to decrease costs, which led to flexible work arrangements such as subcontracting and temporary work. These types of arrangements made labor more substitutable, reducing the capacity for collective action.[46] Globalization and spatialization, along with technological advances, provided opportunities for employers to run away from unions by moving jobs offshore to low-wage countries with nonunion environments, as well as to areas within the United States with right-to-work laws.

Moreover, changes in industry and occupation structures led to declines in traditional union strongholds and increased types of work that had a weaker history of unionization. For example, the decrease in manufacturing industries and the expansion of nontraditionally union-ized service sectors hampered union organizing. In addition, the pro-portion of workers in historically unionized blue-collar occupations began declining in the late 1960s, while the percentage of white-collar occupations—which were not usually unionized in the past—increased.

Ideological changes toward greater individualism also deempha-sized collective solutions and encouraged workers to take more personal responsibility in their relations with one another and with employers. Because of increased competitive pressures and threats of outsourcing and offshoring, unions in some sectors were unable to improve their members' well-being via collective bargaining, thereby increasing the attractiveness of individual solutions to workers.

These sources of union decline were reinforced by the rise of coordi-nated antiunion business strategies: a union-avoidance industry emerged in the United States in the 1970s which utilized management consultants and tactics such as captive-audience meetings and one-on-one discus-sions with supervisors to discourage workers from joining unions.[47] These tactics are still used, but in recent years there has been an increase in more coercive and retaliatory tactics such as plant closings (both threatened and actual), discharges, surveillance, alteration of benefits and working conditions, and other unfair labor practices, particularly in globalized and restructured companies.[48] Additionally, the National Labor Relations Board (NLRB), which oversees union representation elections, has been underfunded since the Reagan administration; it has thus been rather ineffective in enforcing labor laws and Wagner Act standards, as well as protecting the rights of private sector workers to organize into unions and bargain collectively with employers.

The decline in unions is not due primarily to workers' not wanting unions, however. For example, the percentage of non-managerial workers in the United States who say that they would vote for a union has increased from 30 percent in the early 1980s to 53 percent in 2005.[49] These statistics demonstrate that the vast majority of workers who would like to be union members are not represented by one, and that the fear of losing their jobs keeps them from trying to oppose employers and organize into unions.[50]

The shrinking of union density characterizes a number of high-income countries: in addition to the United States, for example, the percentage of union members has also fallen since 1980 in the United Kingdom, Germany, France, the Netherlands, and Denmark, among others.[51] However, the impact of a decline in union density on a reduction in workers' collective power is much greater in the United States than in these other countries, due to a lack of other industrial relations institutions in the United States that provide collective bargaining coverage to nonunion workers. In other words, the gap between union density and the coverage rate (that is, the share of workers who benefit from a collective agreement) is much smaller in the United States than in these other countries. In France, for example, union density is lower than in the United States (8 percent in 2007), but 98 percent of French workers were covered by some form of collective agreement in 2007, as compared with 14 percent of workers in the United States.[52]

These changes have contributed to a post-union bargaining environment in the United States in which unions have had little place and structural ability to gain a foothold for bargaining with employers. The decline of unions in the private sector is thus an important reason why job quality may have declined in recent years for large segments of the labor force. Unions are less able to preserve job security for their members and to provide them with increasing levels of economic compensation. In addition, declining union power reduces the spillover effect of unions by which they indirectly create better jobs for nonunion employees because employers maintain good working conditions to avoid unionization.

The Growing Distance Between Employers and Workers

The structural changes described here have produced an increasing divergence between employers and workers in their economic experiences and their life chances, as well as in their political attitudes and preferences. This is reflected in the division between top managerial occupations and other occupations. Peter Cappelli (1999, 236–37) describes the situation:

> In the traditional workplace, the most important division was between white-collar and blue-collar workers, supervisors and the management above them on one side and hourly frontline workers on the other. This division was reflected in labor law. . . . The restructuring of the workplace has made a mockery of that division. . . . Managerial employees are now

just as much at risk as their frontline counterparts. The more important division in the workplace that has emerged in recent years is between the top executives and everyone else.

The relative decline in worker power is reflected in the growing gap between company profits and employee compensation; whereas wages and productivity both grew in the postwar period, creating a strong middle class in the United States, the profits of organizations have not been shared with America's working families since the 1970s.[53] Despite the strong productivity growth in the United States during this period, economic compensation—including wages and employer-provided health benefits—has not kept pace for nonsupervisory workers and, in some cases, has declined, unlike the situation with the postwar social contract.[54] The disjuncture between employers' and employees' interests is illustrated in figure 2.3, which shows that the gap between productivity and compensation began to widen in the late 1970s and has grown ever since. Indeed, the 2000s have seen a historically large gap between productivity growth and compensation.

Figure 2.3   Productivity and Hourly Compensation Growth, 1973 to 2009

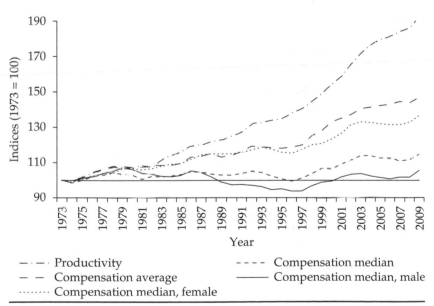

Source: Author's update of Mishel, Bernstein, and Shierholz (2009), figure 3O. Used with permission of the Economic Policy Institute.

Lawrence Mishel, Jared Bernstein, and Sylvia Allegretto (2005, 34) argue that the findings in their book's hundreds of tables and figures describing the state of working America can be reduced to one observation:

> When it comes to an economy that is working for working families, growth in and of itself is a necessary but not a sufficient condition. The growth has to reach the people: the bakers need to benefit from the bread they create each day of their working lives.

The growing gap between productivity and compensation can be traced to the removal of the institutional protections that had enabled workers to share in the profit gains that were made in the 1990s. Workers consequently became more vulnerable to market forces and their attachments to their employers more tenuous and discontinuous. The United States is unique in this respect; it is the only advanced society in which the incomes of the majority have not risen in the 1980s and 1990s, despite steady increases in productivity.[55]

In sum, since the 1970s, workers' situations have worsened while many companies have prospered.[56] This phenomenon has been called the paradox of job quality in an affluent society: employers have benefited as a result of these policies, while workers have not shared in the fruits of success. The United States is not alone in this contradiction; other liberal market economies, such as Britain, have also experienced similar effects.[57] Hence, where jobs are headed might not be the same as where the economy is headed, and the old adage, "What's good for General Motors is good for the country" may not be true anymore, if it ever was at all.

Employers' Responses and Corporate Restructuring

The growth in foreign competition and internationalization of production, along with the increased rapidity of technological change, helped to create a macroeconomic context that pressured employers in the 1980s to restructure their organizations in the face of growing price competition in order to become more flexible—and hopefully more efficient and effective—to respond better to these changes. Corporate restructuring was motivated by profit considerations as well as by institutional reasons, like the attempt to be considered more legitimate to stakeholders by adopting structures that were generally regarded as permitting greater flexibility. The decline of unions facilitated organizations' ability to restructure in order to achieve greater flexibility (and vice versa).

This situation is fairly typical of liberal market economies, which coordinate their economic activities via hierarchies within firms and competitive market arrangements between firms. In these economies, employment dynamics are shaped heavily by employers' efforts to come to grips with changes in their need to elicit commitment from employees, along with skill formation, corporate governance, and inter-firm relations.[58]

The institutional pressures on firms exerted by macrostructural forces—and employers' responses to them—are the central drivers of change in job quality. The decline in the power of unions and the breakdown of the capital-labor accord—along with the reduction in government intervention in the labor market and the ideological shifts toward more individualism—together gave employers considerable freedom to abandon their social contract with labor and instead seek to preserve their profits; employers' strategies and the decline of worker protections are interrelated and mutually reinforcing forces.

In their search for greater flexibility, American companies looked to countries such as Japan, Sweden, Italy, and Germany for alternative models of how to organize production. The models from which they drew insights included Japanese management approaches such as the use of quality circles, the assignment of responsibility to workers to solve problems and work in teams, and the utilization of a peripheral labor force of temporary and part-time workers to buffer a core of protected workers; patterns of subcontracting among firms such as those found in certain regions of Italy; and managerial strategies often associated with Germany that enhanced flexibility in labor utilization and deployment.[59]

The Search for Flexibility

Employers' search for greater flexibility was accompanied by organizational restructuring, which took two main forms. Firms' competitive strategies can be categorized generally as the distinction between "high-road" and "low-road" responses to the need for greater flexibility:

> Some firms may choose to compete for larger shares of standardized products produced by low wage workers carrying out relatively simple tasks. Other firms may choose to tailor production to a high value-added, high quality product at the upper end of the same market. Both strategies may prove successful in generating profits, but with quite different consequences for workers' wages. (Levy and Murnane 1992, 1374)

Noneconomic outcomes, such as autonomy and control over work and schedules, were equally affected.

The distinction between high-road and low-road strategies distinguishes between "post-Fordist," high-performance work organizations that invest in workers and seek to elicit their participation, and "neo-Fordist" organizations that treat workers primarily as costs rather than assets and rely on coercion, or the "stick" strategy, to elicit workers' cooperation and effort through fear rather than commitment.[60]

The relative weakness of the U.S. labor movement, along with a deregulated environment characterized by weak market standards and labor market institutions, made it relatively easy for employers to adopt low-road strategies. Hence, it is not surprising that the majority of American corporations took such a low-road strategy in the 1980s and 1990s.[61] By contrast, the use of low-road strategies was less common in countries with stronger labor movements and more inclusive labor market institutions, such as Denmark, France, and the Netherlands.[62] This variation by country underscores the importance of institutions for employer strategies. I discuss the impact that these two flexibility-seeking strategies of organizing work have on job quality later on, in chapter 4.

Downsizing

Related to the adoption of a low-road strategy was the practice of company downsizing that began in earnest during the recession of 1982 to 1983, the most severe economic downturn since the 1930s—that is, before the Great Recession of 2007 to 2009.[63] Downsizing refers to dismissing workers for reasons other than poor performance; employers sought to reduce their fixed labor costs by shedding workers.[64] Layoffs became increasingly common, and blue-collar occupations bore the brunt of the downsizing movement in the early 1980s.[65] In the latter part of the 1980s and in the 1990s, these layoffs were extended to managerial and white-collar workforces—a departure from past practice—as well as the service sector. While the incidence of job loss among white-collar workers increased in the early 1990s compared with the early 1980s, layoffs actually decreased among blue-collar workers in this period.[66] Moreover, before the 1980s, layoffs had involved temporary periods of unemployment; now they became relatively permanent. Partly in response, the U.S. Department of Labor's Bureau of Labor Statistics started collecting data on "worker displacements" in the early 1980s.

The downsizing of the organization's formerly "permanent" workforce was facilitated by new information technologies, which eliminated the need for some layers of middle management and provided an infrastructure that enabled outsourcing and offshoring. Technological advancement permitted the automating of some routine jobs in manufacturing and in clerical operations, while creating conditions for disintermediation of work in other occupations (for example, managers now did what their secretaries used to do for them). This encouraged employers to get rid of their least-skilled workers in order to hire workers who were better trained and able to work with new technology.[67]

Moreover, President Clinton's administration disconnected the Democratic Party from its New Deal concern for security and full employment by stressing growth—and generating lots of jobs regardless of their quality—at the expense of security. Clinton pressed for the North American Free Trade Agreement (NAFTA) in 1993 and the General Agreement on Tariffs and Trade (GATT) in 1995, both of which encouraged layoffs of American workers by facilitating the movement of jobs to low-wage countries.

Layoffs or involuntary terminations from employment have always occurred and, not surprisingly, have fluctuated with the business cycle. A big change from the past was that layoffs now occurred for reasons of profit maximization rather than survival. Healthy companies laid off workers and justified this as an "unfortunate necessity"—a reflection of the changing norms of the employment relationship.[68] By 1996, laying off workers was regarded as a legitimate corporate tactic and a basic component of the employer strategy of restructuring.[69] Companies have continued to downsize even in good times; while downsizing and layoffs were once legitimate responses to profit pressures, they now have become a way of increasing short-term profits by holding down the wage bill (and the price and quantity of labor) and transferring income from labor to capital.

While downsizing increases profits, there is not much evidence that it has actually resulted in greater productivity or that this strategy improves performance in the medium or long run. Some critics have argued that downsizing has become excessive, since it has not proved to be useful either for the company or for the health of its workers.[70] Indeed, "corporate downsizing remains the most pervasive yet unsuccessful organizational improvement strategy in the 1990s business world" (Cameron 1993).

Conclusions

This chapter has outlined the macrostructural forces operating since the mid-1970s that have transformed the employment systems characteristic of the relative prosperity and security of the post–World War II period in the United States into polarized and precarious employment systems. Some of these forces—such as globalization and technological change—are challenges faced by all high-income nations. Others, such as labor market deregulation and the decline in union power, are more variable and depend on a country's labor market institutions. The absence of a commitment to strong labor market institutions in the United States accelerated the decline of union power and enabled employers to restructure employment systems, enhancing their own flexibility without providing workers with the security to cope with these changes.

═ Chapter 3 ═

New Workers, New Differences

HE LABOR force in the United States has changed in important ways since the 1970s. The proportion of women in the workforce grew, as did the number of dual-earner families. The share of nonwhite workers in the workforce expanded, while the percentage of foreign-born laborers nearly tripled. The workforce has gotten older on average, and education has emerged as the main divider among workers with bad jobs versus those with good ones.

These changes in the labor force play an important supporting role in the macrostructural transformations discussed in the previous chapter that explain the growth of polarized and precarious work. For example, increases in the share of vulnerable groups (such as blacks and Hispanics) have helped to stimulate the growth of low-wage jobs and insecure jobs. In addition, increased numbers of women in the labor force have contributed to the growth of dual-earner couples, thus creating greater demand for flexible schedules and control over the time workers spend on the job. Greater diversity among workers in their market power, skills, and education helps to generate inequalities in their earnings, autonomy, advancement, security, and other job rewards. And, of course, the influence is reciprocal: time on the job, wages, autonomy, and other job characteristics influence inequalities inside families.

In this chapter, I discuss changes in labor force characteristics in terms of major demographic groups defined by education, gender, family, immigration status, race, and age. These are the major dimensions that differentiate people as to whether they work for pay at all, their reasons for working, where they work, and the kinds of jobs in which they work. At the same time, there are also inequalities in job quality *within* many of these groups. The ability of workers with certain levels of education to attain high-quality jobs differs for men and women, for example, and for Hispanics, whites, and blacks. The effects of age on job quality are also likely to differ for these gender-race groups. Inequalities in job quality are complex and vary within gender, race, and age as well as region and other structural demarcations.[1]

40

Education

The educational level of the labor force in the United States has steadily increased over the past thirty years, a continuation of a trend over the course of the twentieth century that saw the average American's level of schooling almost double.[2] Figure 3.1 shows the growth in the percentages of men and women in the workforce with some college education as well as those with a college degree or more, in comparison with the decline in workers who had a high school education or less. The percentages of men and women who have at least a college degree increased from 16 and 11 percent in 1970 to 33 and 36 percent in 2008, respectively. By contrast, the percentages of men and women with less than a high school diploma decreased from 38 and 34 percent in 1970 to 11 and

Figure 3.1   Educational Attainment of the U.S. Labor Force, 1970 to 2008 (Age Twenty-Five to Sixty-Four)

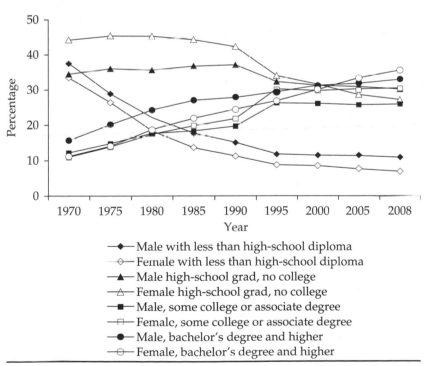

—◆— Male with less than high-school diploma
—◇— Female with less than high-school diploma
—▲— Male high-school grad, no college
—△— Female high-school grad, no college
—■— Male, some college or associate degree
—◻— Female, some college or associate degree
—●— Male, bachelor's degree and higher
—○— Female, bachelor's degree and higher

Source: Author's figure based on data from U.S. Department of Labor (2009).

7 percent in 2008, respectively. The gap in college education for men and women has reversed since 1970, with a higher percentage of women than men now graduating from college.

The growth of education was stimulated by pressures from workers and their families as well as from the demands of the changing structure of work. Workers increasingly realized that investing in education and human capital was their best ticket to success in the labor market and that those without educational credentials were more and more at a disadvantage in the competition for jobs. Moreover, the vast expansion of the knowledge economy and postindustrial society—fueled by the advances in information and communication technologies and the growing prevalence of complex work with data and people, as opposed to the production of goods—increased skill requirements for large numbers of jobs and put a premium on educational credentials for workers filling these jobs. The availability of more highly educated workers both encouraged and facilitated employers' efforts to create jobs that are more complex and skilled, but it has also advanced employers' ability to demand higher credentials regardless of a job's intrinsic skill content. It is debatable what proportion of the jobs that were created during this period actually required the skills provided by higher education and what proportion instead reflected employers' preferences—whether rational or irrational—for people with higher educational credentials.[3]

The expansion of education helped make it the "great divider" among people in general and members of the labor force specifically in the latter part of the twentieth century in America. Claude Fischer and Michael Hout (2006) observe that

> education and age replaced gender and marital status in determining who worked, how many hours they worked, who had the best job, who got paid the most, and how people felt about their jobs . . . During this vast expansion [of schooling in the twentieth century], the least-educated gained more schooling at about the same pace as the most-educated did; in this sense, educational inequality did not increase. Yet educational attainment increasingly divided Americans economically, socially, geographically, and politically. (6–7, 241)

There are growing gaps in both earnings and noneconomic aspects of job quality between people with different amounts of education. A worker's educational attainment has become a key determinant of earnings (see chapters 4 and 6, this volume). Workers with higher levels of education are generally more likely to have good jobs. The rise in educational levels has also enhanced workers' expectations of what constitutes a good job: workers with more education (especially younger workers) are more apt to want jobs that provide greater opportunities for autonomy and control, in addition to being well paid (and so, as I note in chapter 9, highly educated workers tend to be more dissatisfied with their jobs since their relatively high expectations are less likely to be met by the reality of their jobs). Demographic groups, such as those defined by race-ethnicity and immigrant status, are also likely to differ in their levels of education and skills, and this helps to explain inequalities among these groups in the quality of their jobs.

The growing role of education in creating inequality in job quality has also helped explain which people have jobs at all. Fischer and Hout (2006) argue that

> after World War II, two big differences marked Americans' unemployment experiences: race and education. African Americans had higher unemployment rates than others with the same education . . . Education's influence on unemployment increased after 1970. High school dropouts had higher unemployment rates than college graduates in every year for which data are available, but the educational gap grew in the 1970s and was even bigger than the black-nonblack gap after the recession of 1989 to 1990. (129)

The flip side of the expansion of educational opportunities has been the growing disadvantages faced by workers with relatively little education. Despite the overall decline in workers with less than a high school diploma (see figure 3.1), there has been an increase in certain groups of workers who have very little education—and hence little market power—especially those making up the large influx of recent immigrants from Mexico, as I discuss later in the chapter.

Female Labor Force Participation

Since the 1970s, the percentage of labor force participants who are women has grown steadily, from under 40 percent to about half of the labor force.[4] In November of 2008, women held 49.1 percent of the nation's jobs (not including farmworkers and the self-employed).[5]

Table 3.1 presents information on changes in the composition of the labor force with regard to gender, race, and age, beginning in 1950 and projected to 2050. In 1950, about 34 percent of women were in the labor force; by 2000, that proportion had increased to about 60 percent. The proportion of women in their prime working years (age twenty-five to fifty-four) peaked at nearly 75 percent in early 2000 and declined slightly to about 73 percent in June 2008. Projections suggest that the labor force participation rates of women are likely to level off over the next several decades.

Table 3.1   Demographic Characteristics of the U.S. Labor Force, 1950 to 2050

	1950	1980	2000	2020	2050
Labor force (thousands)	62,208	106,940	140,863	164,681	191,825
Total labor force participation rate, age sixteen and older	59.2	63.8	67.2	65.1	61.5
Men					
Percentage of labor force	70.4	57.5	52.4	51.9	52.3
Labor force participation rate	86.4	77.4	74.7	70.3	66.8
Women					
Percentage of labor force	29.6	42.5	46.6	48.1	47.7
Labor force participation rate	33.9	51.5	60.2	60.3	56.6
Race					
White					
Percentage of labor force	—	87.5	83.5	79.5	74.9
Labor force participation rate	—	64.1	67.4	65.0	61.4
Black					
Percentage of labor force	—	10.2	11.8	13.3	14.1
Labor force participation rate	—	61.0	65.8	65.0	59.8
Asian and other					
Percentage of labor force	—	2.3	4.8	7.3	10.9
Labor force participation rate	—	64.6	66.5	66.4	64.9
Hispanic origin[a]					
Percentage of labor force	—	5.8	10.9	16.0	23.7
Labor force participation rate	—	64.0	68.6	67.9	63.8

Table 3.1   (*Continued*)

	1950	1980	2000	2020	2050
Age					
Sixteen to thirty-four					
Percentage of labor force	42.0	51.0	38.6	38.6	39.3
Labor force participation rate	61.9	74.0	75.7	77.8	76.7
Thirty-five to fifty-four					
Percentage of labor force	40.8	35.0	48.5	41.1	41.9
Labor force participation rate	67.0	77.6	83.8	85.3	84.9
Fifty-five and older					
Percentage of labor force	17.2	14.1	12.9	20.3	18.8
Labor force participation rate	43.0	32.8	32.3	36.3	30.2

Source: Author's reproduction of Toossi (2002, tables 3 and 4).
[a]Persons of Hispanic origin may be of any race. Percentages of whites, blacks, and Asians or other add up to 100 percent (deviations from this due to rounding).

By contrast, labor force participation rates of men have decreased significantly over this entire period.[6] The labor force participation rate of men in their prime working years peaked at 96 percent in 1953 and decreased to 86.4 percent in June of 2008. The explanation for the decline in labor force participation (for both men and women) in the last part of the first decade of the twenty-first century was the downturn in the economy, not women staying home to raise their children.[7]

There are a number of reasons for the increase in female workers, including the growth in families headed by women, due in part to greater divorce rates; the decline in the birth rate; the increasing educational attainment of women; the availability of jobs in the service sector and in white-collar occupations; and the stagnation of wages for men, which made it difficult for one wage-earner to support a family. In addition, political policies in the United States—such as the replacement of welfare by workfare programs in the mid-1990s—made it essential for people to participate in paid employment, often forcing them into low-wage jobs. Women composed a large portion of workers entering the labor force during this period.

Women's employment in the United States has increased most rapidly among married women; between 1970 and 2005, the labor force participation of married women increased from about 40 percent to over 60 percent, and both spouses were employed in nearly 60 percent of all married-couple households.[8] There were also substantial increases in the employment of married women with children; between 1970 and 2005, the proportion of married women who had children under the age of eighteen in the labor force increased from nearly 40 percent to nearly 70 percent. By 2005, over 60 percent of married women with children under the age of six were in the workforce, as were nearly three-quarters of those with school-age children (ages six to seventeen).[9]

These dramatic increases in the employment of married women with children are recent developments. The oil price shocks and resulting stagflation in the 1970s led to a long period of falling real wages for men without a college degree. Men's wages fell from 1973 through the mid-1990s and threatened the purchasing power and living standards of most families (see chapter 6, this volume). As the standard employment relation—which had provided men with rising wages over their working lives—began to unravel over the past three decades (see chapter 5, this volume), the subsequent stagnant or declining wages of men fueled the rapid entry of married women into paid employment. Married couples staved off a decline in the family's standard of living primarily by increasing family hours of work (see chapter 8, this volume).

The notable increases in labor force participation rates and educational attainments that women have experienced over the past thirty years have enabled them to take advantage of the growth of professional and technical occupations, as well as employers' increasing demand for high-skilled workers. Greater numbers of women are now also committed to a career and do not view their labor force participation as merely a supplement to their husbands' income. This expansion of career-minded women has led to greater demands for jobs that pay well, provide opportunities for meaningful work, and act as stepping stones to better jobs.

Work continues to be gendered, even though gender is no longer the primary basis for differentiating workers regarding job quality or quantity. And, as shown in later chapters, men generally have better-quality jobs than women, as reflected in the persistent wage gap in earnings and men's greater autonomy and control over their jobs.[10] As in the past, women continue to be excluded from some good jobs and are often assigned to relatively low-paying jobs that do not provide much opportunity for advancement. Part-time jobs are more likely to have these characteristics, and women are about three times more likely than men to work part-time. This reflects in large part women's greater family responsibilities. However, the percentage of part-time workers who are women does not appear to have increased much during the past thirty years.

There is also considerable inequality in job rewards by educational groups *within* genders, and this within-group inequality is complex; for example, Leslie McCall (2001) demonstrates that labor market characteristics such as insecurity and casualization have different effects on the gap between college-educated and non-college-educated women than on the gap between these groups for men.

Dual-Earner Families

The growth in women's labor force participation has had important effects on the structure of families and family dynamics. The proportion of dual-earner couples in the labor force increased since the 1970s, as did the labor force participation of women with children. Figure 3.2 illustrates the decline over this period in the traditional "male breadwinner–female homemaker" model (in which the husband is the sole breadwinner) that was dominant in the United States during the post–World War II period[11] and the rise in married couples (in which both husband and wife work)

Figure 3.2   Dual- Versus Single-Earner Families, 1970 to 2007

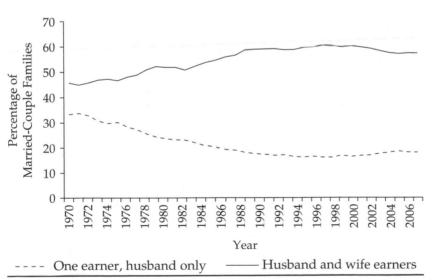

Source: Author's figure based on data from U.S. Department of Labor (2009, table 23). Married-couple families by number and relationship of earners, 1967–2007.

in the labor force. In three-quarters of dual earner couples, both partners work full-time.[12]

The change from a single male breadwinner–female homemaker model to a dual-earner model in which men and women have to share responsibility for homework has not only transformed the family but has affected the way people think about their jobs, such as what they need and want from paid employment. This change has also created greater interdependencies between work and family, so it is not possible to comprehend the consequences of changes in work without taking into account family structures, and vice versa.[13]

The growth of dual-earner families has challenged employers' views about the ideal worker that were built around the model of a person who could focus the bulk of his energy on work because he had a wife at home to take care of family responsibilities and community obligations. Joan Williams (2000) describes this ideal, "unencumbered" worker who behaves in the workplace as if he or she has a spouse at home full-time, performing all of the unpaid care work that families require. This "gold standard" employee works full-time throughout the year, is available to work overtime as required by the employer, and takes no time off for child bearing or child rearing. The expectation is that personal problems will not be brought into the workplace. Conflicting demands are expected to be resolved in favor of the requirements of the job. Indeed, workers in the United States can be—and frequently are—marginalized and even fired if their care responsibilities interfere with their jobs.[14]

The fact that nearly every available adult in the United States is now in paid employment (or looking for paid work) has had a profound effect on the ability of families to meet the personal needs of working adults or to care for children, the sick, and the elderly. Despite the increase in the percentage of women in the labor force, social supports for work and many of the institutions and policies governing the workforce remain largely unchanged; they were put in place during the New Deal in the 1930s and were designed to fit the industrial structure and types of families of that period. Unemployment insurance and social security laws were written to protect families dependent on the wage of a male breadwinner. Not until 1993 did women have the legal right to take time off from work for the birth of a child. But parental leave is still generally unpaid, limited to twelve weeks, and not available to the large numbers of women and men who work in establishments that employ fewer than fifty workers. In contrast to most other industrialized countries, workers in the United States do not have rights to paid vacation leave, sick leave, or parental leave. Mandatory overtime is common, and there is no legal maximum number of hours of work in a day or a week.

Much of the stress and anxiety facing working families in the United States arises from the recent rapid changes in the paid employment of women, especially mothers, combined with slower changes in the norms and institutions that support paid market work and unpaid care work. As Ralph Gomory and Kathleen Christensen describe it, "In today's two-career family, there are three jobs, two paid and one unpaid, but still only two people to do them."[15] Dual-earner families have had to increase their working time in order to keep up with their income needs.[16] Being a member of a dual-earner family influences the kinds of things a worker values in a job, such as greater flexibility with regard to scheduling and work hours, in order to maintain the care work required at home. On the other hand, having a working partner who has health insurance for the household makes this reward a less vital component of what constitutes a good job for such persons.

Immigration

The expansion of globalization and internationalization of production (described earlier in chapter 2) has accelerated labor mobility as well as the movement of products, services, and capital across national borders. A key aspect of international labor mobility is immigration. Levels of immigration and the size of the foreign-born population in the United States have generally increased steadily since World War II, especially after the 1965 amendments to the U.S. Immigration and Nationality Act, which replaced the national quota system with the current family- and employer-based preference system.[17]

The levels of immigration and its impacts on labor markets depend on a nation's institutions and laws. Labor force considerations have played a lesser role in immigration policies in the United States than in other countries; for example, family reunification factors have driven immigration in the United States more than labor market considerations. Yet there are numerous cases where demand for labor has influenced immigration policy, both encouraging immigrants to enter the country (as a source of workers during the Civil War or as unskilled workers for mass-production factories in the early twentieth century) and at times discouraging them (as with the Chinese Exclusion Act of 1882).

The proportion of immigrants in the U.S. civilian labor force has exceeded their share of the total population since 1970. The share of foreign-born in the labor force has nearly tripled since 1970, from 5.3 percent to 14.7 percent. The share of foreign-born persons in the U.S. population more than doubled from 1970 to 2005, increasing from 4.8 percent of the population in 1970 to 12.1 percent in 2005.[18] The percentage of immigrants in the labor force increased sharply in the 1990s.

The geographic origins of immigrants have also changed since the 1970s, thereby enhancing the racial and ethnic diversity in the U.S. labor force. The share of immigrants coming from Europe declined from about 60 percent of all immigrants in 1960 to 15 percent in 2000.[19] Over three-quarters of immigrants to the United States today come from Asia, Latin America, and the Caribbean. The fraction of immigrants from Asia rose to one in four by 2000, from one in twenty in 1960;[20] over half of immigrants in 2000 came from Latin America, up from less than 10 percent in 1960.[21]

Overall, the proportion of foreign-born persons age twenty-five or older who were college graduates in 2008 was about the same as that of native-born persons (18 percent and 16 percent, respectively). Increases in highly educated and highly skilled immigrants, such as those from Asia, have helped employers expand the number of high-skill jobs. This contradicts the common perception that the surge in immigration in the past few decades has engulfed the United States with low-skilled foreign laborers. Indeed, nearly 10 percent of foreign-born persons in 2000 were in executive, administrative, and managerial occupations (compared with 15 percent of native-born persons), and nearly 14 percent of foreign-born persons were in professional occupations (compared with about 16 percent of native-born persons).[22] Moreover, in fourteen of the twenty-five largest metropolitan areas (including Boston, New York, and San Francisco), more immigrants were employed in white-collar occupations in 2008 than in construction, manufacturing, or cleaning jobs.[23]

Much of the current interest in the labor market consequences of immigration stems from the low educational attainment of many of the recent immigrants, especially those from Mexico. Mexicans have dominated the growth in immigration since the 1970s and are now the largest single group of immigrants in the United States: they made up over 30 percent of total immigrants in 2007, compared with less than 8 percent in 1970. The percentage of male Mexican immigrants in the labor force increased from 0.5 percent in 1970 to nearly 7 percent in 2007, while the percentage of female Mexican immigrants grew from 0.3 percent to 3.3 percent.[24]

Mexican immigrants have especially low levels of education: in 2008, more than 40 percent of Mexican immigrants had less than a ninth-grade education, far exceeding any other group (Central American immigrants followed next, with one-third having less than a ninth-grade education). An additional 40 percent of Mexican immigrants had at least some high school education or were high school graduates. Fewer than 4 percent were college graduates.[25] These low-educated immigrants are at a competitive disadvantage in the labor market given the increase in jobs that require at least a high school diploma. Compounding their disadvantage is the fact that many are undocumented and have poor English language skills.

The increase in low-educated Mexican immigrant labor has provided a large supply of workers who have comparatively few alternatives in the labor market and are therefore more willing to work for low wages and less willing to challenge their employers.[26] Immigrant workers with relatively few labor market options tend to be more compliant toward their employers and thus are more likely than native-born workers to take on low-wage jobs that are more difficult and dangerous and offer no benefits.[27] Additionally, low-skilled immigrants with few job prospects—like all workers with little market power—are more likely to be satisfied with low-paying jobs than persons who have invested in education and expect to be rewarded for these investments.[28]

The increase of low-skilled immigrants is associated with the growth and persistence of low-skill, low-wage jobs in industries such as farming, restaurants, hotels, day-care centers, meatpacking, and construction. Immigrants have much higher employment rates in the United States—and much lower wage rates—than in countries like Denmark, where unions have been able to police wage levels at the lower end of the labor market. On the one hand, the growth of low-wage jobs in the United States has encouraged the flow of low-skilled immigrants to seek to fill these jobs, as Saskia Sassen (1998, 45) notes:

> The most important reason for the continuation of large inflows among the new migrant groups has been the rapid expansion of the supply of low-wage jobs [especially in the service sector and the downgraded manufacturing sector] in the United States and the casualization of the labor markets associated with the new growth industries, especially in the major cities.

On the other hand, the enlargement of a low-skilled, relatively uneducated, and often undocumented immigrant population has encouraged employers to continue to create low-skill, low-paying, and generally bad jobs to take advantage of this labor supply.

A major question that arises in debates about the labor market consequences of immigration—especially the influx of low-skilled immigrants—is its impact on the quality of jobs held by native workers. Some economists argue that Hispanic immigrants generally exert downward pressure on wages and reduce job opportunities for low-skilled American citizens.[29] Others maintain that immigration does not have a negative effect on the wages of native workers.[30]

The impact of immigration on native workers is complex and depends in part on whether immigrants are substitutes or complements to native workers. When immigrants substitute for native workers in a particular local labor market (such as nonunion construction jobs), the greater supply of labor might exert a downward pressure on wages for those jobs.

By contrast, when immigrants take jobs that natives do not want or for which they are not qualified, then more immigration might create jobs for native workers (such as in restaurants and other service industries that cater to the growing immigrant population).

These substitution and complementarity mechanisms are likely to vary by geographic area, since the immigrant population is not evenly dispersed around the country. For example, low-skilled immigrants are likely to have more negative effects on natives in local labor markets where there are already large numbers of unskilled native workers.[31] Beginning in the 1990s, Hispanic immigrants have begun to settle in new receiving states (such as North Carolina) where they have been responsible for reenergizing local economies and indirectly generating jobs among American workers.

Immigrants in the United States have traditionally been assimilated into the labor force. Nevertheless, new immigrants face different structural circumstances than they did in the past, so assimilation is much more problematic. In particular, the economic transformations discussed in chapter 2 have led to fewer opportunities for those with less education and skills to experience upward mobility, while strengthening the segmentation between good and bad jobs.[32] Barriers to assimilation also include discrimination against Mexicans, which has risen since the 1990s, when politicians increasingly began to demonize this group as representing threats to America's workers, security, culture, and way of life.[33] Indeed, the prospects for upward mobility of these groups are sufficiently problematic that Frank Bean, Susan Gonzalez-Baker, and Randy Capps (2001, 694) conclude that

> the key sociological research question for the future is thus the extent to which sufficient economic opportunities are emerging that provide pathways for later generations of immigrant and other ethnic groups to move out of low-paying jobs in disadvantaged sectors of the labor market.

Race and Ethnicity

The U.S. labor force has become more racially and ethnically diverse since the 1970s. Whites constitute the vast majority of labor force participants, but the proportion of white workers in the labor force has decreased from 88 percent in 1980 to 84 percent in 2000 and is projected to decline further, to 75 percent, by 2050 (see table 3.1). The labor force participation of white women has leveled off since 1994, and white men's participation has declined slightly due to the availability of early retirement programs and shifts in the economy, among other factors.

Hispanics had the most dramatic increase among any racial-ethnic group, representing less than 6 percent of the labor force in 1980 and increasing to nearly 11 percent in 2000, with a projected share of nearly a quarter of the labor force by 2050.[34] Hispanic men's labor force participation rates have held steady at around 90 percent (this statistic is not shown in table 3.1), while labor force participation rates for Hispanic women are increasing due to opportunities for better education, higher divorce rates, and the growth of single-parent households. The increase in Hispanics in the labor force is in large part attributable to the recent waves of immigration (both legal and undocumented) to the United States from various Latin American countries, coupled with their relatively high fertility rates.[35]

The proportion of black or African American workers in the labor force increased slightly, from about 10 percent in 1980 to about 12 percent in 2000, and is expected to increase to about 14 percent by 2050. The fastest-growing nonwhite racial group in the United States is made up of Asians and other races, whose representation in the labor force more than doubled between 1980 and 2000 (from 2.3 percent to 4.8 percent) and is expected to represent about 11 percent of the labor force in 2050 (see table 3.1).

Whites and blacks generally work in different kinds of occupations and workplaces; this racial segregation is related to inequality in their job rewards. Whites are much more likely to be managers and supervisors, for example, and are more likely to work in white-collar, clerical occupations. Blacks, on the other hand, are more apt to work in service occupations and less-skilled, blue-collar occupations such as operatives and laborers.[36] In these jobs, blacks accumulate less skill and on-the-job training than whites who have similar levels of initial human capital, thereby making it more difficult for them to move into higher-level jobs over the course of their careers.

Race also interacts with gender. The overall participation rate for blacks has grown from 60.2 percent in 1973 to nearly 66 percent in recent years; this increase is almost entirely due to the growing participation of black women in the labor force. Black women and men also had different trajectories with regard to job quality in the twentieth century: black women obtained better jobs, while the progress of black men stalled midcentury. The proportion of black men in the labor force has declined over the past thirty years, due in part to a decline in traditional manufacturing industries and to higher incarceration rates. In 2004, nearly 20 percent of black men in their prime working years (twenty-five to fifty-four) were no longer in the labor force. By contrast, the percentage of black women in their prime working years in the labor force has steadily increased because of better education, which gives them more access to jobs, as well as an increase in households in which black women are the sole breadwinners.

The degree of racial occupational and workplace segregation declined from 1970 to 1980 but essentially stopped after 1980 (unlike occupational sex segregation, which continued to decline after 1980).[37] Researchers have also found some disturbing evidence of resegregation after 1995 in old economy sectors such as mining, construction, and durable and nondurable manufacturing. The lack of progress in integrating racial groups at work reflects the general pattern of government deregulation and the removal of institutional protections, which I described in chapter 2.

Unemployment rates by race reveal another dimension of black disadvantage: unemployment rates for black high school graduates and dropouts were about double those of comparable nonblacks between 1970 and 2000 (the unemployment rates of black and nonblack college grads were similar to each other).[38] These rates also underestimate black joblessness because they do not count prisoners; for example, the unemployment rate among African American high school dropouts would be 50 percent higher if prisoners were counted as unemployed.[39]

The racial gap in the quality and quantity of jobs is due to various factors, including the connection between race and education, segregation, higher incarceration rates, and lower life expectancies.[40] Minorities are more likely to experience disadvantages in acquiring the qualifications they need to compete for good jobs. Educational differences create discrepancies among the races and among blacks, as the comparison between the unemployment rates of college- and non-college-educated blacks suggests. The notion that educational and skill differences may explain racial differences in job quality and unemployment was introduced forcefully in *The Declining Significance of Race*, by William Julius Wilson (1978), who argued that class, primarily stemming from educational differences, has replaced discrimination as a major source of disadvantage for blacks.

But black-white race differences are not simply a product of educational inequality. Donald Tomaskovic-Devey, Melvin Thomas, and Kecia Johnson's (2005) analysis of longitudinal data from the National Longitudinal Study of Youth (NLSY) show that the gap between whites versus blacks and Hispanics is greatest at the highest levels of education.[41] This suggests that blacks and Hispanics are less able than whites to translate their educational attainments into higher-quality jobs due to discrimination and other structural factors. These findings imply that pre-labor-market investments in education and other human capital–enhancing attributes are not sufficient to explain racial differences in earnings and careers. Rather, differences in job quality are due to human capital attributes that are formed after entry into the labor market, such as experience, tenure, and on-the-job training. These forms of human capital reflect the hiring, promotion, and personnel practices of employers, which in turn contribute further to the race gap in job quality.

There are several structural reasons for patterns of racial occupational segregation and inequality in job quality. One is employment discrimination against blacks and Hispanics. A variety of explanations have been offered for this; some suggest that employers may have a "taste" for discrimination or believe that blacks and Hispanics are less productive or have fewer "soft" skills, such as motivation or "appropriate attitudes," and this leads employers to "statistically" discriminate against them. Furthermore, discrimination occurs even if people are not overtly prejudiced. For example, Devah Pager and Lincoln Quillian's (2005) study of the relations between hiring attitudes and behaviors provides a succinct but powerful description of employment discrimination; they find a low correlation between employers' expressions of their willingness to hire black ex-offenders and their actual rates of hiring them.

Another structural disadvantage for blacks and Hispanics is a lack of social capital, such as access to social networks and contacts. This keeps nonwhites—especially blacks—from finding out about and applying for many jobs. Network-based recruitment that favors members of the in-group leads to disparate employment outcomes, regardless of educational attainment, as Deirdre Royster (2003) shows in her analysis of the exclusion of black men from blue-collar jobs due to the dominance of white networks.

The "spatial mismatch" hypothesis also explains the structural disadvantage of locality. Minorities are more likely to experience disadvantages in finding desirable places to live. Douglas Massey and Nancy Denton (1993) detail the extent of segregation and race-based housing discrimination and its consequences. Minorities, especially blacks, live mainly in the inner cities and are unable to move closer to the jobs for which they are qualified. Inequalities in the housing market due to racial segregation spill over and cause inequalities in people's job opportunities. This hypothesis attributes the occurrence of racial inequality to frictions or constraints in housing and labor markets, not primarily to discriminatory behavior on the part of employers in denying jobs to blacks.[42]

Age

As table 3.1 indicates, the proportion of the labor force between the ages of sixteen and thirty-four increased from 42 percent in 1950 to 51 percent in 1980 but then declined fairly dramatically to 39 percent between 1980 and 2000. By contrast, the proportion of people age thirty-five to fifty-four increased sharply between 1980 and 2000, from 35 percent to 49 percent. The decline in the younger age group, coupled with the rise of workers in the thirty-five–to–fifty-four age group, is due in large part to the aging of the sizable cohort of baby boomers, who were born after the end of World War II.

The labor force participation rates of workers ages sixteen to thirty-four and thirty-five to fifty-four also increased since 1950. However, the labor force participation of older workers (fifty-four and over) has declined since 1970. In particular, older men have been more likely to leave the labor force in the past half-century: 80 percent of elderly men (over sixty-five) were retired in 2000, compared with 50 percent in 1950.[43]

The aging of the baby boom cohort will lead to an increase in the age of the labor force over the next several decades, especially if workers are less able to retire because of economic circumstances. The largest gains are likely to occur in the proportion of workers who are fifty-five and older (who made up 13 percent of the labor force in 2000 and are projected to be 19 percent in 2050). The aging of the U.S. population will slow the growth of the labor force, unless other factors—such as immigration—pick up the slack.

The aging of the labor force has made it more likely that workers will be underqualified for many of the jobs that are available, as older peoples' skills are more apt to become outdated due to technological changes and reorganizations taking place within workplaces.[44] It has also made retirement security a bigger factor in evaluating the quality of jobs, and it will increasingly put more pressure on government entitlement programs like Social Security. Smaller numbers of young labor market entrants may also limit future economic growth, which depends on the increase in the labor force along with an increase in productivity (that is, the amount each worker can produce in a given period). So, a major challenge for the future is to create good jobs for workers over fifty years of age and to prepare these workers for the new jobs.[45]

An increase in older workers will also impact younger workers, who have a particularly hard time finding jobs—not to mention good jobs—during recessionary periods like that of 2007 to 2009. Poor economic circumstances—such as inadequate Social Security, diminishing company pensions, and vanishing 401(k) savings plans—have led older men and women to take and stay in jobs that would otherwise have gone to younger people. So, young people are relegated to bad jobs, as well as being unemployed, underemployed (as in involuntary part-time work), overqualified, and often discouraged. Among other things, this hurts the ability of young workers to make the transition to adulthood. An increase in older workers' labor force participation also contributes to a ready supply of labor that, along with more low-skilled immigrants (see earlier discussion) has helped to expand the pool of workers who are likely to be at risk for taking low-skill, low-wage, and insecure jobs.

Implications for Job Quality

Decisions by employers to pursue particular human resource strategies or to design jobs in certain ways are facilitated or constrained by the availability of workers with particular skill levels or commitments to work. The changes in the labor force described in this chapter have several important implications for job quality.

First, education has emerged as the great divider between persons with good jobs and those with bad jobs. The workforce has become more polarized along education and skill lines due to the increasing number of highly educated college graduates, as well as the expansion in the population of low-skilled workers, such as immigrants from Mexico with weak English skills and less than a ninth-grade education. As the significance of educational divisions has grown, determinants of job quality such as gender, race, age, and region became less important over the century, though "the evidence for the declining significance of gender, ancestry, and nativity is stronger than for the declining significance of race" (Fischer and Hout 2006, 248).

Second, workers with relatively low skills and education—such as nonwhites, the foreign-born, and older workers—are more vulnerable than others to the structural changes described in chapter 2. This has encouraged employers to create jobs that pay poorly and are generally of low quality, since they now have access to a pool of workers who are willing (or forced) to work for low wages and in poor conditions: women, young people, older workers, less-educated workers, immigrants. Bad service jobs in industries such as health care, leisure and hospitality, and retail trade pay low wages and do not provide pension and health coverage; these occupations are often populated by women and especially by blacks and other minorities who have relatively low skills and little collective power. Minorities are also more likely to be unemployed and displaced from their jobs than whites. And older workers are more likely to see their skills become outdated and obsolete and thereby suffer from the effects of outsourcing and industrial restructuring.

These workers typically have low skills and human capital, can count on little or no financial support when not working, have constrained mobility (including substantial responsibility for child or elder care), and often face discrimination by employers. The higher incidence of low-wage and generally low-quality work among these disadvantaged groups is more likely in less-inclusive institutional systems such as the United States, in which individual differences in bargaining power tend to give rise to a dualistic labor market.[46]

Third, the growth in labor force diversity has increased the variety of job rewards that workers seek to obtain from their jobs. The increase of women and the associated proliferation of dual-earner families in the labor force, along with the growth in educational attainments, have altered the kinds of rewards that people feel are important in their jobs. This growth has also shaped workers' expectations for the kinds of rewards they feel entitled to obtain. In particular, many workers are now more likely to place greater importance on having more control over their work schedules and flexibility in their work times.

Some changes in the composition of the workforce—such as the increase in dual-earner families—have created mismatches between many labor force members and their needs, on the one hand, and workplace practices and labor market institutions and policies, on the other.[47] Changes in the organization of work have not kept pace with new family structures, for example. Moreover, many of our laws governing labor and employment were constructed on the assumption of a social contract between business and labor, whereby workers exchanged their effort and loyalty for relatively well-paying, secure jobs.

Our depiction of the changes in labor force composition in this chapter complements our narrative of transformations in the structural and institutional contexts of work outlined in the previous chapter. Together, these stories set the stage for our account of the correlates and consequences of polarized and precarious employment systems and the implications for changes in job quality.

— Part II —

Inequality in Job Quality

Chapter 4

Dimensions of Polarity

OLARIZING FORCES operate on both the demand side and supply side of the labor market. As discussed in chapter 2, a myriad of social, political, and economic forces have contributed to the polarization of job quality, including macrostructural influences such as globalization, the growth of price competition, the expansion of the knowledge economy, and the deregulation of markets. These forces motivated employers to search for more flexible employment systems and to restructure work. They also led to the decline of union power and the removal of institutional protections. Moreover, as outlined in chapter 3, workers have become more diverse and polarized in terms of their vulnerability to the growing marketization of employment relations; this has enabled some workers to be more successful than others in the labor market, continuing to stratify the labor market along racial and ethnic lines. Workers with more education and valuable occupational skills, in particular, have greater opportunities to move freely from one company to another and can take advantage of supply and demand mechanisms within labor markets.

These demand- and supply-side forces have led to a growing division in both economic and noneconomic job rewards, as I elaborate in chapters 6 through 9. The main mechanisms linking these labor market forces to polarization in job quality is the divergence in different kinds of work structures—that is, the institutions, regularities, and arrangements that characterize work in industrial societies. In addition to creating greater divergence among individuals, the general forces discussed in the last two chapters have led to polarization in a variety of work structures: service industries, occupations, organizations, and employment relations. In this chapter, I outline the nature and explanations of growing inequality in each of these work structures and thereby set the stage for a subsequent assessment of polarization in the various types of job rewards.

Polarization Within Service Industries

The growth of service industries is one of the hallmarks of the organization of work in the past thirty years and underlies many of the concerns about the growth of bad jobs, as discussed in chapter 2. The fear that

America was becoming deindustrialized and losing its high-wage manufacturing industries due to economic restructuring and the expansion of services industries was linked to the growth of earnings inequality, especially in the 1980s.[1] Large increases in service sector "McJobs" were taken as evidence that the growth of services and the decline of manufacturing were producing more low-wage jobs. Service industries are likely to remain a growing sector of the economy in the future, as high technology and information and knowledge services as well as personal services industries will continue to expand.

Jobs in service industries are not necessarily worse than blue-collar manufacturing jobs, however. The distribution of earnings is similar in manufacturing and service industries, indicating that the equation of manufacturing industries with high-wage jobs and service industries with low-wage jobs is overly simplistic.[2] The overall average earnings for nonsupervisory workers in manufacturing and services were also similar in the early years of this century. Moreover, the legendary alienation associated with factory jobs—a central theme in the literature on job quality and a major concern of workers in the 1960s and the early 1970s— may mean that the decline of such work is not necessarily a bad thing.

Unlike the case in traditional manufacturing industries, though, relatively low-skilled service workers are less apt to be able to obtain good jobs that are economically well compensated and relatively secure. The service sector jobs that pay well require at least a college education; this differs from the case of the comparatively low-skilled yet high-paying unionized manufacturing jobs that were available during the postwar period.

The growth of the service sector over the past three decades has led to an expansion of both high-skill, high-quality jobs and low-skill, poor-quality jobs. Financial and business services are often extremely well paid, for example, while retail and some personal service industries are not. Good jobs tend to be found in information- and knowledge-intensive fields, which produced over 9 million jobs from 1973 to 1987—nearly 30 percent of all jobs that were created during that period in the United States. Poor-quality jobs are generally found in retail sales and personal services industries and include janitors, housekeepers, sales clerks, and restaurant servers (the low-wage service sector generated 11.2 million jobs—also about a third of jobs in the United States from 1973 to 1987).[3] These trends in the growth of high- and low-wage service jobs continued into the 1990s[4] and beyond and are likely to increase in the future. The continued expansion of both good and bad jobs underscores the structural— rather than cyclical—nature of polarization in service industries.

It is likely that there is greater polarization in job quality within service industries than in manufacturing industries.[5] Most service jobs tend to be either extremely well paid or poorly paid, with relatively few jobs in the middle-income range.[6] While there is divergence among wages within manufacturing industries—for example, chemical workers are paid well, but apparel workers are not—traditional manufacturing was characterized by a preponderance of middle-income jobs due largely to the influence of unions, which were able to obtain protections and wages for their workers based on principles of seniority and collective bargaining rather than on individuals' market power.

Polarization of the Occupational Structure

Sociologists (but usually not economists) often argue that the occupational structure—that is, the relative size and average wages of different occupations—is central to explanations of inequality.[7] Recent descriptions of stratification systems, such as those based on disaggregate structuration, contend that members of detailed occupational categories are fairly homogeneous in terms of their life chances, and so economic inequalities should lie primarily between occupations, not within them.[8]

Sociologists have examined trends in the occupational structure since 1900 by looking at changes in occupational inequality in terms of Duncan's Socioeconomic Index (SEI). This measure ranks occupations on the basis of their average education and income and is highly correlated with measures of the "overall goodness" of occupations, such as prestige.[9] Fischer and Hout (2006) show that the mean SEI score for workers age twenty-five to fifty-four increased steadily over the course of the twentieth century, as occupations became more specialized and were involved in the production of services rather than goods. Moreover, they found that the gap or dispersion in SEI among occupations did not change much from 1900 to 1950, but the polarization of occupations increased from 1950 to 1970 and remained fairly wide thereafter (the trends were similar for men and women).

Changes in the relative sizes of occupational groups result from the broader trends in the restructuring of work and organizations that have occurred since the 1970s in the United States, such as the acceleration of technological innovations and globalization, discussed in chapter 2. Other trends continue long-standing patterns, like the shift from manufacturing to service industries, which was accompanied by the replacement of manual occupations by white-collar workers over the course of the twentieth century.[10]

Figure 4.1 provides a basic overview of changes within the occupational structure of the United States since the 1970s; it shows the percentage of people who worked in each of the major occupational groups in the United States in 1970 and 2000. I have arranged these major occupational groups in three clusters according to their overall levels of job

Figure 4.1   Occupational Distributions in the United States, 1970 and 2000

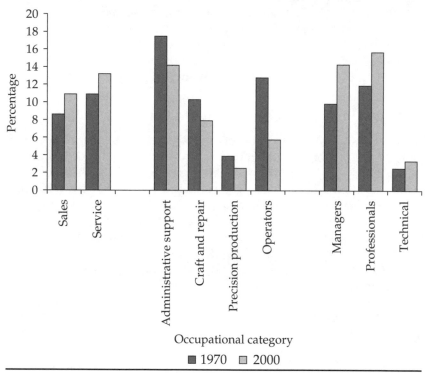

Occupational category

■ 1970   ▨ 2000

Source: Author's calculations based on data from 1970 and 2000 U.S. Censuses (Ruggles et al. 2010).

quality: on the left side of the graph are occupations generally regarded as those with the lowest-quality jobs (which have expanded from 1970 to 2000); occupations with medium-level job quality (which have declined in size) are located in the middle; and on the right side are occupations with by and large the highest-quality jobs (which have also increased in size). This pattern has continued in the post-2000 period, with jobs growing at both the top and bottom of the occupational structure.[11]

This figure illustrates the polarization of occupations—that is, the expansion of occupations at the top and bottom of the occupational hierarchy and the decline of those in the middle. Occupations that are generally regarded as good jobs, such as managers and professionals, have grown; there has also been an increase in poorly rewarded sales and service occupations. On the other hand, there has been a decline of many of the middle-class occupations of yesteryear that used to provide relatively steady, moderate earnings while requiring relatively little skill (for example, administrative support and semiskilled blue-collar occupations such as an assembly-line operative).

A number of writers have described this divergent pattern of occupational change as characterized by a "barbell" or "hourglass" pattern. Douglas Massey and Deborah Hirst (1998) found empirical support for an hourglass pattern of growth in both high- and low-paying occupations in the period of 1969 to 1989 for men but not for women; this represents a change from the 1949-to-1969 period, which exhibited an "escalator" pattern whereby people worked in progressively higher-paid occupations. Erik Olin Wright and Rachel Dwyer (2003) examined the growth and decline of jobs of varying quality during the economic expansions in the United States since the 1960s. They concluded that there was a growth of jobs in the top and bottom quintiles in the 1990s and a decline of those in the middle quintile. The expansion in the 1990s differed from the pattern of job growth in the 1980s, when there was a sharp increase in inequality due to increases at the top and bottom, but there was not a sharp decline in the middle.[12] Moreover, David Autor, Lawrence Katz, and Melissa Kearney (2006) showed that the share of total hours worked by members of both high-wage and low-wage occupations increased during the 1990s, while the employment shares of middle-wage occupations declined.[13]

There is considerable heterogeneity within these major occupation groups, however, so this scheme should be viewed only as heuristic. In particular, the quality of jobs within the same occupation may differ depending on the organizations in which the jobs are performed. Thus, the work activities (and rewards) of a physician may differ considerably depending on whether he or she works in a research lab, is a heart surgeon at a private clinic, or is a solo ob-gyn with a private practice in a rural area. Moreover, some sales occupations (such as those in financial services) are very highly paid, especially in recent years, while other sales occupations (such as cashiers) receive relatively low earnings.

Managers

The proportion of managers in the United States has increased since the 1970s, from about 10 percent of the labor force in 1970 to more than 14 percent in 2000.[14] The percentage of managers and administrators is higher in the United States than in other high-income countries: these occupational groups constituted a higher proportion of nonfarm employment in the United States in 1989 among nine countries analyzed by David Gordon (1996), and their proportion was more than three times higher than Germany's and Japan's.

The increase in managerial occupations has been especially marked among women, particularly white women: the proportion of white female managers increased from about 3 percent in 1970 to more than 8 percent in 2000, and from about 10 percent to nearly 30 percent of all managers.[15] The growth of women managers partly represents a new sex segregation principle, as women increasingly manage other women, especially in larger workplaces in the expanding service sectors of the economy. It also partly reflects a real integration of women—white women in particular— into managerial roles, side by side with white men.

The growth of management occupations is due in part to the expansion of service industries, such as the finance sector and the education and health sectors. Accordingly, specific types of management occupations that experienced high increases during this period include financial managers; managers in education and health; insurance underwriters; personnel, human resources, training, and labor relations managers; management analysts; and marketing and advertising managers.

The growth of management occupations in the United States since the 1970s seems at first blush to be inconsistent with the conventional wisdom and perceptions popularized by academics and business journalists— especially in the late 1980s through the mid-1990s—about the decline of middle management. This also appears to contradict arguments presented elsewhere in this book that downsizing and organizational restructuring have drastically reduced the layers of middle management and that there has been a trimming of the managerial component of organizations.

This apparent paradox can be explained by reference to the changing nature of managerial work. The organizational restructuring described in chapter 2 resulted in a decline in activities done internally within organizations and an expansion of external relations with other organizations, customers, partners, competitors, and investors. Moreover, managers are increasingly expected to lead and empower their subordinates rather than to exercise authority by means of command and control, especially in manufacturing and production workplaces.

These changing functions have deemphasized administrative activities within organizations. Marshall Meyer (2001), for example, demonstrates that the number of management positions increased at a much faster rate than administrative support positions between 1980 and the mid-1990s (see also figure 4.1, which shows a decline in administrative support positions) and in comparison to the workforce as a whole.

Managers are thus now more likely to be involved in strategic activities associated with organizations than in internal administrative functions. This is, in part, a consequence of the decline in the average size of organizations and the associated reductions in the amount of internal coordination required, along with the necessity for establishing and maintaining greater connections among organizations.[16] Technological advances such as computerization shaped the organization of work, making it easier to monitor and coordinate workers and reducing the administrative component of management work. This facilitated both downsizing and outsourcing and made it more feasible to substitute machines for labor and to implement new systems of management and control.[17]

The range of activities that managers are expected to do has expanded considerably from simply exercising command and control over their subordinates. Managers must now be able to anticipate and address the escalating demands placed on organizations by external constituencies such as customers, investors, and other companies. In addition, managers must increasingly negotiate relations with more knowledgeable, empowered workers within and across organizations.

Professional and Technical Occupations

The proportion of professional occupations has also increased since 1970. This growth has been especially striking among women, who have moved out of clerical occupations and into professional and technical occupations, along with managerial occupations. Professional gender integration is driven by two major factors: the educational advancement of women and the growing importance of educational certification for access to professional jobs.

This increase in the percentage of professional occupations generally reflects the expansion of the postindustrial service economy, as well as the new economy's greater emphasis on knowledge and skill. The growth of professions in the service sector (such as in health and education) is illustrated by the especially marked increases in specific occupations such as health and therapy (for example, physical therapists), veterinarians, registered nurses, physicians' assistants, special education teachers, psychologists, and social workers. The expansion of some professions also directly reflects the growing importance of knowledge and technological innovation, as seen in the particularly large increases in professional occupations, such as computer systems analysts and administrators, biological scientists, and medical scientists.

The increase in the percentage of technical occupations has been more modest; the proportion of the labor force classified as technical occupations is much smaller than all other occupational groups except for precision production. There has been some growth in technical occupations, however, which also is a manifestation of the expansion of the knowledge economy and the postindustrial society. Stephen Barley (1996) has described this expansion of technical workers as a reflection of the growth of the horizontal division of labor that results from the greater specialization of occupational activities. Technical occupations that have seen particularly big percentage increases include dental hygienists, radiological technologists, and other health technologists and technicians;

airplane pilots and navigators (though the proportion of air traffic controllers has decreased since 1990); computer software developers; and legal assistants and paralegals.

Sales and Service Occupations

The growth of the service economy has also led to the expansion of occupations that are often regarded as less desirable than managerial and professional occupations—in terms of pay or working conditions, for example. Two general occupational categories consisting of such bad jobs that increased during this period were sales and service occupations.[18] Many of these sales and service jobs are in very low-wage service industries such as retail trade and temporary services. There are, of course, often wide variations in job quality within these broad occupational categories. In particular, sales occupations in the finance sector were very highly paid by the end of the 1990s and continuing into the present century. In addition, a large proportion of some of these occupations are performed part-time, which helps to explain why the workers are paid lower wages.

Sales occupations with particularly big percentage increases between 1970 and 2000 include real estate sales, financial sales, and cashiers. These are all occupations found in the expanding service sector of the economy. Service occupations with large increases consist of guards, watchmen, and doorkeepers; cooks and chefs; nursing aides, orderlies, and hospital attendants; attendants at amusement and recreation facilities; welfare service aides; child and day care workers; public transportation attendants; and restaurant and food service occupations (such as assistants to waiters and waitresses).

The Declining Middle Occupations

Many of the occupations that have declined in size since the 1970s formed the backbone of the middle-class lifestyle during much of the postwar period. Some of these shrinking occupations, such as clerical workers, are classified as white-collar administrative support. Others are blue-collar occupations and are represented by the unionized, fairly high-paying, and often relatively low-skill occupations in mass-production industries, such as autos and steel.

The waning of these middle-class occupations reflects, in part, the downsizing of manufacturing organizations that led to a decrease in blue-collar occupations primarily in the 1980s and in white-collar occupations in the 1990s. Moreover, many of these jobs have suffered from the effects of a combination of trade and advancing technology and have been outsourced and sent overseas; these include blue-collar workers who were left behind when their manufacturing plants moved, as well as white-collar workers in technical and computer-related occupations, whose jobs were not previously at risk but which were offshored in the past decade.

Administrative support occupations that have experienced especially big percentage declines since 1970 include secretaries and administrative assistants, typists, file clerks, bookkeepers, accounting and auditing clerks, telephone operators, postal clerks (usually excluding mail carriers, a group whose size has remained fairly constant), stock and inventory clerks, meter readers, statistical clerks, and general office clerks. By contrast, the percentage of workers in some administrative support occupations has increased: teachers' aides, receptionists, customer services representatives and investigators, and bill and account collectors.

The proportion of craft and repair occupations declined in size from the 1970s to the 1980s, but has remained fairly constant since 1990. Examples of craft and repair occupations that have been reduced in size include automobile mechanics and their apprentices; farm and heavy equipment mechanics; household appliance and power tool repairers; telecommunication installers; repairers and linemen; precision makers, repairers, and smiths; office machine repairers and mechanics; millwrights; carpenters; electricians; plasterers; plumbers, pipe fitters, and steamfitters; and structural metal workers.

The precision production occupations that declined in size include tool and die makers and die setters; machinists; boilermakers; precision grinders and filers; patternmakers and model makers; dressmakers and seamstresses; tailors; shoe repairers; bookbinders; and butchers and meat cutters.

The growth of the knowledge economy is reflected more in the sharp decline in operatives (which are regarded as semiskilled) than in skilled, blue-collar occupations such as craft and repair and precision production. Low-skill and semiskilled blue-collar occupations were especially vulnerable to routinization by computers and other technological advances, which permitted employers to substitute capital for labor (see chapter 7, this volume).

Operative occupations that experienced big percentage declines include lathe, mill, and turning machine operators; punch and stamping press operators; drilling and boring machine operators; metal platers; sawyers and sawing machine operators; typesetters and compositors; textile operatives; textile sewing machine operators; shoemaking machine operators; painting machine operators; motion picture projectionists; welders and cutters; and assemblers.

Sources of Occupational Polarization

Occupational polarization results from a growing divergence in both occupational skills and power. First, occupations vary in their skills— that is, occupational activities differ in their degree of complexity and require different amounts of training time to perform them adequately. The skill level of an occupation is often measured by the average education level of its incumbents and by occupation-specific skills not captured by broad educational categories.

Technological changes and skill differences help to explain the growing polarization between high-skill occupations such as managers, professionals, and technical workers, on the one hand, and lower-skill, white-collar and blue-collar occupations, on the other. For example, the increasing use of computers has permitted managers to routinize (and de-skill) middle-level occupations, thereby reducing the wages associated with these jobs.[19] This increases inequality in both wages and autonomy between high-end jobs and routinized, middle-level jobs. Routinizing middle-level jobs also reduces inequality between these positions and low-end jobs, which are less amenable to computerization.

A second causal factor producing occupational polarization is the growing difference in the collective market power of occupational groups that enable some to exert greater control over their own work jurisdictions. Such collective market power may be derived from craft unionism, which historically organized workers in the same occupation. Craft unionism was a source of market power for occupations as disparate as highly skilled craftsmen and lower-skilled workers such as waitresses.[20] The actions of organizations, such as professional associations, may also contribute to such control. Unions and professional associations help occupations adopt and maintain institutional mechanisms of social closure such as licensing, educational credentialing, and voluntary certification.[21]

Occupational licensing has become a particularly important form of social closure in the United States in recent years. Licensing grew from about 4.5 percent in the 1950s to more than 20 percent of the workforce in the early 2000s, a period when unions declined from about a third to less than 13 percent of the workforce.[22] More than eight hundred occupations are licensed in at least one state, and approximately fifty are licensed in all states. Some of the largest licensed occupations are accountants, doctors, dentists, elementary school teachers, secondary school teachers, and cosmetologists.

In the United States, licensing controls entry into the occupation and restriction of mobility across states. Licensing increases the quality of workers in the occupation, as well as the quality of service, by diminishing the number of low-quality practitioners through testing and regulatory requirements. The licensing of particular occupational activities can also lead to the creation of job ladders or internal labor markets between firms. These occupational internal labor markets enable workers to move from one firm to another along job ladders that are associated with the progressive development of skill and knowledge.[23]

Finally, an important group of occupations—managers—are able to obtain power by virtue of their control over organizational assets, such as supervisory authority over other people, and sometimes their control of physical and monetary capital. The power of individual managers will differ depending on the size and resources of their organizations. The growing interdependence among organizations gives managers greater opportunities to develop network relationships across organizations, thereby providing them with sources of social capital that they can use to enhance their earnings, their opportunities for advancement to other companies, and other job rewards (I discuss this later in this chapter in further detail).

Within-Occupation Differences

In addition to differences between occupations, there has also been a growing polarization in job quality within occupations for part of the period since the mid-1970s. Institutional changes spurred by the need for flexibility (see chapter 2, this volume)—such as externalization of employment, decline in firm size, and increase in subcontracting within an industry—were especially salient for increasing income inequality within occupations in the 1970s and 1980s. They also helped to mediate the effects of macro-level factors on the increase in income inequality. As noted earlier, the broad category of sales occupations includes both high-end and low-end jobs: cashiers working for minimum wages as well as real estate brokers who can earn millions of dollars in commissions.

In the next two sections, I discuss polarization related to the organization of work. I first consider differences *between* firms in the employment and labor market strategies that organizations adopted in response to the competitive pressures discussed in chapter 2. These strategies represent the organizational-level changes and restructuring that resulted from their efforts to enhance flexibility. Next, I discuss differences *within* firms in the nature of the micro-level employment relations that are associated with these forms of work organization—that is, the growing division between a core of permanent workers and a periphery of more temporary workers.

The Polarization of Organizations: Corporate Restructuring via High-Road Versus Low-Road Strategies

Most firms in the United States responded to the economic transformations of the past four decades by utilizing "low-road" strategies: cutting costs by de-skilling jobs and subcontracting jobs as much as possible, as discussed in chapter 2. Some American firms, albeit a minority, adopted various forms of "high-road" labor market strategies, however. These firms sought to compete by making investments in their employees, thereby considering them as human resources rather than simply labor costs of production to be minimized.

Distinguishing between high-road and low-road strategies is, of course, an oversimplification. Many organizations used some combination of low-road and high-road strategies for different groups of workers. Such "core-periphery" or "flexible firms" use contingent workers to buffer their most valuable, core workers from fluctuations in supply and demand.[24]

Low-Road Strategies

Organizations that adopted low-road strategies emphasized cost cutting and relied on the "sticks" of coercion rather than the "carrots" of the high-road strategies.[25] The goal of these organizations was to reduce wages and to use market mechanisms to maximize profits. These organizations sought to obtain "numerical" flexibility by using nonpermanent employees that have been called variously, "contingent" (Barker and Christensen 1998; Freedman 1985; Polivka and Nardone 1989), "market-mediated" (Abraham 1990), "externalized" (Pfeffer and Baron 1988), and "nonstandard" (Blank 1998; Casey 1991).

This strategy extended the popular just-in-time production philosophy to labor and treated workers in the same way as raw materials—that is, to be added only as needed. The use of market-mediated employment relationships such as subcontracting is a modern-day manifestation of phenomena that occurred long ago; these practices were common in the United States more than a hundred years ago.[26]

Low-road organizations saw human resource policies that emphasized the internalization of labor and fixed labor costs as problematic because of the increased rapidity of change in markets and technology; swift changes meant they would need to alter production levels and skills more quickly. These organizations reduced their permanent workforce and cut out the fat, so as to become "lean and mean," using contingent workers obtained through temporary help agencies, hiring workers directly for a fixed period of time, and contracting arrangements with other companies.[27]

Organizations that have taken the low road to restructuring have tended to create longer work weeks and high stress levels for survivors, and layoffs and unemployment for those who are terminated. Workers in these organizations also tend to have fewer skills and less control over work, in addition to lower wages.

High-Road Strategies

Other organizations sought to achieve functional flexibility by adopting high-road strategies that sought to elicit the discretionary effort of their employees through the use of high-performance or high-involvement work systems. These generally provided workers with higher wages, more skills and training, greater control over their work, and the ability to participate in decisions—thus leading to more opportunities for advancement to higher-skill jobs within internal labor markets.[28] Along with these changes in work organization, high-performance work systems also included a set of associated human resource practices such as pay-for-performance, which gave workers a stake in the success of the company, as well as the assurance of employment security (or at least the promise of gaining skills that would enhance employability elsewhere).

It is difficult to assess precisely the proportion of U.S. organizations that have adopted high-performance systems.[29] Osterman (1999) reports that in the 1990s, between 20 and 33 percent of establishments had adopted substantial elements of such systems. Moreover, he found that 80 percent of establishments that had such systems in place in 1992 still had them in 1997. Organizations that adopted elements of high-road strategies tended to be relatively large and were often public or quasi-public organizations that were subject to government regulation or influence (such as hospitals and banks). These organizations were frequently in knowledge-intensive industries and occupations, and they often experienced labor shortages. The use of high-involvement work organizations was a strategy that was also particularly useful in high-value-added manufacturing operations, where it made sense to invest in human resources as opposed to cutting labor costs. However, such systems were also adopted in many service organizations, such as Southwest Airlines.[30]

Corporate restructuring toward the model of high-performance work organizations contributed to growing inequality in earnings. In such organizations, pay is typically tied to performance, thus shifting the risk to workers.[31] This in turn made pay less secure since wages vary by individual and organizational performance, as opposed to being governed by seniority and by efforts to maintain an equitable wage structure between jobs within the organization.[32]

The Core-Periphery Model

Still other organizations sought to obtain functional and numerical flexibility simultaneously. Writers have used various labels to refer to organizations' labor utilization strategies that combine numerical and functional flexibility, including the "core-periphery" model, "core-ring" configuration, "shamrock" organization, "two-tier" organization, and the "attachment-detachment" model.[33] The core-periphery model is illustrated by Japanese organizations and by Procter and Gamble, among many others.

In the core-periphery model, organizations distinguish between their core competencies and those that are more peripheral to their missions. A core of highly skilled, functionally flexible workers on fairly permanent contracts is buffered by a periphery of outsourced, temporary, part-time, and contract workers. Core, or "permanent," workers are able to acquire more firm-specific human capital, leading to higher earnings. Core-periphery models imply the use of a combination of hegemonic and despotic regimes of control within one organization.[34] According to Louis Uchitelle, "Many companies bent on cutting labor costs have adopted this corporate dichotomy, taking advantage of the growing acceptability of layoffs to peel off the outer layers" (2006, 115).

A 1996 study of high performance and flexible staffing practices based on a representative sample of U.S. organizations shows evidence of establishments' simultaneous use of numerical and functional flexibility practices.[35] Table 4.1, based on data from this study, cross-classifies 669 establishments by their use of these two flexibility strategies.[36] Nearly three-quarters (479 out of 669) of establishments used some combination of numerical flexibility strategies, such as direct hire temporaries, temporary help agencies, or contract companies. The columns of the table indicate the number of establishments that used between zero and four high-performance work practices.[37] If we consider establishments that use two or more of these practices as having functional flexibility, then 42 percent (281 out of 669) fit this description; if we use one or more high-performance practices as the criterion, then 67 percent (447 out of 669) are in this category.

Cross-classifying establishments by their use of both numerical and functional flexibility indicates that 36 percent (242 out of 669) use both forms of flexibility (using two or more high-performance work practices as the criterion of functional flexibility), while about half (333 out of 669) use numerical flexibility strategies as well as at least one high-performance work practice. These data suggest that between one-third and one-half of U.S. establishments had adopted some form of core-periphery labor utilization strategy.

Table 4.1   Models of Labor Utilization (1996 National
             Organizations Survey)

Flexible Staffing Arrangement	Number of High-Performance Work Practices					N
	0	1	2	3	4	
No[a]	76	75	25	12	2	190
Yes[b]	146	91	154	70	18	479
Total numbers of establishments (weighted)	222	166	179	82	20	669

Source: Adapted from Kalleberg (2003), with permission.
[a]Establishments use only full-time or only full-time and part-time workers.
[b]Establishments use full-time or part-time workers along with some combination of direct-hire temporaries and employment intermediaries.

Additional evidence about the popularity of the core-periphery model is provided by the fact that over half of the managers who responded to this survey said that they "agreed" or "strongly agreed" with the statement, "Your human resource management strategy divides the workforce into permanent and nonpermanent employees."

The Polarization of Employment Relations: Standard Versus Nonstandard Work Arrangements

The polarization between organizations that have adopted high-road and low-road labor market strategies is paralleled at the individual, micro level by the divergence between standard employment relations enjoyed by regular, "permanent" members of the organization's core and the nonstandard employment arrangements for temporary and peripheral workers.[38]

Nonstandard work arrangements depart from standard employment relations in several ways: administrative control over the employee is often maintained by another organization (such as a temporary help agency or contract company), and there is no norm of continued employment with the employer. Nonstandard work arrangements include temporary and contract work, involuntary part-time work, self-employment, and independent contracting. These arrangements are often equated with work that is "contingent" on the employers' needs and preferences.[39]

The growing use of nonstandard work relations has fueled a rising division between organizational insiders in the core and outsiders in the periphery. This gap between organizational insiders and outsiders is associated with greater inequality in earnings and especially in the receipt of fringe benefits like health insurance and retirement plans. The use of nonstandard workers, especially temporary workers, also puts downward pressure on the earnings of permanent workers, much in the same way as an industrial reserve army of unemployed people did in earlier periods of capitalism.

The expansion of nonstandard work arrangements such as contracting and temporary work has increased earnings inequality in part by increasing dramatically the penalty for insecure employment; for example, workers who have been displaced from their jobs are much less likely to find jobs that pay as much as their previous jobs, if they are fortunate enough to find jobs at all. Such displacement has shifted more people to the lower end of the income distribution, contributing further to the increase in inequality.[40] Nonstandard work arrangements are also disorganizing; they undermine the capacity of workers to act collectively. This hinders the capacity of labor to assert claims to wages, even in tight labor markets.

Contingent jobs—especially temporary and part-time work—are often seen as being associated with bad jobs.[41] However, aside from a general increase in insecurity, the differences in the quality of jobs associated with nonstandard work arrangements are complex. Workers in some nonstandard arrangements do very well financially, such as some freelance independent consultants and contractors, temp agency nurses, and other professionals.[42] While workers in these often "high-end," nonstandard arrangements are less likely to have fringe benefits than workers in standard arrangements, many earn higher wages than regular full-time workers in standard jobs[43] and have greater flexibility and control over their schedules, and thus may prefer to work in these arrangements.

On the other hand, temporary-help agency employees, on-call workers and day laborers, and part-time and other nonstandard laborers consistently have lower pay and no insurance or pension benefits compared with regular full-time workers. Moreover, relatively few workers in these particular nonstandard arrangements express a preference for working in these jobs.[44]

Job quality within certain kinds of nonstandard arrangements also became more polarized over the past four decades, and so it is no longer possible to equate all contingent work with bad jobs. Temporary work, for example, has been used for high-skill as well as low-skill jobs. Some employees of temporary help agencies are paid wages similar to those of regular employees. Moreover, independent contractors and contract company employees include both high- and low-paying jobs. For example, contingent jobs are found among professional workers (such as college instructors, computer programmers, managers, and even doctors) as well as in relatively low-skill, white-collar and blue-collar occupations (for example, administrative, clerical, secretarial, and laborer jobs and jobs in wholesale and manufacturing industries).

The distinction between standard and nonstandard work arrangements is also an important form of polarization even in relatively inclusive employment regimes. In Germany, for example, a growing dualism and polarization stemmed from changes in social norms, such as those associated with the rise in female labor force participation. Polarization in Germany also arose from the retrenchment of protective institutions; greater numbers of employers exited and opted out from collective bargaining agreements, and unions made concessions due to rising unemployment. The forms of dualism also vary among countries. The tendency toward dualism in Germany, for example, is strongest between regular employees and mini-jobbers; in the Netherlands, inequalities are strongest between part-time and full-time employees; and in France, it is between civil servants and contract workers in public hospitals.[45]

In response to the growing polarization between standard and nonstandard workers, the European Union has issued directives that provide for equal treatment and nondiscrimination against nonstandard work. Toward the end of the 1990s, there were two such directives—one for part-time workers and one for fixed-term contracts.[46] By contrast, there are no specific regulations in the United States (other than general antidiscrimination laws); thus part-time work is extensively used by employers in some sectors (such as retail) as an exit option, since fringe benefits are lower for part-timers.

In practice, workers in nonstandard work arrangements are often disadvantaged in Europe as well as in the United States. In France, for example, almost 30 percent of all unskilled, blue-collar workers are employed on temporary contracts, and they often do not receive much legal protection. Many are on less-protected contracts (such as seasonal or derogatory fixed-term contracts), and employers do not always follow their legal obligations—for example, in hotels and retail, where unionization is low. The Netherlands has a high proportion of laborers from temporary help agencies, and these temporary workers have fewer rights than permanent workers.[47]

Polarizing Workers

Workers can acquire power relative to employers and other workers either collectively or individually, as discussed in chapter 2. Earlier, I argued that there has been a decline in collective union power and a related erosion of institutional protections for workers due to the rollback of the government regulations and labor market standards that unions once helped to establish. On the other hand, my discussion of occupational licensing points to a type of collective worker power that has been on the increase, though this type of power is available to only about a fifth of the labor force.

The growing importance of market mechanisms and the low levels of collective power have made it more and more necessary for each person to look out for him or herself in the labor market. The ideological shifts toward greater individualism that I discuss in chapter 2 illustrate the reality that people are now, more than ever, "on their own." In the new market-mediated employment relationships, workers' success depends primarily on themselves, not on collective sources of power such as unions or on protections afforded by labor laws or other government regulations. Marketization has impacted different groups of workers in different ways, however: some persons are able to take advantage of the greater opportunities for achievement in the market, while others are especially vulnerable to market forces and insecure employment relations.[48]

A way of differentiating workers with regard to their ability to take advantage of labor market opportunities is their degree of *market power*, or the extent to which they are able to control the terms of their employment, as opposed to being vulnerable to the market. The sources of workers' market power or degree of control over their employment situations are rooted in their possession of skills that are in high demand and are highly valued and marketable (human capital), as well as their network connections and memberships in various kinds of social groups (social capital), which allow them to learn about and acquire good jobs. Workers who have high human and social capital are likely to be more sheltered from the market because they hold a strong bargaining position due to their greater skills or various sources of job property rights. Such workers have more chances to become free agents and to develop their careers by exploiting the growing opportunities in the emergent "winner-take-all" labor markets for their valued skills. By contrast, workers without valued skills and social capital are less able to protect themselves from the market and thus are more vulnerable to it. This situation is analogous to the ideology of social Darwinism, popularized by Herbert Spencer and William Graham Sumner at the turn of the twentieth century, which applied Darwin's idea of survival of the fittest to the human economic and social realm.[49]

The differential ability of workers to take advantage of labor market opportunities has created a polarization between the market "winners," who have benefited from the growth of good jobs—and may also have gotten "rents," or better jobs than they deserve based on their skills and performance—and the market "losers," who have experienced a decline in job quality, including reduced opportunities for earnings and wage growth, less control over their work activities and schedules, and greater work intensification.[50]

The Growing Importance of Skills and Education

The greater importance of skills for labor market success is rooted in a number of the changes in work that I have discussed in chapter 2. In particular, the development of new technologies (such as computers) has reinforced and contributed to the growing gaps between high-skilled and low-skilled jobs and workers. The expansion of knowledge-intensive industries has generally placed a premium on knowledge and skills, emphasizing differences among jobs in their skill and education requirements. Semiskilled jobs have become routinized as employers have used technology, particularly computers, to replace people with machines whenever possible.[51]

The increasing importance of education as a differentiating factor within the labor force is consistent with this greater emphasis on skills. General, portable skills that can be used in a variety of settings have become especially important in the new economy due to the rapidity of technological change, while firm-specific knowledge and skills have arguably become less valuable.

The growing salience of education is reflected in the rise in the college premium—relative to high school—in the 1980s and 1990s, which I discuss further in chapter 6.[52] More education also offers some limited protection from uncertainty. Insecure employment is strongly patterned by education, for example, since those with higher levels of education have lower displacement rates, as we will see in chapter 5.[53]

The growth of precarious work has made educational decisions risky, however. The uncertainty and unpredictability of future work opportunities makes it hard for students to make plans for their education; they must decide, for example, which is the best subject to major in to ensure occupational success. Moreover, parents' economically precarious situation (even for those who are employed full-time) may make them less able to invest in their children's education, so children themselves may need to provide more of their educational costs, leading to greater debt upon graduation from college—that is, if they are able to attend college at all.[54] Opportunities to learn and maintain job skills to keep up with changing job requirements are also perilous, and many workers will be hard pressed to identify ways of remaining employable in a fast-changing economic environment in which skills become rapidly obsolete. Unlike workers of the 1950s and 1960s, workers are more likely to need to engage in lifelong learning and to return to school again and again to retool their skills as they shift careers.

Although educational attainment cannot guarantee a good job, higher levels of education make acquiring a better job more likely, and the lack of education is certainly a major disadvantage in the new labor market. Investments in education have been described as being more like buying stocks than buying a meal ticket, since education often comes with debt and exposes workers to big risks if the field in which they are trained loses demand.[55]

Social Capital

Another important source of market power is a person's social capital. This is an umbrella concept that is generally defined as the resources embedded within social relationships.[56] It refers to the ability of actors to obtain benefits by virtue of their membership in social structures, such as social networks.[57]

Social capital is both an individual asset and a resource that is controlled by the collective.[58] It is acquired by membership in organized groups such as unions. While the decline in unions has removed this source of protection from the market for most workers in the private sector, unions are still a source of social capital in the public sector. Other sources of social capital are organized groups, such as occupational associations and other licensing bodies, that provide workers with valuable credentials and greater market power.

Workers also acquire power in and protections from the labor market by acquiring social capital such as network connections, which help persons to locate and obtain good jobs. There is now an extensive empirical literature in sociology on the importance of social networks in acquiring information about jobs and being hired in them; the vast bulk of these studies focus on the supply side of the labor market, adopting the point of view of the worker and the worker's social relations.[59]

Sociologists have long documented that people tend to associate with those who are similar to them. Social ties thus tend to be homophilous and reinforce one's advantages and disadvantages in the labor market. For example, the extent to which one has well-developed social networks that are effective in job acquisition is closely related to one's race; whites are generally better able to secure good jobs based on their network contacts. In this way, differences in social capital serve to perpetuate racial inequality.

Conclusions

In this chapter, I have outlined how social and economic forces associated with several different types of work structures have led to greater polarization among jobs and workers. The dynamics of polarization associated with different work structures affect some types of job rewards more than others. For example, the polarization of the occupational structure is intimately related to the growth of earnings inequality. On the other hand, the divergence between high-road and low-road organizational restructuring has direct implications for the polarization in the degree of autonomy and control workers have over their jobs and tasks. Moreover, the growing polarization among occupations within service industries is apt to be linked closely to inequality in the degree of flexibility that workers have over their work schedules.

In the next chapter, I consider the other major change in the nature of employment systems since the 1970s: the growth of precarious employment relations.

= Chapter 5 =

Precarious Employment
Relations

T HE CHANGES in macroscopic and mesoscopic work structures and
contexts discussed in chapter 2 have transformed the rules, laws,
and shared norms that govern the microscopic employment relationships between employers and their employees. Employment relations
have become more precarious and uncertain, and workers have generally
become more insecure. This trend has permeated throughout the occupational structure and the life course, affecting both young and older workers. At the same time, there are important variations in the nature and
extent of this increase in precarious work and insecurity. As I discuss in
chapter 3, whether these changes have been a source of opportunity or
vulnerability for employees depends on their education, skills, gender,
family situation, race, immigration status, and age.

This chapter provides an overview of the main changes that have taken
place in employment relations since the mid-1970s. I first describe the
transformation from closed to market-mediated or open employment
relationships and the dimensions of these open employment relations. I
review the idea of social and psychological contracts and the difference
between precarity and uncertainty. I then summarize some of the empirical evidence on whether there has been a transformation of employment
relations. This evidence includes the growth and institutionalization of
nonstandard employment relations, the decrease in job stability, a decline
in firm internal labor markets, growth of long-term unemployment,
greater perceptions of insecurity that are unrelated to the business cycles,
and the shifting of risks from employers to workers. Taken as a whole,
these objective and subjective indicators suggest strongly that there has
been a growth of precarious work in the United States since the 1970s.

Changing Employment Relations

Employment relations represent the dynamic social, economic, psychological, and political relationships between individual workers and their
employers.[1] Employment relations are the main means by which workers

in the United States have obtained rights and benefits associated with work with respect to labor law and social security. These relations differ in the relative power of employers and employees to control tasks, negotiate the conditions of employment, and terminate a job.[2]

Employment relations are useful for studying the connections among macro-, meso-, and micro-levels of analysis because they explicitly link individual workers to their workplaces and other institutions wherein work is structured. Employment relations are embedded in other social institutions, such as the family, education, politics, and the health care sector. They are also intimately related to gender, race, age, and other demographic characteristics of the labor force.

The Growth of Market-Mediated, Open Employment Relationships

The combination of corporate restructuring driven by employers' search for greater flexibility and profits and the decline in collective worker power, along with the erosion of institutional protections for workers, led to a growing marketization and individualization of employment relations in the United States. Employment relations have become increasingly market-mediated since the 1970s; market solutions have been substituted for administrative rules, and market mechanisms are now more likely to affect employers' decisions regarding employees' job security and earnings. Labor market mechanisms have also become the main source of judgment about a worker's economic value and exert a greater influence on firms' internal administrative policies regarding how much control workers are able to exercise over their jobs.[3] Labor market mechanisms also increasingly influence the movement of workers from one firm to another.

Market-mediated employment relations are often called "open" employment relationships since they are based on free market forces and competition and are associated with relatively weak labor market institutions, standards, and regulations.[4] The centrality of market mechanisms makes individuals' resources—education, human capital, experience, and social origins, for example—more vital sources of their power in labor markets. Open employment relations may be contrasted with "closed" employment relations, which are characterized by strong institutional protections derived from unions or firm internal labor markets.

The growth of market-mediated employment relations has altered two key features of the employment relationship. First, open employment relationships sever the psychological contract between employers and employees in which stability and security were exchanged for loyalty and hard work: the employee would exchange his or her loyalty and commitment in return for employers' promises of job security, earnings growth, and opportunities for advancement.[5] The psychological contract was characterized by mutual trust and expectations about each other's obligations and duties. Employers are now more likely to terminate the employment relation if business conditions warrant cutbacks through practices such as downsizing, in an attempt to enhance effectiveness, short-term profitability, and other outcomes, as discussed in chapter 2. Employees too are more likely to leave the firm in order to take advantage of better job opportunities elsewhere. Evidence of the breakdown of the psychological contract is provided by anecdotes in which employers reportedly tell their workers that their only real source of security is "employability," or their ability to find a job elsewhere.[6]

Second, the market-mediated or open employment relations are characterized by a breakdown of the post–World War II social contract between capital and labor. This collective arrangement between business and unions, which I discussed in chapter 2, stabilized employment relations, providing workers with job protections in the form of job property rights or closed employment relationships.[7] This led to greater job security for workers and provided progressively greater earnings and opportunities for advancement in the post–World War II period of economic growth in the United States. The dissolution of the social contract—reflected in the decline of unions, which enabled employers to have freer rein to change the terms of the employment relation—also helped to disband the psychological contract.

The demise of the old psychological and social contracts is reinforced by a normative context that legitimizes a more individualistic relationship and a decline of collective power. There is also a general decline in job security for all workers due to shifting norms of the employment contract. Employers are now less likely to be able to promise their employees security since their organizations are themselves more insecure. Employers may also not be inclined to offer employees security in exchange for loyalty and hard work since norms regarding the nature of the employment relationship have changed, and there are more options for employers to hire workers on an as-needed basis, such as through temporary help agencies and contract companies. There has thus been a decrease in the norm of lifetime employment with an employer.

The extent to which employment relations have become marketized or externalized beyond the boundaries of the firm has sometimes been overstated and misunderstood. Not all employment relations have become externalized, of course, and there are still numerous examples of the persistence of closed employment relations, such as the numerous professional employees or unionized workers who have long-term contracts with employers. Moreover, the kinds of changes discussed here have also led to a transformation of the relations between employers and employees *within* firms. Patrick McGovern and his colleagues (2008), for example, outline the changes that have taken place in the internalization—as well as the externalization—of employment relations in the United Kingdom—and to some extent in the United States—as a result of increasing pressures on employers to enhance their flexibility. The growth of high-performance work practices, discussed in the last chapter, illustrates some of these changes in internal organizational arrangements.

Second, the growth of open employment relations is not new, since these relationships were common prior to the institutionalization of social protections enacted during the New Deal in the 1930s. Indeed, the use of subcontracting, contingent work, unchecked managerial discretion in employment decisions, and pay increases were common in the United States in the early 1900s, before the development of modern internalized employment practices.[8] So, too, were practices such as making security contingent on performance and the absence of a psychological contract that traded security for loyalty. Moreover, even after the economy recovered after World War II and there was greater stability in the 1950s, this prosperity generally excluded nonwhite males, who were often in precarious employment relations.

Dimensions of Market-Mediated Employment Relationships

The new open or marked-mediated relationship between employers and employees has several notable characteristics.

First, employment relations have become more precarious and insecure. Insecurity for workers is the "dark side" of employers' attempts to increase their flexibility. Employment relations are now "less like marriage and dating than serial monogamy" (Cappelli 1999, 35). The decline in job security is generally assumed to have begun in the late 1970s and 1980s, due to the slowdown in economic growth; jobs were generally more insecure from the 1980s to the present than in the 1970s. This decline in job security should be evaluated in context, however. Compared with the Great Depression, for example, the state of the labor market was not so bad in the period beginning in the mid-1970s—at least until the Great Recession of 2007 to 2009 and its aftermath. What makes the current period of insecurity especially problematic, though, is that it represents a discontinuity with the thirty-year period of shared prosperity in the United States following World War II. The growth of job insecurity is especially problematic in this country since Americans have traditionally placed great importance on the search for job security and the belief in opportunity;[9] moreover, the absence of a strong safety net makes the experience of unemployment especially challenging.

Second, job insecurity and the macro forces that have led to it—such as globalization and technological innovation—have increased the uncertainty that both employers and workers face when planning their futures. Paul Krugman calls this the "age of anxiety."[10] Michael Mandel (1996, 160) argues that job insecurity is "the single largest cause of uncertainty in the high-risk society" and is calculated as the odds of losing a job times the economic and psychological impact of actual job loss. And John Gray (1998, 110) describes America as "a society in which anxiety pervades the majority. For most Americans, the ledge of security on which they live has not been so narrow since the 1930s."

Employees' decisions about which skills and occupations they should invest their time and resources in are accompanied by employers' hesitation about what kinds of training to provide. The lack of continuity of employment relationships works against generating an ongoing social relationship between an employer and employee. This uncertainty also makes it difficult for people to create a life narrative out of work, resulting in a sense of aimlessness and inadequacy, which "corrodes one's character" and loosens the bonds of human beings to one another.[11]

The greater insecurity and uncertainty in employment relations have spread to the labor force as a whole, creating an equality of insecurity and uncertainty.[12] Aside from U.S. Supreme Court justices and tenured faculty members, virtually all jobs are now more unstable as insecurity permeates the entire occupational structure. Even good jobs that pay well and provide opportunities for control and intrinsic rewards have become more insecure and stressful.[13] Protections that white-collar workers have historically thought they had are now under attack, as evidenced in the increased numbers of layoffs of white-collar workers. The popular media has profiled many people who formerly had good jobs—such as those in middle management positions or with professional jobs at dot-com startups—who have become unemployed. All of these jobs are likely to have gotten more insecure and unstable, though low-skilled workers are particularly vulnerable.[14]

This equality of insecurity differs from previous eras, when precarious work was often described in terms of a dual labor market, with unstable and uncertain jobs concentrated in a secondary labor market.[15] Indeed, precarity and insecurity were used to differentiate jobs in the primary as opposed to secondary labor market segments. Now, precarious work has spread to all sectors of the economy and has become much more pervasive and generalized: professional and managerial jobs are just as precarious these days as low-end jobs.

The growing pervasiveness of job insecurity and uncertainty is not restricted to the United States; it constitutes a global challenge. All industrial countries are faced with the basic problem of balancing security (due to precarity) and flexibility (due to competition), the two dimensions of Polanyi's (1944) "double movement." Moreover, the widespread nature of job insecurity is not unique to the United States. In Britain, for example, job insecurity was restricted to blue-collar workers, ethnic minorities, and nongraduates until the mid-1970s. This polarization had either been reduced or had completely disappeared by the mid-1990s; for example, professionals in Britain went from having high security in the mid-1980s to high insecurity in the mid-1990s.[16]

While all workers are likely to experience uncertainty, people differ in their vulnerability to precarious work depending on their personality dynamics, levels and kinds of education, age, family responsibilities, type of occupation and industry, and the degree of welfare and labor market protections in a society.[17] The consequences of job insecurity are especially severe for people who do not have the marketable skills that employers value or that would help them to find new jobs if they are laid off, as I discuss in chapter 4. Moreover, as noted in chapter 3, minorities are more likely than whites to be unemployed and displaced from their jobs, and older workers are more likely to suffer from the effects of outsourcing and industrial restructuring. Hence, not everyone may be equally anxious due to uncertainty; those whose skills are in demand may even see the growth of precarious and uncertain work as a chance to take advantage of the expansion of opportunities in a more open labor market.

The third feature of the market-mediated or open employment relationship is a transfer of risks away from employers and toward workers—a move that is seen by some writers as the key feature of precarious work.[18] The growth of contingent work illustrates aspects of the growth of the "risk society." Globalization and other sources of pressures on employers have encouraged them to shift risks associated with the employment relationship (such as fixed costs) to employees, and they have been able to do so due to declines in worker protections. Employers have also shifted to employees the responsibility for acquiring skills that may make them more employable in other organizations. In addition to this, corporate restructuring has tended to make job security (as well as other job rewards, such as wages) more contingent on performance. This has made middle managers, in particular, go from being one of the most secure occupations to one of the least, as organizations continue to downsize their ranks and cut out supervisory positions.[19]

These basic changes in the nature of employment relations—the growing influence of labor market mechanisms, insecurity, uncertainty, and risk-shifting from employers to employees—help to explain changes in the quality of jobs for various groups within the labor force. Labor market mechanisms contributed to making some workers' skills more valuable (and rewarded) than others. These mechanisms, along with the insecurity and uncertainty they help create, also made earnings more unstable and volatile. The shifting of risks from employers to employees also accounts for the decline in employer-provided health insurance and the transition from defined-benefit to defined-contribution pension plans.

Evidence of Growth in Precarious Employment Relations

There is widespread agreement that work and employment relations have changed in important ways since the 1970s. Still, there is some disagreement as to the specifics of these changes. Studies of individual organizations, occupations, and industries often yield different conclusions than do analyses of the economy as a whole. Peter Cappelli (1999, 113) observes that

> those who argue that the change [in labor market institutions] is revolutionary study firms, especially large corporations. Those who believe the change is modest at best study the labor market and the workforce as a whole. While I have yet to meet a manager who believes that this change has not stood his or her world on its head, I meet plenty of labor economists studying the aggregate workforce who are not sure what exactly has changed.

The prominence in the media of examples such as automobile manufacturing and other core industries where precarity and instability have certainly increased might account for some of the differences between the perceived wisdom of managers and the results obtained from data on the overall labor force.

The lack of availability of systematic, longitudinal information on the nature of employment relations and organizational practices also makes it difficult to evaluate just how much change has really occurred. The U.S. government and other agencies such as the International Labour Organization often collect data on phenomena only after they are deemed to be problematic.[20] For example, the Bureau of Labor Statistics' (BLS) Current Population Survey (CPS)[21] did not count displaced workers who are involuntarily terminated from their jobs until the early 1980s, and did not systematically collect information on different nonstandard work arrangements and types of contingent work until 1995.[22] Moreover, the Current Population Survey's measure of employee tenure changed in 1983, making it difficult to evaluate changes in job stability using this measure. There is also a paucity of longitudinal panel data on the same organizations and employees—information that might otherwise shed light on the mechanisms that are producing precarity and other changes in employment relations.[23]

Moreover, a key dimension of precarious employment relations—job insecurity—is difficult to measure directly, though it can be studied indirectly in various ways using a variety of data sets and population definitions.[24] Labor economists have tended to focus on job stability and instability, utilizing indicators such as job displacements and involuntary job loss, unemployment, and employer job tenure. Sociologists and psychologists have focused more on subjective measures, such as workers' perceptions of their job security and fear of job loss. Analysts employing these different approaches have often come to divergent conclusions.

Despite these limitations on available quantitative data, the evidence from a variety of diverse indicators—both objective and subjective—that are reviewed in the following sections nevertheless generally support the view that there has been an increase in overall job insecurity in the labor force during the past quarter century in the United States.

The Growing Importance of Nonstandard Work Arrangements and Contingent Work

The expansion of nonstandard work arrangements—and the associated decline in social and psychological contracts—are in themselves evidence of a general increase in job insecurity.[25]

Data from a representative sample of U.S. establishments collected in the mid-1990s indicated that over half of them externalized or outsourced some of their activities to various employment intermediaries.[26] Examples of outsourcing in specific sectors illustrate the pervasiveness of this phenomenon: food and janitorial services; accounting; routine legal work; medical tourism; military activities (for example, the use of mercenary soldiers like the employees of Blackwater in Iraq); and immigration enforcement duties (which were outsourced to local law enforcement officials as a result of Homeland Security's 287(g) program).[27] The key threat of outsourcing is that virtually all jobs are vulnerable to it, including high-wage, white-collar jobs that were once seen as safe. Moreover, a large portion of jobs can also be offshored, except perhaps those that cannot be delivered electronically or are notably inferior if so delivered, such as jobs requiring personal contact (for example, home health care, maids, hospital care workers, and massage therapists).[28] The other kinds of work that are unlikely to be digitized and therefore outsourced are high-end jobs such as teaching elementary school or selling mansions to millionaires.[29]

The temporary-help agency sector increased at an annual rate of over 11 percent from 1972 to the late 1990s. Its share of U.S. employment grew from under 0.3 percent to nearly 2.5 percent in 1998; by contrast, total non-farm employment grew at a rate of 2 percent during this period.[30] When the stock bubble burst in the early 2000s, the percentage of temporary-help industry employment fell slightly (to 2 percent of private employment) but increased again as the economy picked up.[31] The proportion of temporary workers remains a relatively small portion of the overall labor force, but the institutionalization of the temporary help industry increases precarity since it makes all workers potentially replaceable by temporary employees.

Nonstandard work arrangements have increasingly spread throughout the labor force in both high- and low-skill jobs.[32] Even the halls of academia are not immune from the temping of America: the percentage of full-time, tenured, and tenure-track faculty in academia declined between 1973 and 2005, while the percentage of full-time, non–tenure-track and part-time faculty increased.[33] Evidently, the occupation Stanley Aronowitz (2001) called "the last good job in America"—the college professor—is becoming precarious too, with likely negative long-term consequences, such as reductions in teacher quality.

The growing importance of contingent and other nonstandard work arrangements led to a clamor to obtain good measures of their incidence and distribution among various occupations, industries, and groups of people in the labor force. Accordingly, in 1995 the Bureau of Labor Statistics began to collect a supplement to the February CPS in order to gather and monitor ongoing data on contingent work every two years.

Figure 5.1 provides estimates from these CPS surveys of the number of employed Americans who worked in four kinds of nonstandard work arrangements: employees of temporary help agencies, employees of contract companies, independent contractors (who are generally self-employed), and on-call workers (who are called to work by employers on an "as needed" basis, such as substitute teachers).

Fewer than 2 million workers were employed by temporary help agencies and contract companies, and the sizes of these groups seem to be relatively constant between the time of the original survey in 1995 and the latest survey in 2005. The number of on-call workers was slightly greater in 2005, with over 2 million workers. The number of independent contractors, on the other hand, appeared to increase over the past six years and now stands at more than 10 million workers. The trends in these nonstandard work arrangements thus appear to be relatively flat, except perhaps for independent contractors. This conclusion is somewhat misleading, however, as the main increases in temporary-help agency employment

Figure 5.1   Trends in Nonstandard Employment Relations, 1995 to 2005

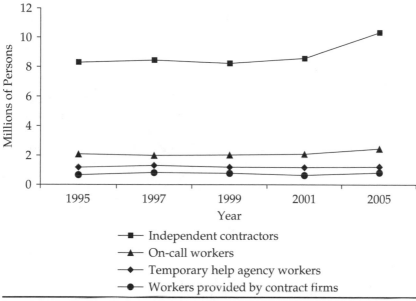

Independent contractors

On-call workers

Temporary help agency workers

Workers provided by contract firms

Source: Author's compilation of data from U.S. Department of Labor (1995, 1997, 1999, 2001, 2005).

and the other forms of nonstandard work are likely to have occurred before 1995.[34]

The overall proportion of American workers in these kinds of nonstandard work arrangements that were in contingent jobs declined from 4.9 percent in 1995 to 4.1 percent in 2005; this was the BLS's broadest estimate.[35] This decline may reflect the tight labor markets in the United States during this period: in periods of relatively low unemployment, employers try to hold on to valued employees by providing them with more incentives to remain. Of course, retention strategies are complicated by the declining trust that employees have in their employers as a result of the greater precarity of employment relations and the deterioration of psychological contracts.

It is also the case that the weak employment protection that characterizes the United States (and other liberal market economies, such as the United Kingdom) is associated with relatively low levels of temporary employment. Employers in these countries have fewer incentives to offer fixed-term, temporary contracts since employment protections for permanent workers are relatively weak. By contrast, in countries where employment protections are strong, such as France and Spain, there are very high levels of temporary workers since employers are reluctant to hire permanent workers that they will have difficulty shedding.

Moreover, we should also keep in mind that the rise of nonstandard work arrangements like temporary work and contracting has been accompanied by a general increase in the insecurity of employment relations for all workers, in both high- and low-skill jobs. Even among workers who continue to work full-time with their employers on standard employment contracts, the greater incidence of downsizing and related human resource practices has made their employment more precarious. In the United States, employment protection is weak for the vast majority of workers who are employees "at will," except for the relatively small number of union members (especially in the private sector) and some well-paid professionals with individual employment contracts.

The Decline in Attachment to Employers

An important indicator of behavioral changes in the nature of employment relations is job stability. This is most commonly measured by employer tenure, or the length of time a person has worked for a particular employer.[36] Studies of employer tenure have generally used data from the CPS.[37] The CPS data contain the most extensive data series on employer tenure—although, unfortunately, changes in the wording of the job tenure question in 1983 made it difficult to infer trends before and after that date.[38] By 1983, the "age of layoffs" was already under way, so comparisons from that date forward are likely to underestimate the decline in tenure.[39]

Early studies often found that employee tenure has remained relatively constant since the early 1970s. This was a surprising and counterintuitive result, since speculation about the consequences of the growth of contingent work arrangements, downsizing, and layoffs would suggest a decline in job stability. Francis Diebold, David Neumark, and Daniel Polsky (1997), using CPS data, found that job retention rates were fairly stable over the 1980s and early 1990s; additionally, the exchange between Diebold, Neumark, and Polsky (1996) and Kenneth Swinnerton and Howard Wial (1996) seemed to support the view that there was not a decrease in job stability during the period of 1979 to 1991. Similarly, Peter Auer and Sandrine Cazes (2003) found that there was a relatively high level of stability in rates of employer tenure in the United States, the European Union, and Japan.

The apparent constancy found in some studies masks divergent trends for different subgroups of the population, however.[40] Men experienced a decline in their median number of years with employers, from

5.9 years in 1983 to 5.1 in 2004. On the other hand, average job tenure has steadily increased for women, from 4.2 years in 1983 to 4.7 years in 2004. For men, about 38 percent had ten or more years of employer tenure in 1983, declining to about 32 percent in 2004; for women, this increased from about 25 percent in 1983 to about 29 percent in 2004.

The importance of education for differentiating workers with regard to their job stability was also reinforced in several studies. Henry Farber (1998a) had that the prevalence of long-term jobs had not declined but that less-educated men were less likely to hold long-term jobs than previously, and there was a substantial increase in the proportion of women who held long-term jobs.[41] Diebold, Neumark, and Polsky (1997) found declines in job retention rates for high school dropouts and high school graduates relative to college graduates (especially for the youngest workers); these groups also experienced the sharpest relative wage declines during the period.

People of different age groups also had different job tenure rates.[42] Job instability increased in the 1990s for white males with long job tenure, blacks, and young adults. There were substantial declines in job tenure for men in their prime working years of thirty-five to sixty-four, but not for women. In 1983, 58 percent of men age forty-five to forty-nine had been with their current employer for ten years or more; by 2004, the comparable figure was 48 percent.[43]

The most recent studies of this topic have concluded that there has indeed been a general decline in the average length of time a person spends with his or her employer. This varies by specific subgroup: women's employer tenure has generally increased, while men's has decreased (though tenure levels for women remain substantially lower than those for men in the private sector). The decline in employer tenure is especially pronounced among older white men, the group that had been most protected by internal labor markets in the past.[44] In a 2005 study, Auer also found that the average employer tenure in the United States declined over the 1990s, and employer tenure was less in the United States than in the other countries studied.[45] By the beginning of January 2005, Neumark, a main proponent of the view that employer tenure rates were stable, had changed his views. He concluded, "I think there are a lot of indications that say the employment situation has changed. . . . We are finding that the people who used to be in the most secure jobs are experiencing less stability."[46]

The Weakening of Firm Internal Labor Markets

The study of job mobility has long been on the forefront of the social science research agenda on the organization of work and social stratification. Theories of labor market segmentation assumed that job immobility was an indicator of whether or not one was placed in secondary labor markets, as disadvantaged workers were trapped in dead-end, bad jobs.

Opportunities for advancement or promotion to better jobs may occur with a given employer or by moving from one employer to another. Within organizations, movement from one job to another constitutes a key indicator of the successful operation of firm internal labor markets (FILMs), the main structures by which employers in relatively large organizations provide "carrots" to motivate workers by promising opportunities for upward mobility. Firm internal labor markets are also useful for transmitting skills by having workers climb job ladders, a practice within firms that is associated with the progressive development of skill and knowledge.[47] The opportunity to participate in firm internal labor markets was a hallmark of the long-term, standard employment relations that exemplified the three decades of economic growth following World War II.

The growing competitive pressures on firms and the rapidity of technological and social changes discussed in chapter 2 suggest that FILMs are likely to have been dismantled along with the dissolution of psychological contracts between employers and their employees and the greater exposure of employment relations to the external labor market.[48] The forces underlying economic restructuring have made it less desirable and feasible for employers to treat their employees as fixed costs and to guarantee them opportunities for long-term employment and opportunities for upward mobility. Consistent with the model of risk-shifting, employers are more likely to encourage their employees to invest in their own training, so as to make them more valuable to the current employer, though this is also likely to make them more employable and attractive to other employers as well.

Some social scientists have questioned the extent to which FILMs were ever the dominant organizational form of employment.[49] For example, some researchers have calculated that organizations need a minimum of five hundred employees to make formal, job evaluation–based compensation systems feasible. The majority of establishments in the United States currently have fewer than twenty-five employees, which is too small a number to sustain elaborate arrangements such as job ladders and seniority-based promotion systems.[50] So, it might be the case that FILMs were characteristic of large firms, but were not the modal form by which careers typically unfolded in the labor force. Cappelli (1999, 114) estimates that about 10 percent of the private-sector workforce is a ballpark figure for the proportion of employees who might have participated in the lifetime-career employment system; these are managerial employees in firms large enough to have reputations. There have been dramatic changes in this segment of the workforce, though the changes in the overall workforce are less striking since most workers never had such long-term, internal employment relations.

Several pieces of indirect evidence suggest that there has, in fact, been a decline in firm internal labor markets. First, there has been an increasing tendency for employers to hire workers from outside the organization rather than to develop the human capital of their employees internally. For example, the proportion of managers hired from the external market rather than being promoted from within the organization has increased dramatically since the 1950s.[51]

Moreover, an analysis of the CPS data shows that since the late 1970s, there has been an increase in the external hiring of experienced men (between the ages of thirty and sixty-five), restricted almost entirely to large firms with more than one thousand employees, especially since the mid-1990s. By contrast, there was little change in the proportion of workers hired by medium-sized firms, as well as a decline in the propensity of the smallest firms to hire from the outside.[52] In addition, Matthew Bidwell (2010) finds that the increase in external hiring is due to the weakening of union pressures, supporting the view that unions play an important role in pressuring firms to construct firm internal labor markets, in part through unions' support of personnel professionals within organizations.

Second, it appears that firm hierarchies are becoming flatter, thereby reducing the number of positions in the organization to which employees are able to move. A study by Raghuram Rajan and Julie Wulf (2006) using panel data on over three hundred large firms found that the number of levels between division heads and the CEO has decreased since the 1980s; more managers report directly to the CEO, and companies have mostly dispensed with intermediate managers.

Third, while most large companies have some sort of bidding and posting system for moving persons among jobs within the organization, these systems tend to be directed by employees (that is, they themselves apply for posted vacancies) and do not appear to display the orderly career movement that characterized employer-directed firm-internal labor markets.[53] A community college president in Michigan has described such advancement as rock climbing rather than a rung-by-rung, clear, linear progression.[54] Such internal bidding systems are consistent with the observation that "career jobs remain, but lifetime guarantees—formal or informal—are gone" (Samuelson 2009, 26).

An Increase in Rates of Involuntary Job Loss?

Another commonly studied measure of job stability or security is the likelihood of a worker experiencing involuntary job loss. This is generally measured by job displacement rates, or the extent to which employees are involuntarily displaced from their jobs. The use of the word *displacement* is a rhetorical, descriptive expression for involuntary job loss that emerged in the 1980s and replaced the term *firing*, and even *layoffs*.[55]

There are numerous anecdotes about people losing their jobs at a faster rate now than before.[56] However, while government statisticians have been tracking indicators of job loss for many years, indicators of job insecurity or instability—the pace at which people have become separated involuntarily, laid off, or displaced from their jobs due to reasons such as downsizing or plant closings (as opposed to performance-related reasons)—were not collected systematically for the labor force as a whole prior to the mid-1980s. The BLS did not start monitoring worker displacement until 1984 as supplements to the CPS, just as it did not begin monitoring contingent work until 1995. That the BLS did not even collect data on permanent job loss until the mid-1980s is very telling, as it indicates that it was widely believed that this was not really a systemic, large-scale problem before then.

Henry Farber (2008) provides an overview of trends in job displacement rates between the early 1980s and 2006, based on analyses of the CPS Displaced Workers Surveys. He shows that job displacement has a strong cyclical component; rates of job displacement decreased substantially after the recession of the early 1980s but then increased in the recessions of the 1990s and early 2000s. However, rates of job displacement were greater in 1993 to 1995—a time of significant economic expansion—than in 1981 to 1983—the worst recession since the Great Depression until the Great Recession of 2007 to 2009. In general, there appears to have been higher displacement rates during expansions in more recent years, which may tend to foster the perception that job displacement is rising overall. Louis Uchitelle, summarizing a BLS report for the period 1999 to 2001, concludes that permanent layoffs no longer dip as sharply in the expansionary periods between recessions.[57] In addition, he argues that their constant presence has generated job insecurity.

Job displacement appears to have increased for white-collar and service occupations, since the displacement risk for blue-collar workers—while higher than for white-collar occupations—has fallen since the early 1980s.[58] The growth in displacement rates for white-collar workers may also have contributed to public perceptions about the pervasiveness of layoffs. Farber (2005) also reports an increase in the negative consequences of job displacement (earnings loss, for example) among previously protected groups of workers, such as those with higher levels of education.

Cappelli's (1999, 115–28) review concludes that the proportion of prime-age males (thirty-five to fifty-four) who were permanently displaced from their jobs almost doubled between the 1970s and the 1990s.

At the same time, he finds evidence that employers were churning their workforces: in the mid-1990s, companies were hiring at the same time they were downsizing.[59] Osterman's (1999, 43–54) review finds that the proportion of people who are unemployed because they quit decreased from 25 percent in 1979 to 21 percent in 1998, while the proportion of permanent layoffs increased from 50 percent in 1979 to 56 percent in 1998. Moreover, the gap in job dislocation between men and women closed in the 1990s.

Farber's (2008) thorough analysis concludes that there is no evidence of an overall rate of job loss in the CPS data, however. What might account for the discrepancy between the relative lack of increase in job loss, as measured by the CPS time series on displaced workers, and the sharp declines in job tenure and incidence of long-term employment, also observed in the CPS and noted earlier in this chapter? A likely possibility is that CPS displacement rates do not identify all the involuntary terminations that occur in a given year.

The BLS worker-displacement data series were established in 1984 to respond to blue-collar layoffs. The question asked back then is the same as it is today: "Did you lose your job because a plant or office closed, your position was abolished, or you had insufficient work?"[60] This question is not likely to include "hidden" layoffs, such as retirements, "voluntary" buyouts taken in anticipation of looming layoffs, temporary work, and contract work. An alternative question suggested by Farber is, "Did your job end against your wishes, and if so, why?"[61] Such a more comprehensive indicator of whether people lost their jobs involuntarily would likely have produced a biennial layoff rate averaging 7 to 8 percent of full-time workers, rather than the 4.3 percent that the BLS reported from 1981 through 2003.[62]

Additional evidence of job displacement comes from panel studies of the same individual over a period of time. A number of panel studies indicate that job displacement rates have increased.[63] Robert Valletta (1999) uses data from the Panel Study of Income Dynamics (PSID) for 1976 to 1993 and finds support for the view that job security has declined. His finding of an increase in the turnover of high-tenured males is consistent with the results reported by Johanne Boisjoly, Greg Duncan, and Timothy Smeeding (1998) and by David Jaeger and Ann Huff-Stevens (1999). Boisjoly, Duncan, and Smeeding (1998) use data from the PSID to show that there was an increasing trend in involuntary separations for men with strong labor force attachments during the period between 1968 and 1992.

Moreover, Stefanie Schmidt and Shirley Svorny (1998) conclude from their review of research on job separations that the proportion of job losses that were involuntary, as compared with quits, increased between the 1970s and the early 1990s. They also conclude that involuntary job loss increased for workers age forty to fifty-five, though this group has relatively low rates of job loss compared with younger workers. In addition, Annette Bernhardt and her colleagues (2001) analyzed two panel samples of young men from two National Longitudinal Surveys of Youth (those entering the labor market between 1966 and 1981 and those entering between 1979 and 1994). In the second panel, they found a more substantial increase in involuntary separation from employment, especially among older groups of young, white men, than in the first panel. Finally, Valletta argues that there has been an upward trend in permanent dismissals as a share of unemployment since the 1970s.[64]

Taken as a whole, the quantitative empirical evidence on the trends in involuntary job loss suggests that job stability has declined since the 1970s, especially for previously advantaged groups such as white-collar workers and prime-age males. While the evidence from the CPS data does not indicate a general rise in displacement rates, the measurement error that is likely associated with the question used to assess involuntary job loss in these data may well result in an undercount of those who have lost their jobs involuntarily. Evidence from panel surveys is more suggestive of an increase in displacement.

The Spread of Long-Term Unemployment

Not having a job at all is, of course, the ultimate form of work precarity.[65] A key issue in unemployment is the rise of permanent, as opposed to temporary, layoffs. Long-term unemployed workers, defined as those who are jobless for six months or more, are most likely to suffer economic and psychological hardships. Uchitelle (2006) vividly documents the damage to peoples' mental health and self-esteem that results from layoffs.

The percentage of unemployed persons who are classified as long-term unemployed has increased enormously since 2000; this gap is the largest it has been since the 1970s.[66] The gap between unemployment rates and the share of long-term unemployment has grown since the 2001 and 2007–2009 recessions; nearly a quarter of the unemployed in the first decade of the 2000s were out of work long-term. Workers are now experiencing more difficulty in getting jobs than in previous periods, and more of them are experiencing the hardship associated with long-term unemployment. In addition, the majority of those who are laid off end up in new jobs that pay significantly less than what they earned before (alternatively, they remain jobless).

The large proportion of unemployed persons who found it difficult to obtain employment after the 2001 and 2007 to 2009 recessions is likely due to low rates of job growth, as well as challenges faced by workers in industries such as manufacturing, whose jobs have been lost.[67]

The Escalation of Perceived Job Insecurity

Still another research strategy for studying trends in job insecurity is to ask workers directly how secure they feel about their jobs with their current employer. This supplements the more objective data on job loss and employer tenure by shedding light on how workers perceive the extent to which their jobs are insecure. Questions of this type ask workers to assess the likelihood that they will be laid off or otherwise lose their jobs. People differ in their perceptions of insecurity and risk.[68] Nevertheless, the growth of precarious employment relations suggests that people in general should be increasingly worried about losing their jobs—in large part because the consequences of job loss have become much more severe in recent years—and less confident about getting comparable new jobs.

We can derive measures of subjective aspects of job insecurity from the General Social Survey, which has asked the following two questions in surveys since 1977 (scores assigned to responses appear in brackets):[69]

1. *Likelihood of losing current job:* "Thinking about the next twelve months, how likely do you think it is that you will lose your job or be laid off?" Possible answers are very likely [4], fairly likely [3], not too likely [2], and not at all likely [1].[70]

2. *Difficulty of finding a comparable job:* "About how easy would it be for you to find a job with another employer with approximately the same income and fringe benefits you now have? Would you say: very easy [1], somewhat easy [2], or not easy at all [3]?"[71]

The first indicator reflects insecurity in one's current position, while the second measures a more general concern about employability security (or the ability to find other employers who are willing to pay for one's skills). The latter (which taps "skill security") is likely to become increasingly important in market-mediated employment relationships.[72] I combine these two indicators into a summary measure developed by Schmidt (1999) that reflects the simultaneous presence of these two aspects of insecurity; this measure is coded "1" if a respondent thinks it is very or fairly likely that she or he will lose the current job *and* thinks that it would be not easy at all to find another comparable job; otherwise it is coded "0." Those who scored "1" perceive themselves at risk of a "costly job loss."

An analysis of the General Social Survey (GSS) data from 1972 to 2006 found that the composite indicators of perceived job insecurity were intimately linked to general labor market conditions.[73] Unemployment levels themselves are closely associated with perceived insecurity: a one-percentage-point rise in the unemployment rate is linked to a 13-percent increase in the odds of perceiving greater risk of job loss, an 18-percent rise in the odds of perceiving greater difficulty in obtaining comparable work, and a 33-percent rise in the odds of perceiving oneself at risk of costly job loss.[74] Schmidt (1999) also observes that these patterns of workers' subjective beliefs are closely related to the unemployment rate and are consistent with the objective data on involuntary job loss rates from the Displaced Workers Surveys.[75]

Notably, the trend in unemployment moved downward from the peak in the recession of the early 1980s until the sharp increase in unemployment during the recession of 2007 to 2009. For this reason, the trend line for job insecurity is likewise downward, with notable variations around it corresponding to business cycles. It should be kept in mind, though, that this analysis ends in 2006, before unemployment increased back to the recession levels of the 1980s.

Once labor market conditions as reflected in the unemployment rate are held constant, structural trends in job insecurity net of cyclical unemployment levels are revealed. The per-year trends in perceived insecurity become positive when the unemployment rate is held constant. Controlling for the unemployment rate, the odds of perceiving greater risk of job loss grow by a factor of 1.5 percent per year between 1977 and 2006, while the odds of being at risk of a costly job loss grow by nearly 2 percent per year. The annual trend indicates no statistically significant change in the perceived difficulty of locating comparable employment, but it too becomes more positive when labor market conditions are held constant. These results confirm that there is an upward trend in perceived job insecurity net of the unemployment rate.[76] Our interpretation of this result is that this increased insecurity reflects the impact of macrostructural conditions that have increased the precarity of employment relations.

How has the estimated growth in job insecurity been affected by changes in labor force composition since the 1970s? During this period, average education rose, while higher-level professional and managerial occupations expanded; because upper-socioeconomic-status (SES) workers have historically been more secure, one might anticipate that these shifts would decrease insecurity levels. Demographically, the labor force has come to include more women, nonwhites, and older workers, as discussed in chapter 3; the increased proportion of nonwhites might raise perceived insecurity, while greater numbers of older workers might decrease it.

The estimated annual trends in insecurity are substantively unchanged after adjusting for changing labor force composition. Indeed, all three estimates are somewhat more positive after this adjustment. This sug-

Figure 5.2   Trends in Overall and Adjusted Perceived Job Insecurity, 1977 to 2006

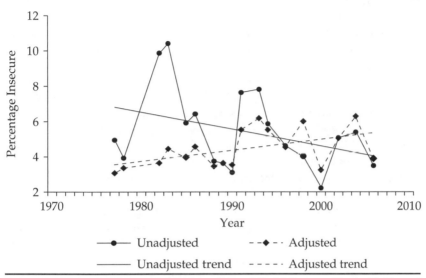

Source: Author's compilation of data from General Social Surveys (Davis, Smith, and Marsden, 2009).
Note: Adjusted for unemployment and labor force characteristics.

gests that the structural forces contributing to the growth in precarious work in the United States during this period led to greater perceived job insecurity, notwithstanding changes in labor force composition that might have been expected to alter such perceptions. Figure 5.2 illustrates this result for the summary insecurity indicator (risk of costly job loss). The upward-sloping dashed line shows the estimated annual trend in perceived insecurity after adjusting for the unemployment rate and sociodemographic labor force characteristics. Holding the unemployment rate constant at about 6 percent (its average annual level for this period), and setting all sociodemographic variables at their mean levels, a rise can be seen in the predicted percentage increase from around 3 percent in 1977 to nearly 5 percent by 2006. Figure 5.2 also shows that perceived insecurity grew dramatically after 1990 relative to the smaller changes before then.

This growth in perceived job insecurity appears to be fairly widespread within the labor force, supporting the view that precarious work has become more pervasive. Some people are more or less vulnerable to job insecurity, of course. Workers of greater socioeconomic status (those with higher education, in white-collar occupations, or with greater family income) express less job insecurity. Nonwhite workers, especially blacks, are more likely to feel insecure in their jobs than whites. Schmidt (2000) also found that the proportion of African Americans who expressed at least a "moderate" fear of job insecurity has been at least twice that of whites for the past two decades. She found the trend in this racial gap for both genders and all adult age groups. Older and full-time workers perceive themselves at lower risk of losing their current jobs but are more apt to expect that it would be difficult to find a job of comparable quality. Perceived job insecurity levels for men and women do not differ significantly. Moreover, the effects of increased precarity are rather general, suggesting that estimated annual rises in insecurity apply across all labor force segments.[77]

Job insecurity grew more rapidly among occupations that had previously been relatively secure (white-collar workers), and economic insecurity increased the most in higher-level (managerial and professional) occupational groups.[78] (Job insecurity is strongly associated with economic insecurity, which also increased since the 1970s once labor market conditions and labor force characteristics are taken into account.) In particular, the trend toward insecurity was stronger among those in white-collar occupations.[79] This result is consistent with the suggestion that precarity grew to encompass formerly secure portions of the labor force during these years. It is also in harmony with Schmidt's (1999) finding that the trends in job security beliefs by occupation mirror the trends in involuntary job loss rates. During the 1990s, white-collar workers and service occupation workers became more pessimistic about keeping their jobs, and white-collar workers became more concerned about costly job losses; meanwhile, blue-collar workers became significantly more optimistic about keeping their jobs but not about costly job loss.

The general increase in perceived insecurity that is net of business cycles and labor force composition supports the notion that there has been a sea change in employment relations in the United States. This is also observed in other liberal market economies such as the United Kingdom:

> What is . . . difficult to explain is why job insecurity has stayed high even as unemployment has fallen and stayed at relatively low rates in the U.K. and U.S. for the past few years. This phenomenon seems to suggest that job insecurity is not simply a passing issue linked to the economic cycle and unemployment, but rather that it has stabilized at higher levels than in the three decades following World War II. (Wichert, Nolan, and Burchell 2000, 3)[80]

Given these results, it is not surprising that high layoffs and volatile earnings make more people anxious and insecure even when unemployment rates are relatively low.[81] These results are also generally consistent with employee surveys that show sharp declines in satisfaction with employment security between 1985 and 1996.[82] These results may help to explain the findings of a 1995 survey by the *New York Times* that showed that 75 percent of respondents felt that companies are less loyal to their workers than they used to be, and 64 percent felt that workers were less loyal to their companies.[83]

Additional Forms of Risk-Shifting from Employers to Employees

Another illustration of risk-shifting from employers to employees is the increase in defined-contribution pension and health insurance plans, in which employees pay more of the premium and absorb more of the risk than employers. Similarly, the decline in defined-benefit plans, in which the employer absorbs more of the risk than the employee by guaranteeing a certain level of benefits, is another form of risk-shifting.[84] I discuss these forms of risk-shifting in more detail in chapter 6.

Conclusions

Job insecurity and instability—and the resulting uncertainty—has increased in the United States since the 1970s. This conclusion is supported by evidence from diverse indicators: the growth of nonstandard, market-mediated work arrangements; the decline in employer tenure; the increase in rates of involuntary job loss for certain groups; the growth in the share of unemployment that is long-term; and the increase in workers' perceptions that they will be laid off or otherwise lose their jobs.

The changes in the employment relationship described and documented in this chapter, together with institutional changes in the organization of work and changes in characteristics of the labor force, have led all jobs to become more insecure and precarious. The growth in job insecurity has permeated the entire occupational structure, reflecting a greater equality of insecurity: professional and technical workers were more likely to have nonstandard work arrangements than they previously were, as were other skilled white-collar and blue-collar workers. At the same time, the evidence also suggests that there are differences in insecurity for different subgroups of the population. In particular, more-educated workers were less likely to lose their jobs involuntarily. The growth of insecurity has redefined the meaning of the psychological contract between employers and their employees; it no longer points to an exchange of effort and loyalty for the promise of a secure job and future advancement with the company.

One might argue that a certain level of insecurity is advantageous in that it motivates people to obtain more skills and to otherwise work harder. While this may be true to a certain extent, job insecurity in the United States is nevertheless problematic because job loss is associated with loss of health insurance and other benefits that are distributed to workers through their employers. Moreover, people are differentially vulnerable to insecurity, and this helps to explain the polarization of the labor force with regard to job rewards. In the next four chapters, I discuss how the growth of polarized and precarious employment systems has contributed to changes and differences in various components of job quality.

= Chapter 6 =

Economic Rewards: Earnings and Fringe Benefits

The lack of middle class income growth since the late 1970s is the defining issue of our time.

—Lawrence Summers[1]

ECONOMIC REWARDS are a key motivation for work; for many workers, they are the main basis upon which they evaluate the quality of their jobs. The economic dimension of work encompasses a variety of concepts related to wages or earnings, as well as fringe benefits. We may think broadly about economic compensation as reflecting a "social wage"—one that includes earnings as well as nonwage benefits such as health care, pension or retirement benefits, annual leave, and sickness leave. These nonwage benefits enhance the economic value of one's job.

This chapter provides an overview of changes since the 1970s in levels of earnings and in earnings inequality for men and women, as well as in earnings mobility and instability, and changes in the availability of fringe benefits such as health insurance and retirement security. The evidence suggests that there has been a growth in both well-compensated and poorly compensated jobs—and a decline in middle class jobs—contributing to an expansion of earnings inequality beginning in the 1970s, along with a growing divergence in the provision of health and pension benefits.

Earnings

Earnings are a central indicator of job quality and have become increasingly important to workers in the United States as economic insecurity has risen. In general, earnings are also positively related to other aspects of job quality, such as relatively high levels of skill; thus relatively high-paid jobs are also more likely to be challenging and to provide opportunities for autonomy.[2]

Figure 6.1   Wages for 20th, 50th, and 95th Percentiles, 1973 to 2009, for Men and Women

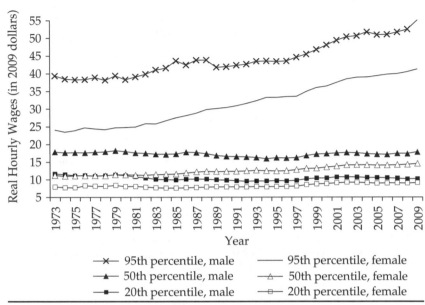

Source: Author's figure based on data from Mishel, Bernstein, and Shierholz (2009, tables 3.6 and 3.7). Used with permission from the Economic Policy Institute.

Figure 6.1 shows the trends in hourly wages[3] from 1973 to 2009 for men and women in the 20th, 50th, and 95th percentiles of the wage distributions.[4]

This figure suggests that wages have increased substantially for those at the top of the wage distributions. Wages for men in the 95th percentile have increased from about $39 per hour in 1973 to about $55 per hour in 2009 (in 2009 dollars), while wages for women in the 95th percentile have grown from about $24 per hour to about $41 per hour.

By contrast, wages have stagnated for most of the labor force since the 1970s, especially for men. Rates of real wage growth in the United States have averaged less than 1 percent per year since 1973, according to data from the National Income and Product Accounts (NIPA) and the Bureau of Labor Statistics (BLS).[5] Median wages for men (50th percentile) have remained stagnant, at nearly $18 per hour, while median wages for women have increased from $11.28 in 1973 to $14.55 in 2009. Wages for men in the 20th percentile have fallen from almost $12 per hour in 1973 to $10 per hour in 2009; while wages for women in the lowest quintile have increased slightly, from about \$8 per hour in 1973 to about \$9 per hour in 2009.

The period of wage stagnation beginning in the 1970s contrasts with the previous two decades, during which incomes rose more than in any other two decades in the twentieth century.[6] Moreover, the gains in income since the 1970s were focused at the top of the distribution, in contrast to the earlier post–World War II period, when gains were more equally shared.[7]

There are a number of reasons underlying the general stagnation of wages for the vast majority of workers over the past quarter century. Layoffs and job insecurity helped to suppress wage pressures during the 1990s, as did the growth in contingent work arrangements. Insecure employment now has a relatively large negative effect on wages, and this also varies among workers with differing amounts of education, as noted in the previous chapter. The lack of growth of wages was also caused by the decline in unionization, which decreased the power of workers to demand higher wages, as I discuss in chapter 2.

A Gender Gap in Earnings

The group that had previously been the most privileged (full-time, non-Hispanic, white males) has suffered the greatest relative losses in the new economy.[8] As the data in figure 6.1 suggest, the economic position of women relative to men has improved since the 1970s. Median wages have been stagnant or decreasing for men, while they have increased for women; the ratio of female-to-male median earnings increased from 63 percent in 1973 to 82 percent in 2007. The earnings profiles for white men and white women converged substantially in the 1990s, as women's wages gained relative to men's, even after adjusting for men's greater experience and number of hours worked. Women, especially those with a college education, have generally seen their situation improve relative to men since the 1980s, a time when their gains were especially impressive.[9] Compared with males, female workers experienced a greater shift away from jobs in the lower-quality contours or clusters of jobs, as well as higher real earnings growth within each job contour.[10]

On the other hand, the gender gap among those with a four-year college degree has widened slightly since the 1990s. This reflects both discrimination and workers' personal choices, as the number of women "opting out" of the labor force and staying home with children rose; the increase was sharpest among highly educated mothers.[11] Moreover, men still earn more money than women. This is due in large part to men and women working in different kinds of occupations and being segregated into different specialties within occupations (female doctors, for example, are more likely to enter family practice or specialize in ob-gyn than pursue more highly paid surgical specialties). Women are also more likely to work in service industries, where wages are lower. Nevertheless, discrimination based on gender is still prevalent, in addition to personal choices to work in particular occupations or industries.

The Racial Gap in Earnings

There are substantial racial gaps in earnings, and these have not narrowed very much since the 1980s. The ratio of mean full-time, full-year earnings for whites to those of African Americans was relatively unchanged from 1983 to 2003 (1.32 to 1.33), based on data from the CPS.[12] At the same time, earnings inequality within race groups increased substantially. This suggests the importance of studying earnings inequality within racial, ethnic, and other demographic groups rather than simply looking at race gaps (or gender, education, or age gaps) in earnings.[13]

Nevertheless, the polarization between high- and low-paying jobs in the 1990s was linked to race, and racial differentials have been unacceptably slow in narrowing.[14] Minorities ended up in worse jobs relative to whites during the 1990s; whites dominated the expansion of employment at the top of the earnings distribution, while the growth at the bottom of the job structure was dominated by jobs that were held by minorities.[15] The declining relative position of employed black and Hispanic men resulted from both a worsening job mix relative to white men and a sharp drop in the quality of low-skill jobs.[16] The decline of unions has been especially harmful to the jobs of black men.

Earnings Inequality

The patterns in growth of earnings for different groups presented in figure 6.1 underscore the increase in earnings inequality in the United States since the 1970s.[17] It is generally agreed that wage inequality for men and women was relatively stable in the United States in the 1970s, increased dramatically in the 1980s (primarily between 1979 and 1985), leveled off in the 1990s, and then increased again in the late 1990s, when it once again stabilized.[18]

The acceleration of income inequality that has occurred since the 1980s contrasts with the earnings pattern of the 1950s and 1960s, when

> mean wages in the United States grew rapidly, and the dispersion around this growing mean changed very little. Starting in the 1970s and continuing into the 1980s and 1990s, these patterns were reversed: mean wages grew slowly, and inequality increased rapidly. (Gottschalk 1997, 21)

Figure 6.2   Change in Wage Inequality from 1979 to 2008, Women

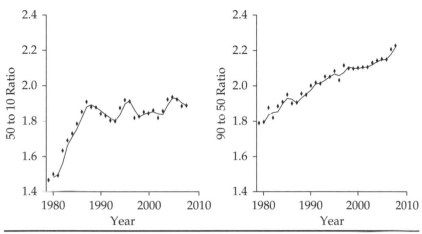

Source: Author's calculations based on data from Current Population Surveys (National Bureau of Economic Research, various years).
Note: Bandwidth = .4.

Overall inequality can be represented by the ninety-to-ten ratio, or the ratio of the wages of the highest 10 percent of wage earners to the lowest 10 percent. This ratio (results not presented) has been consistently larger for men than women since the 1970s but has increased for both groups since then; the ratios between the top and bottom deciles (ninety-to-ten) increased from 1.28 to 1.55 for men and from 1.16 to 1.44 for women between 1973 and 2007.[19]

Figures 6.2 and 6.3 show the increase in inequality at various points in the wage distributions for women and men from 1979 to 2008. Graphs are presented for the top half of the wage distribution (the ratio of the 90th percentile to the median, or 50th percentile) and the bottom half (the ratio of the median to the 10th percentile). These graphs indicate that the trend in wage inequality in the top half of the wage distribution (ninety-to-fifty) is very different from that in the bottom half (fifty-to-ten).

The ratio between the 90th percentile and the median has increased steadily since 1979 for both men and women. The growing disparity between the salaries of top managers and workers illustrates a rising gap in the top half of the wage distribution, between the highest earners and those in the middle. The ratio of the average total direct compensation of the CEOs of large firms to the average hourly compensation of production or nonsupervisory employees (who make up about 80 percent of payroll employment) was about 27 in 1973. This ratio shot up

Figure 6.3   Change in Wage Inequality from 1979 to 2008, Men

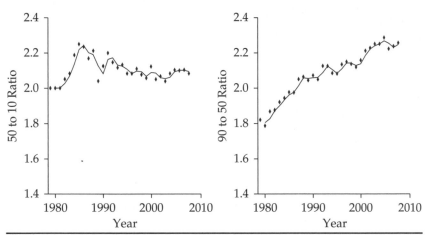

Source: Author's calculations based on data from Current Population Surveys (National Bureau of Economic Research, various years).
Note: Bandwidth = .4.

dramatically during the boom years of the second half of the 1990s, reaching nearly 300 by the time the high-tech bubble burst in 2000 and then falling to 143 a few years later before rising again to its current level of 275.[20] These ratios are much higher than those in other industrial countries. For example, Mishel, Bernstein, and Heidi Shierholz (2009, table 3.42) report that the ratio of CEO pay in the United States was far larger than in any of the other thirteen advanced countries for which there were comparable data over the period between 1988 and 2005; the next highest ratio was for the United Kingdom, another liberal market economy, while the lowest was for Japan. Compounding these large growing inequalities in recent years has been a regressive tax system that has favored the unearned income of the wealthy over the earned income of jobholders.

Trends in inequality in the bottom half of the wage distribution differed from those at the top. The ratio between the median and the lowest-paying jobs for women (the bottom 10 percent of the wage distribution) increased in the first half of the 1980s and has leveled off since then. For men, median wages have actually declined relative to the 10th percentile since the 1980s.

Therefore, it is the increase in jobs with very high wages—the top 10 percent, or even the top 1 or 5 percent—that is primarily responsible for driving the overall increases in wage inequality in the United States since the mid- to late-1980s.

Explaining the Increases in Wage Inequality

It is important to distinguish among explanations of the ninety-to-fifty gap and those that help account for the fifty-to-ten gap and explanations that might address both. Different mechanisms generate inequality at the top and bottom of the wage distributions, and these diverse processes suggest different policy strategies to reduce inequality. In addition, explanations of wage inequality need to take into consideration differences in the patterns of changes in inequality in various time periods: the increase in inequality in the 1980s occurred fairly consistently throughout the wage distribution, while the growth in inequality since the 1990s was concentrated at the top.

The most prominent explanation of the growth in wage inequality in the 1980s in the economics literature was the theory of skill-biased technical change (SBTC). This view held that changes in inequality were driven by fundamental technological advances, especially the growing use of computers, which produces a bias in favor of high-skilled workers.[21] New information technologies created high demand for skilled labor while reducing the call for unskilled workers. The economic winners in the labor market were those who were able to acquire more valuable human capital. The SBTC hypothesis helps to explain the growth in demand for workers with high levels of education and the deterioration of wages for less-skilled workers during the 1980s.[22]

An extension of the liberal, up-skilling theory advanced by Clark Kerr and his colleagues in the 1950s, the SBTC hypothesis maintains that the requirements of sophisticated technology and the knowledge society have increased the number of high-skill jobs.[23] It suggests that there has been a growing gap between high-skill occupations such as managers, professionals, and technical workers, on the one hand, and low-skill, white-collar and blue-collar occupations, on the other. Incumbents of low-skill occupations are disadvantaged, since many of these low-skill jobs can be computerized or outsourced to low-wage areas of the world. The declining demand for low-skill jobs in the United States has led to an oversupply of unskilled workers.

The SBTC explanation is compatible with the dramatic widening of the gap in wages between more- and less-educated workers that occurred in the United States between 1973 and the late 1980s.[24] The college wage premium (the wage gap between college and high school graduates) exploded in the 1980s, growing about fourteen percentage points for both men and women. This would be consistent with the growing importance of educational differences as bases of cleavage in job quality, as I discuss in chapters 3 and 4. Growth in the college wage premium then slowed after 1989.[25]

The SBTC hypothesis is better able to explain the growth in inequality throughout the wage structure during the 1980s than the rising inequality at the top since the 1990s. Nevertheless, certain facts are difficult to reconcile with the hypothesis that SBTC was the sole driver of growing wage inequality, even in the 1980s.[26] One challenge is that wage inequality did not increase very much in other advanced industrial economies such as France, Germany, and Japan, despite the technological changes that also occurred in these countries during this period. Another objection to the SBTC hypothesis is the recognition that institutions matter for wage setting: inequality tended to be greater in liberal market economies such as the United States, Britain, and Canada, which have relatively weak unions and decentralized patterns of wage-setting, whereas inequality was relatively low in countries such as France and Germany, which have relatively centralized wage-setting mechanisms and stronger unions. For example, the decline in unionization accounted for about 20 percent of the growth in inequality among males in the United States in the 1980s. Moreover, the decline in the value of the minimum wage in the 1980s increased inequality at the bottom of the wage distribution.[27] In addition, Claudia Goldin and Katz (2008) contend that the demand for skills is not sufficient to explain increases in the college wage premium, which is also due to changes in the supply of college graduates.

Furthermore, the view that computers increased economic inequality by raising the demand for high-skilled workers in the 1980s—while automating many routine tasks and thereby reducing the demand for low-skilled workers—was challenged by a study by David Card and John DiNardo (2002). They argue that the growth in inequality (mainly in the early 1980s, and mainly for the fifty-to-ten ratio) reflects the deep recession of 1981 to 1982 (the deepest recession since the Great Depression, until the Great Recession of 2007 to 2009), along with the fall of inflation. To compete, companies held down the wages of their least-skilled, least-mobile, and youngest workers; this was made possible by high unemployment (9.7 percent in 1982). DiNardo and Jörn-Steffan Pischke (1997) provide another challenge to the technological argument by using German data to show that while the wage differential associated with working with computers is about the same in Germany as in the United States, the same wage differential is also associated with laborers who work with a pencil or work sitting down. This finding suggests that it is not primarily technological change that generated wage inequality.

To adjudicate between SBTC and alternative theories, it is useful to examine trends in residual inequality in wages after taking into account human capital variables and labor force characteristics.[28] The SBTC hypothesis predicts that inequality will increase both within and between educational levels, for example. Within-education inequality increases because of the greater demand for skills, some of which is unobserved to the researcher and varies among workers with the same level of education. Workers who are best able to adapt to the new technologies earn a wage premium, leaving less adaptable workers with the same level of education behind.[29]

Overall, there was a rise of residual inequality in the 1970s and 1980s that was consistent with the predictions of SBTC: Katz and Autor (1999) found that residual inequality explained around 60 percent of the increase in inequality between 1963 and 1995; and Chinhui Juhn, Kevin Murphy, and Brooks Pierce (1993) and Daron Acemoglu (2002) found significant increases in residual inequality since the late 1970s after controlling for individual-level predictors of wages such as education, experience, and demographic categories.

However, residual inequality slowed or ceased during the 1990s, which suggests that the SBTC explanation is less useful as an explanation of growing wage inequality during that period.[30] Thomas Lemieux (2006) shows that after 1990 there is no longer a trend in residual inequality after adjusting for changes in the proportion of workers within different education and experience categories. This suggests that the increase in wage inequality since the 1990s is the result of changes in the demographic composition of the labor force or other institutional changes (such as the polarization of occupations), rather than an underlying process of skill-biased technological change.

Occupational Wage Inequality

About two-thirds of the increase in wage inequality in the United States since the early 1990s was due to occupational differences between jobs, according to Ted Mouw and Arne Kalleberg's analysis of CPS data (2010b). Much of the growth in inequality over this time period is due to differences across aggregate groups of occupations ("big classes"), especially for men.[31]

Occupational differences in wage inequality are not necessarily inconsistent with explanations based on human capital and differences in skills, however. As discussed in chapter 4, occupations differ in the level and type of skill they require, and so it could be that changes in labor force composition or an increase of within-education residual inequality contribute to the growth of wage inequality in the occupational structure. For instance, one of the reasons why the variance of wages increases with education is that specialized training encourages workers to move into heterogeneous occupations.[32] The growth of occupational polarization could thus reflect, in part, technological changes,[33] and this would help to explain why wage inequality increased in the top half of the wage distribution but remained steady or declined at the bottom half, as figures 6.2 and 6.3 show.

But occupational differences in skills and labor force composition are not sufficient to account for wage differences among occupations. Indeed, a substantial amount of occupation-level wage inequality remains even after controlling for measures of human capital (like education and experience) and other labor force characteristics (such as gender), which also vary by occupation.[34] That there is occupational inequality in wages due to factors other than skill level shows that low-wage jobs are not always low-skill jobs. Some low-skill jobs pay well, as is the case with some relatively low-skill unionized manufacturing jobs; on the other hand, some high-skill jobs pay poorly, as is the case with teachers in some states.[35] Moreover, differences in skill levels do not account very well for variations in low pay across advanced industrial economies: the United States ranks relatively high on skill indicators (such as average years of formal schooling and the proportion of population holding qualifications above the upper-secondary level of education), but it has the highest incidence of low pay.[36]

Inequality in occupational earnings is also generated by differences in occupational power, as outlined in chapter 4. Mechanisms of social closure contribute to earnings differences above and beyond levels of technical complexity, for example.[37] The earnings of regulated occupations in the United States are generally 10 to 12 percent higher than for nonregulated occupations, or 4 percent more for occupations that are regulated in some states but not others. Licensing enables occupations to exert market control by restricting competition for their jobs and protecting their job property rights; this serves to increase the rents associated with these jobs, regardless of their skill levels.[38] Licensing also drives up prices for services due to better-trained and qualified workers and, often, greater technological advances and innovations associated with regulation.[39]

The importance of occupational power for generating polarization in wages is vividly illustrated by the expansion of inequality in the top half of the wage distribution since the 1990s. The great increase in the salaries of top managers or financial sales occupations reflects the growing financialization of the economy much more than any increase in demand for particular skills or human capital on the part of incumbents of these occupations. The significance of occupational power is also reflected in institutional changes such as deunionization, which resulted in wage stagnation in the middle of the occupational structure, thus contributing to the decline in wage inequality in the bottom half of the occupational structure in the 1990s.

In this chapter I examine processes generating wage inequality in different parts of the occupational structure, since different mechanisms are operative in high-wage as opposed to low-wage occupations. A more detailed assessment is also warranted since overall occupational wage inequality is produced primarily by changes in relatively few occupations. For example, 18 percent of the increase in wage inequality from the early 1980s to the early 2000s is due to changes in just three occupations: increases in the size of relatively highly paid occupations of computer systems analysts and managers "not elsewhere classified" and decreases in the middle-wage occupation of secretaries. In addition, the top ten occupations with the largest positive effect on inequality accounted for nearly one-third of the overall increase in inequality from 1983 to 2002.[40] These results indicate that trends in occupational inequality are sensitive to the impact of a relatively small number of occupations.

High-Wage Occupations

Certain high-paying jobs have become increasingly well paid.[41] Much of the growth of inequality at the top end of the wage distribution since the 1990s was driven by changes in capital markets, along with the consequences of the deregulation of the financial sector, which together led to the growing financialization of the economy over the past several decades. These changes, in turn, led to transformations in wage-setting institutions, such as the changing norms of managerial compensation and the implementation of pay-for-performance reward schemes for top managers. An explanation based on social norms that removed barriers to high managerial salaries in the United States would help account for why managers' relative compensation increased so much in the United States but not in countries where these norms were still in place.[42]

Thomas DiPrete, Gregory Eirich, and Matthew Pittinsky (2010) suggest that increased inequality at the top of the wage distribution is being driven, not by the market, but rather by enacted or imagined market signals. They argue that "market-like" compensation schemes that track perceived or real performance are driving organizational compensation practices rather than actual labor market signals. Their analysis shows that the overall increase in mean CEO compensation since the early 1990s—which exceeded 100 percent when adjusted for inflation, far surpassing the 15 percent increase in U.S. industries as a whole—was due to the ability of a few executives to "leapfrog" to very high compensation levels. These high levels then became established as competitive benchmarks for other companies and spread throughout the wage distribution. This underscores the power of networks and occupational groups to set wages, rather than the behavior of individual managers or market-based rewards for actual skills.

Other institutional explanations also help account for why some managerial occupations received increasingly higher economic rewards. In particular, a larger component of executive compensation was given in the form of stock options, and so compensation has been increasingly pegged to a firm's performance in the stock market. This would help to explain the dramatic rise in executive compensation in the 1990s, discussed earlier in this chapter. The rationale behind linking compensation to stock prices was to motivate top executives to work hard to increase company performance and profits, though the relationship between compensation and performance is not always that close; executive compensation has often continued to rise relative to the earnings of other employees, despite downturns in firm performance.

Low-Wage Occupations

From a social policy point of view, the most problematic aspect of the rise in occupational wage inequality has been the creation of large numbers of poor-quality, low-paying jobs. Conclusions about the extent to which there has been an expansion of low-wage jobs depend, of course, on how one measures them.[43] A cross-national study of high-income economies showed that the United States had the highest level of low-wage employment in the 1970s (about 25 percent of the labor force earned less than two-thirds of the gross hourly median wage), and that this proportion has remained consistently high since then. By contrast, the United Kingdom, the Netherlands, and Germany have moved closer to the U.S. level; the Danish level has remained consistently low; and the French level has fallen since the late 1990s.[44]

The relative stability in the high incidence of low-paying jobs in the United States contrasts with the widening of wage dispersion since the 1980s. The persistence of low-wage jobs, combined with the decline of middle-level occupations, also helps to account for the decline in wage inequality (especially among men) in the bottom half of the wage distribution since the 1990s.

The creation of large numbers of low-wage jobs reflects institutional forces such as deunionization. The declining power of unions and relatively weak labor market institutions enabled managers to take the "low road" to cut costs, as argued in earlier chapters. American corporations have adopted an increasingly coercive and aggressive stance with their employees, and this has been aided by the growth of nonstandard work and declining union power. Moreover, more managers have put the squeeze on frontline workers' wages in order to enhance their own compensation.[45]

The erosion of the value of the federal minimum wage has also contributed to the spread of low-wage jobs. Introduced in 1938 as part of the Fair Labor Standards Act, this statutory wage level sets a minimum floor that applies to almost all employees (although since the middle of the first decade of the 2000s, more than half of the U.S. labor force has been covered by a state minimum wage that exceeds the federal level). The level of the federal minimum wage has increased periodically, but its purchasing power has been eroded over time such that its current value ($7.25) is well below its historic peak in the late 1960s: in 2007, the minimum wage was worth 34 percent of an average worker's hourly wage, compared with about 50 percent in the late 1960s. The low level of the federal minimum wage has strongly affected the wage gains of low-wage workers, especially low-wage women workers.[46]

In addition to these institutional effects, the expansion of low-wage jobs also reflects the growth of service jobs such as those in health care, hotels, retail, child care, and elder care. It is much more difficult to increase wages by increasing productivity in these services (compared with manufacturing industries, for example), and the lack of productivity growth helps to keep wages low in them. Economists refer to the difficulty in raising productivity in many service industries (such as personal services) as Baumol's disease, after economist William Baumol.[47] Improving productivity in many personal services—unlike in manufacturing—is either impossible (for example, reducing the time it takes to play a concert) or undesirable (such as increasing class size to raise student output per teacher input). Hence, prices of personal services, such as education, will rise relative to the costs of manufactured goods and nonpersonal services,[48] and employers are motivated to keep wages low in order to make profits in the personal service sector, unless the services are subsidized by the government, as are many health care jobs.

In addition to institutional forces, changes in labor force composition are another reason for the expansion of low-wage jobs; as David Gordon argues, "There are too many unskilled workers and too few with sufficient skills" (1996, 9). Employers in the United States have kept costs down in personal service jobs by hiring people with few qualifications and then paying them low wages. Their ability to do this has been facilitated by the availability of low-skilled workers who are constrained to take these low-wage service jobs, such as immigrants and others with less education. In turn, the availability of low-skill jobs facilitated the absorption of rising numbers of immigrants into the labor market.[49]

Table 6.1 illustrates the structural nature of the problem of low-wage jobs by ranking the top ten occupations with the largest projected job growth between 2006 and 2016.[50] Projecting to 2016, the wages are low in eight of these ten, and in five, the wages are very low (up to $21,200). The latter five are below the poverty line for a family of four.

A substantial number of the jobs expected to be created in the near future are in low-paying personal services. Many of these services involve things that people need, such as health care, day care, elder care, and so on. These kinds of jobs are also difficult to digitize since they involve physical contact with customers, and therefore are unlikely to be outsourced.[51] The expansion of these kinds of personal services is part of the structural transformation of the economy and will not be altered much by swings of the business cycle.

Personal services such as home health care are typically provided by the private sector in the United States; they are very expensive if they are performed by highly qualified people. Consumers are not able and often unwilling to pay for the true value of these services (especially once they have gotten used to not doing so). How we remunerate these kinds of personal service jobs is a social choice, however; we do not have to let private markets make these decisions. Personal and other services can be delivered at many different levels of quality. If we want higher-quality services, we will need to upgrade these jobs and hire workers with greater skills to do them. Personal service jobs tend to be low-skill in the United States because we have defined them that way, paying them low wages and recruiting people with relatively few qualifications to do them. If we insisted on higher standards of quality for, say, child care, then we could require those jobs to be more highly skilled and pay qualified people more. Other countries have upgraded the quality of these kinds of personal service jobs by putting them in the public sector and supporting them publicly though taxation (as in Sweden, for example). Since many of these personal service jobs are paid by public funds one way or another, their levels of compensation are ultimately social and political decisions, requiring only the will to upgrade them.

Since much of our economic growth in recent years has been in these low-wage jobs, social policies and business strategies are needed to reverse the growth in these low-paying jobs; market solutions are insufficient. While the government can increase the federal minimum wage in these jobs to $7.25, as it did in July 2009, or perhaps even a dollar or two more, it cannot increase the wage dramatically (say, to $17.00) unless it mandates quality standards for jobs (which will tend to force wages up) or subsidizes them via taxation or in some other way (such as creating jobs in the public sector or giving private employers greater tax deductions or credits for providing personal care services).

Table 6.1 Top Ten Occupations with Largest Job Growth, 2006 to 2016

Occupation Title	Employment		Change		Rank by 2006 Median Annual Wages[a]	Most Significant Source of Postsecondary Education or Training
	2006	2016	Number	Percentage		
Registered nurses	2,505	3,092	537	24	1	Associate degree
Retail salespersons	4,477	5,034	557	12	4	Short on-the-job training
Customer service representatives	2,202	2,747	545	25	3	Moderate on-the-job training
Food preparation and serving workers	2,503	2,955	452	18	4	Short on-the-job training
Office clerks, general	3,200	3,604	404	13	3	Short on-the-job training
Personal and home health care aides	767	1,156	389	51	4	Short on-the-job training
Home health aides	787	1,171	384	49	4	Short on-the-job training
Postsecondary teachers	1,672	2,054	382	23	1	Doctoral degree
Janitors and cleaners, except maids and housekeeping	2,387	2,732	345	15	4	Short on-the-job training
Nursing aides, orderlies, and attendants	1,447	1,711	264	18	3	Postsecondary vocational award

Source: Author's adaptation of data from Dohm and Shniper (2007, table 3).
[a]Quartile rankings: 1 = $46,360 or more (very high), 2 = $30,630 to $46,300 (high), 3 = $21,260 to $30,560 (low), 4 = up to $21,200 (very low). Wages are for wage and salary workers. Numbers are in thousands of jobs.

Earnings Mobility

Wage stagnation and growing wage inequality might be offset to some extent if workers are able to improve their economic situation by moving into higher-paying jobs.[52] Sociologists generally study the opportunity for advancement to better jobs by means of the concept of occupational mobility, which they have traditionally regarded as a primary indicator of social advancement and the "openness" of societies. Economists usually analyze mobility by focusing on movement from one employer to another.

There is a considerable amount of anecdotal and qualitative-ethnographic evidence that the degree of upward mobility within firms has generally declined in the United States over the past three decades.[53] Moreover, declines in promotion rates for particular occupational groups, such as managers, have been especially visible. Cappelli (1999, 226), for example, reports on a study of General Motors that found that promotion rates were dramatically reduced for managerial employees during the company's period of downsizing and restructuring.

Some quantitative studies of the broader labor force have also found that upward earnings mobility has declined, especially for men (the empirical evidence on this topic for groups other than white males is sparse). Bernhardt et al. (2001, 148), analyzing two panel surveys of young men, found that upward mobility (defined as long-term wage growth) has deteriorated for young men who entered the labor market in the 1980s.[54] The finding that there was a decrease of opportunities for economic mobility for white males in the 1980s and 1990s (as compared with the 1960s and 1970s) is consistent with the story of the dismantling of firm internal labor markets (see chapter 5). They also found that there were fewer opportunities for men in the more recent cohort to improve their wages by job hunting, suggesting that one of the traditional paths to good wages—an initial period of job hunting, followed by stable employment—has been blocked. Moshe Buchinsky and Jennifer Hunt's (1999) analysis of data from the NLSY between 1979 and 1991 also found that mobility declined significantly over the years, especially at the lower end of the wage and earnings distributions.

In general, there seems to be slightly less movement across income quintiles than there was a few decades ago.[55] One reason for this might be the slowdown in economic growth during the past several decades. Cappelli and Monika Hamori (2005), for example, argue that there are huge advantages to working in a growing firm in terms of career opportunities. The implication is that as organizational growth has slowed, so have opportunities for upward mobility.

While a number of studies suggest the rate of mobility has decreased, others have found that it remains essentially unchanged.[56] Maury Gittleman and Mary Joyce (1996) used matched data (between two years) from the Current Population Surveys from 1967 to 1991 and did not find much change in short-term wage mobility, year to year. Daniel McMurrer and Isabel Sawhill (1996a), on the basis of a review of a number of mobility studies, conclude that there is little evidence that economic mobility has changed substantially over time. In any event, the evidence on earnings mobility, taken as a whole, suggests that the recent increases in inequality have not been offset by greater opportunities for advancement.

Earnings volatility is closely related to downward mobility. The political scientist Jacob Hacker has argued that earnings have become more unstable and volatile from year to year, especially in the 1990s, and especially for people with less education. He suggests that

> over the past generation the economic *instability* of American families has actually risen much faster than economic *inequality*—the growing gap between rich and poor that is often taken as a defining feature of the contemporary U.S. economy. (Hacker 2006, 2)

In a similar vein, the economist Paul Osterman, writing in the late 1990s, summarizes his analyses of several national data sets by the observation that

> these dismal earnings patterns [especially for men] are not offset by mobility. People are not moving in large numbers from the bottom of the earnings distribution to the top over the course of their careers. (1999, 71)

And the British economist John Gray, also writing in the late 1990s, concludes that

> even for those whose incomes have risen, personal economic risk has increased perceptibly. Most Americans dread a mid-life economic dislocation from which—they suspect—they may never recover. Few think now in terms of a lifelong vocation. Many expect, not without reason, that their incomes may fall in future. These are not circumstances which nurture a culture of contentment. (1998, 111)

The extent of earnings volatility differs among members of the labor force. Insecure employment is strongly patterned by education, and individuals with relatively few labor market resources are more sensitive to structural turbulence.[57] Young, less-educated, and black workers encounter greater instability in earnings (defined as year-to-year fluctuations) than older, more highly educated, and white workers.[58] In recent years, individuals with at least a college education are more likely to experience upward mobility than members of any other group; this is a significant change from the 1970s, when income increases were more evenly distributed across educational levels.[59] Moreover, though the income volatility of less-educated workers was relatively high, the rate of increase in income volatility during the 1990s was greater among college-educated workers.[60]

Job Mobility and Wage Inequality

An important theoretical question for understanding the underlying mechanisms in earnings or wage mobility is the extent to which increases in wages are due to job mobility (changes in occupations or employers) as opposed to wage growth in the same job. The shift from closed to open, market-mediated employment relations described in chapter 5 might be interpreted to suggest that job mobility should be increasingly important as a source of earnings attainment, as workers seek to capitalize on their resources, especially by changing employers.

However, Mouw and Kalleberg (2010a), using longitudinal data from the PSID, found that the majority of the increase in wage inequality for men in the United States from 1977 to 2005 is due to differential rates of wage growth within firms. The effect of job loss accounts for 39 percent of the increase in wage inequality during the average eight-year period between 1977 and 2005, compared with the 52 percent that is attributable to wage changes for workers who stay with the same employer. That within-employer wage growth accounts for most of the increase in wage inequality raises serious questions about the validity of arguments that assume that greater employment instability was primarily responsible for the observed growth in wage inequality.[61] While employer mobility or job displacement can have a big effect on individual wage trajectories, the growth in wage inequality among men in the United States over the past three decades appears to be happening largely within firms rather than through the movement of workers across firms. This strongly points to organizational sources of increased inequality rather than the result of market mechanisms. This is consistent with DiPrete, Eirich, and Pittinsky's (2010) argument that organizational compensation schemes are driven by market-like signals rather than actual labor market signals.

Some of this within-employer inequality may result from growing divergence among employers in profitability and other factors associated with their ability and willingness to pay high wages to their employees. Some employers are able and increasingly likely to reward their own workers based on differences in their skills, in order to persuade them to remain in the firm and not to take advantage of the greater opportunities to move to other firms. This is consistent with explanations that posit a decline in firm internal labor markets: firms may be forced to pay market wages for capable workers if those workers can threaten to move to other firms without suffering a wage penalty due to the loss of firm-specific human capital or because of seniority-based pay scales, assuming there is enough of an increase in job mobility–induced inequality to make these threats credible. Whether employers actually decide to pay such wage premiums to their workers depends a lot on whether all employers switch at once (a Nash equilibrium type of situation) or whether only some do while others do not.

The growing divergence among employers may also reflect the decisions by some to respond to greater price competition by adopting high-road versus low-road forms of work organization, as I have discussed in earlier chapters. High-road firms rely on highly skilled workers and elicit their commitment by means of pay-for-performance schemes and promises of job security. Evidence for this explanation is suggested by Lemieux, W. Bentley Macleod, and Daniel Parent (2006), who found that performance-related compensation policies help to explain the increase in wages above the 80th percentile. Low-road firms, by contrast, rely more on cost-cutting devices such as low wages and designing jobs to minimize the training and skills involved, as I have argued earlier.

Workers in low-wage jobs who change jobs generally experience an increase in wages, which moves them closer to the mean and reduces inequality. Thus, Fredrik Andersson, Harry Holzer, and Julia Lane (2005) found that low-wage workers in the period 1993 to 1995 who changed employers during the subsequent six years generally fared better than those who tried to move up within the same firm, mainly because they found employers who paid more, though their findings do not speak to changing mobility patterns over time. This is not inconsistent with Mouw and Kalleberg's (2010a) analysis, which shows that employer changes are more strongly related to reducing inequality at the bottom of the wage distribution. Moreover, Andersson, Holzer, and Lane (2004) also affirm the importance of within-firm wage growth as they conclude that the best strategy is for workers to move to a higher-wage firm with chances of within-firm wage growth and then remain at that firm.[62]

Health and Pension Benefits

The United States stands out among the world's major economies in its distribution of key benefits through employers as part of the employment relationship rather than as a right of citizenship through social legislation. The most prominent of these employee benefits are health insurance and retirement pensions. Many workers consider a "real job" to be one that provides health insurance and pension benefits, and these benefits have come to occupy a central place in workers' economic compensation packages. As the labor force has changed, particularly to encompass more dual-earner families (as I discuss in chapter 3), workers' needs for other fringe benefits arose, such as flexible schedules, parental leaves, and other ways of helping them balance their work and family lives (see chapter 8).

Company-funded pensions were initially designed to encourage workers to remain with their employers and develop their skills and then leave when their effectiveness declined. They first came into use among the railroads (by 1916, more than 50 percent of all railroad employees had pension coverage) and were later adopted by banks, public utilities, and manufacturers. Welfare capitalism solidified this attempt to secure long-term employment during World War I.[63] While the passage of Social Security in 1935 provided workers with a source of retirement income, the relatively low dollar amounts provided by Social Security forced many workers to depend on pensions from their employers.

The rise of industrial unions during the next several decades extended and reinforced this employer-centered system, and as new benefits such as health insurance were added to attract workers, these too were distributed through employers.[64] The imposition of wage and price controls during World War II prevented employers from raising wages, so instead they offered additional economic "fringe benefits," such as health insurance, to attract workers. These fringe benefits became institutionalized after World War II, particularly in large, unionized companies, as unions came to regard them as a central goal in collective bargaining. A likely unintended consequence of this employer-centered system has been to contribute to the lack of a national health insurance scheme in the United States, as the government became accustomed to the idea of the employer-centered system. In the mid-1960s, the passage of Medicare to provide health care coverage for retirees, and Medicaid for the poor, provided some health benefits for these groups but did not cover those who were neither poor nor of retirement age. The provision of health insurance and pension benefits has become an increasingly important issue as the labor force has gotten older, thus requiring more access to health care.

The employer-centered model worked fairly well while the economy was growing and jobs were relatively stable, at least for those fortunate workers who worked for the large employers that could afford to provide these benefits, as opposed to smaller employers whose profits were not sufficient to do this. However, this model became much less viable as the economic pressures on employers to cut costs mounted and workers could no longer count on having a secure job; the demise of the private welfare system in the United States was represented vividly by the 2009 bankruptcy of General Motors, once the nation's most powerful company.

In the United States, a high proportion of average labor costs (about 37 percent in 2000) are nonwage costs (these are lower for low-wage workers since they generally have lower nonwage benefits, like health care and paid time off). This proportion is not that much lower than in Germany (43.3 percent) or France (45 percent), but unlike those countries, many social benefits in the United States are not legally regulated, so employers can pay low-wage workers social wages below the average. Only 76 percent of employees in the United States receive paid holidays, and only 57 percent get sick pay (again, these are lower for low-wage employees). Therefore, the gap in social wages between low-paid workers in the United States and those in other high-income, industrial countries is greater than the difference in private wages alone.[65]

Together, cost pressures and employers' desire to shift fixed costs and risks of employment to employees—facilitated by the decline in worker protections discussed in chapter 2—have led to a decrease in the proportion of workers in the United States who receive health insurance and pension benefits from their employers.[66] Employers facing cost pressures and looming bankruptcy are increasingly seeking to roll back prior commitments regarding health insurance and, especially, pension guarantees. Among those who receive pension benefits from their employers, there is also a movement from defined-benefit plans to defined-contribution plans, as employers have sought to shift the risks of employment to workers. Supported by ideologies that tout the "ownership society" and market mechanisms as solutions to labor market problems, these shifts have put the burden on workers to provide for their own lives.

The share of all private-sector workers (age eighteen to sixty-four, who worked at least twenty hours per week and twenty-six weeks per year) who received health insurance coverage from their employers fell from 69 percent in 1979 to 55 percent in 2006, a drop of fourteen percentage points.[67] These figures do not take into account the decline in the quality of health insurance coverage during this period, including the rise in the share of health insurance premiums and higher deductibles that employees have been asked to pay as employers increasingly pass onto workers the higher costs of health insurance premiums.[68] Nearly 20 percent of the U.S. population spent more than 10 percent of their after-tax income on health services (including premiums for health care) in 2003, up from about 16 percent in 1996. The percentage of total compensation that was spent by employers on health insurance premiums increased from 3.2 percent in 1979 to 7.2 percent in 2006; this is one reason for the decline and stagnation of wages and salaries and a major motivation for employers' unwillingness to protect their employees' health benefits.

The passage of the Patient Protection and Affordable Care Act in March of 2010 was a major step toward comprehensive health reform.[69] This law, and changes made to it in subsequent legislation, was designed to expand health insurance coverage, control health care costs, and improve aspects of health delivery. It did not propose to change the employer-centered model (political opposition derailed a so-called public option that would have provided more universal coverage) but rather built on the current system and emulated many of the features of the 2006 Massachusetts health reform. Among the reforms contained in the law were prohibiting health insurance companies from denying coverage or claims based on preexisting conditions; expanding Medicaid eligibility; and providing incentives to businesses to provide health care coverage and to workers to purchase insurance.

Pension coverage has also declined since the 1970s; in 1979, over half of private sector workers (50.6 percent of workers ages eighteen to sixty-four, who worked at least twenty hours per week and twenty-six weeks per year) received some pension plan coverage from their employers, while in 2006 only 42.8 percent of workers had some employer-provided pension coverage.[70] The kinds of employer-provided pension coverage also changed, as figure 6.4 illustrates. In 1980, about 40 percent of these

Figure 6.4   Share of Pension Participants in Defined-Contribution and Defined-Benefit Plans, 1980 to 2004

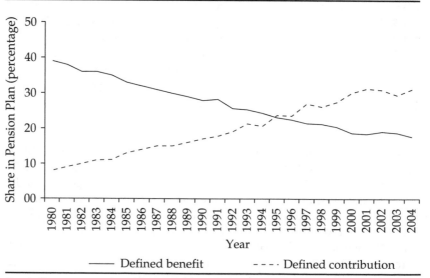

Source: Figure is reproduced from Mishel, Bernstein, and Shierholz (2009, figure 3J), used with permission from the Economic Policy Institute.

private sector workers had defined-benefit plans, in which they were guaranteed a fixed amount of payment based on pre-retirement and years of service, regardless of market conditions. By contrast, less than 10 percent of these workers were in defined-contribution plans in 1980. By 2004, less than 20 percent were in defined-benefit plans, in which employers (and often employees) make contributions, but the post-retirement payouts depend on how well these funds fared in the market. By 2004, a larger proportion of these private-sector employees were in defined-contribution plans. These plans reflect deterioration in the quality of pension plans, since they fluctuate with market conditions; in these plans, workers bear more of the risks of market fluctuations than do employers.

Inequality in Fringe Benefits

A growing polarization of fringe benefits has accompanied the increasing divergence in wages that I have discussed. The distribution of benefits became significantly more unequal from 1973 to 1996.[71]

Employers differ in the extent to which they provide pension or retirement benefits. Public employers generally provide higher pensions than private employers. This results in part from the greater density and power of unions in the public than in the private sector, as I note in chapter 2. A number of private employers, due to budget pressures, are reevaluating previous commitments regarding pension benefits.

Declines in employer-provided health coverage and pension benefits were greatest among those at the bottom of the stratification system. The proportion of private sector workers (age eighteen to sixty-four, who worked at least twenty hours per week and twenty-six weeks per year) with a college degree or more and who had employer-provided health insurance dropped from about 80 percent in 1979 to about 67 percent in 2006, while the percentage of high-school graduates in this group who had employer-provided health insurance decreased from about 70 percent to about 50 percent. The proportion of male workers in this group with employer-provided health insurance dropped more (from about 75 percent to 58 percent) than did the proportion of women workers (from 60 percent to 51 percent).[72]

Some employees in companies that offer health benefits are unable to obtain them due to stricter eligibility criteria and higher premium contributions, deductibles, and co-pays. Between 1987 and 2001, for example, the rate of uninsured workers in large companies (with more than one thousand employees) increased by 57 percent, even though the percentage of large companies that offered such benefits increased to more than 99 percent in the early 2000s.[73] This has created inequality in health insurance coverage among workers within the same company; about 25 percent of people without health coverage in the early 2000s worked (full-time or part-time) in companies with five hundred or more employees.

Moreover, the proportion of private sector workers (age eighteen to sixty-four, who worked at least twenty hours per week and twenty-six weeks per year) with a college degree or more who had employer-provided pension coverage dropped from about 61 percent in 1979 to 57 percent in 2006, while the percentage of high-school graduates in this group who had such coverage fell much more, from slightly over 50 percent in 1979 to 37 percent in 2006. The proportion of male workers in this group with employer-provided pension coverage dropped substantially (from 57 percent to 44 percent), while the proportion of women workers with employer-provided pension coverage remained fairly constant over this period (at about 41 percent).[74]

There has been a steady decline in the availability of fringe benefits such as health insurance and pension benefits for all workers but especially for those in blue-collar and service occupations and in nonstandard work arrangements. Blue-collar and service workers experienced the largest decrease in benefits.[75] Farber (1997) demonstrates the increasing inequality in benefits between high- and low-skilled occupations; his findings show that there has been a decline in the rate of employer-provided health insurance coverage, as well as in real wages for low-skilled workers, but there has been little change in the quality of jobs for higher-skilled workers. He also finds that there has been a substantial decline in health insurance benefits for newly created jobs during the period between 1979 and 1996.

The growth in nonstandard work arrangements—especially temporary work and independent contracting, which typically have few health insurance and retirement benefits—has also contributed to the polarization of fringe benefits. Indeed, the ability of employers to avoid paying fringe benefits to nonstandard workers constitutes a major reason for the expansion of this type of employment relationship. Part-time work also provides relatively few benefits, though the proportion of workers in this kind of employment has remained fairly steady for the past several decades.

Economically Compensated Good and Bad Jobs

A way of defining "good" and "bad" jobs with regard to economic compensation is to combine wages and fringe benefits to create a single indicator. Arne Kalleberg, Barbara Reskin, and Ken Hudson (2000), for example, define bad jobs as those that do not provide either health insur-

Figure 6.5   **Good Jobs and Bad Jobs over the Business Cycle
as Percentage of Total Employment, 1979 to 2006**

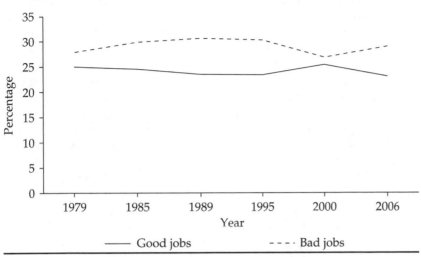

Source: Author's figure based on data from Schmitt (2007, table 1).

ance or pension benefits and that pay in the bottom quintile of the wage distribution (less than $6 per hour in 1995). Their analysis of data from the 1995 CPS showed that one in seven jobs were bad in all three of these dimensions, and only four in ten were not bad in any of these three dimensions. In addition, they found that male and female temporary-help agency employees, on-call workers and day laborers, and part-time workers are consistently more likely than regular full-time workers—and workers in the other nonstandard arrangements—to have low pay and to lack insurance and pension benefits.

A more recent and elaborate analysis of March CPS data using this approach is provided by John Schmitt (2007), who used information on these three dimensions of economic compensation to define two categories of jobs; "good jobs" are those that paid at least $17.00 an hour (the inflation-adjusted male median earnings in 1979) and also had employer-provided health insurance and pension coverage; while "bad jobs" are those that paid less than $17.00 an hour and provided neither health insurance nor pension coverage. Schmitt then examined the share of good and bad jobs generated by the U.S. economy during the last three business cycles up to 2006.[76] His results are graphed in figure 6.5.

The data in figure 6.5 indicate that the share of workers with good jobs in the U.S. economy has remained relatively constant since the late 1970s, varying between about 23 and 25 percent of all workers. This constancy results from a fairly continuous decline in the share of men with good jobs (from 37.7 percent in 1979 to 27.2 percent in 2006) and an offsetting increase in the share of women with good jobs (growing from 10.2 percent in 1979 to 18.7 percent in 2006). The share of good jobs created by the U.S. economy remained essentially unchanged during this period, despite an almost 70 percent increase in the gross domestic product per person since the late 1970s. The main reason for the lack of growth in good jobs despite substantial economic growth is the drop in jobs offering health insurance and pension coverage, rather than stagnant or declining wages.[77]

The trend in bad jobs is also relatively flat over this period, ranging from 28 percent in 1979 to 29 percent in 2006, with slight increases in the late 1980s and the middle of the first decade of the 2000s. The relative constancy in bad jobs also reflects an increasing share of men in bad jobs and a declining proportion of women in bad jobs since the late 1970s. The proportion of bad jobs in the U.S. economy is slightly higher than the share of good jobs throughout the period from 1979 to 2006.

The polarization of good as opposed to bad jobs has been especially evident since 2000, when the share of bad jobs increased rather sharply while the proportion of good jobs declined. Polarization was also evidenced by the growing disparity between good and bad jobs from the late 1970s to the mid-1990s. By contrast, the economic boom of the late 1990s was associated with a convergence in job quality, as good jobs increased and bad jobs declined. The proportion of good jobs fell during the most recent economic expansion, underscoring the weakness in the creation of good jobs in this economic cycle relative to previous cycles. The share of jobs paying more than $17.00 per hour actually rose slightly during the first decade of the new century (in constant dollars), again highlighting the large drops in employer-provided health and pension coverage as the explanation for the decline in good jobs and the rise in bad jobs.

Conclusions

This chapter has provided an overview of the changes in the economic aspects of job quality in the United States since the 1970s. Wages have stagnated for most men, while wages for most women have increased, narrowing—but not eliminating—the gender wage gap. In addition, the volatility of wages has increased, while opportunities for earnings mobility have been stagnant or have decreased. In general, employer-provided health insurance and pension benefits have been reduced.

Men and women with very high-paying jobs have seen their wages increase dramatically, especially since the 1990s, a pattern that is primarily responsible for generating income inequality during this period. The gap between the highest-paid persons and everyone else stems mainly from the financialization of the economy and the ability of highly paid occupational groups to extract higher wages. On the other hand, there has been little increase in inequality between men and women who earn median and very low wages. Education has played a major role in differentiating workers with regard to their wages and their ability to obtain valued benefits such as health insurance and pension benefits.

= Chapter 7 =

Control over Work Activities
and Intrinsic Rewards

THE DEGREE of control that workers have over their work activities is an important aspect of employment relations and a central component of job quality. This chapter examines trends in three closely related concepts that refer generally to an employee's degree of control: autonomy over work activities, or task discretion; participation in wider group decision-making; and intrinsic rewards.

These interrelated concepts have been of great interest to sociologists, economists, and psychologists. Their interest has been encouraged in large part by the wide array of consequences associated with control over work and intrinsic rewards for both organizational and psychological functioning. Control over work activities is also intimately related to the skill levels associated with jobs. Indeed, some writers see autonomy or task discretion as one aspect of skill, the other component being the complexity of tasks;[1] workers with more complex and in-demand skills are apt to have greater control over their work activities. Workers who are able to exercise control over their work activities are also more likely to obtain intrinsic satisfaction from their jobs.

Examining trends in these noneconomic aspects of work in the United States is hampered by the paucity of good longitudinal panel surveys that ask comparable questions for diverse samples of workers over long periods of time. In contrast, countries such as Britain and Australia, for example, have systematically collected data on noneconomic features of employment relations and job quality since the 1980s. The analyses reported in this chapter are thus based on less-than-ideal data and on several pieces of evidence that nevertheless tell a consistent story.

Studying trends in noneconomic job rewards is also difficult because such rewards are more subjective than economic rewards, like earnings or fringe benefits. While social scientists generally rely on individuals' self-reports for information on economic rewards too (thereby introducing a subjective element into seemingly objective rewards, since similar levels of these rewards might be described differently from one individual to the next), some noneconomic rewards are inherently much more subjective. In particular, intrinsic rewards are explicitly defined as subjective evaluations of jobs.

However, even intrinsic rewards are rooted in objective features of jobs—such as task structure, complexity of the task, and length of training time—that can, in principle, be verified by neutral observers. Such objective referents are essential if social policies aimed at improving the quality of jobs will be based on conclusions about the distribution and trends of job rewards. There is considerable evidence to suggest that people are able to describe the characteristics of their jobs and their immediate working environments fairly accurately in social surveys. As Melvin Kohn and Carmi Schooler (1973, 99) note, survey methods are useful for "studying the immediate conditions of a man's own job—what he does, who determines how he does it, in what physical and social circumstances he works, subject to what risks and rewards."

In this chapter, I discuss trends in three main indicators of worker control: autonomy and control over work activities; participation in decision-making in the workplace; and intrinsic rewards. I provide an overview of the social science research related to each of these noneconomic job rewards and how they have changed since the 1970s. I then present the results of analyses of comparable data from the 1970s and the first decade of the 2000s that address whether and how the average levels and the dispersion or polarization of these noneconomic rewards have changed over this period.

Autonomy over Work Activities

Autonomy over work tasks has been defined as "the degree to which the job provides substantial freedom, independence, and discretion to the individual in scheduling the work and in determining the procedures to be used in carrying it out" (Hackman and Oldham 1975, 162). The concept of work autonomy has also been called "self-direction," "conceptual autonomy," and task discretion, or the "degree of initiative that employees can exercise over their immediate work tasks."[2]

Autonomy and control over the content of work was the central dimension underlying job quality for Karl Marx, who felt that people needed to control both the conception and execution of their job tasks in order to be able to develop fully their "essence" and "humanness" by cultivating their own particular competences and skills. He argued that the possibility for self-development at work could only be achieved through performing meaningful and fulfilling work activities. The view that the capitalist—or detailed—division of labor resulted in a separation of conception from execution (and thus a decline in workers' discretion) has formed the critique of the division of labor since the days of Adam Smith; this theory was the basis of Marx's critical appraisal of capitalism as a system of production.[3] Marx viewed control over work in objective terms; he regarded workers who did not have such control as being "self-estranged" and "alienated," whether or not they were happy with their work.[4] Whether workers actually felt alienated did not change the fact that they were alienated in an objective sense; workers who were satisfied despite not having control over their work were considered by Marx to be victims of "false consciousness."

Max Weber (1947) assumed that a decline in workers' control over their work activities would be a normal by-product of bureaucratic organization, regardless of the economic system in which these organizations are found. The division of labor in modern organizations requires interdependence, which generally reduces the freedom of individual workers to exercise discretion over their work tasks. As organizations came under pressure to be less bureaucratic in order to adapt to turbulent environments (discussed in chapter 2), some organizations created structures, called "high-performance work organizations," that enabled workers to exercise greater autonomy. Both sociological and economic theories of work organization emphasize the advantages for employers of lowering transaction costs or solving agency problems in turbulent environments by adopting governance structures in which workers have more autonomy and control over their work tasks.

Sociologists studying social stratification have traditionally viewed autonomy as a key dimension that defines class position in modern societies. John Goldthorpe (1980), for example, regarded autonomy as a central criterion defining middle-class location, and he identified the service class of professional, administrative, and managerial employees as the group that has decision-making authority within the labor process. The question of changes in autonomy is thus related to the debate about the definition of and trends in the middle class. Goldthorpe's emphasis has shifted somewhat over the years, and he now stresses security and long-term career prospects rather than the relevance of autonomy and skill.[5] Nevertheless, his categories are still de facto largely skill-based classes.

James Breaugh (1998, 119) summarizes the evidence confirming the importance of having control over work tasks for individuals:

> During the past 30 years, the importance of work autonomy has been well-established. For example, meta analyses (e.g., Spector 1986) have shown self-reports of autonomy to be related to such important variables as employee turnover, performance, and satisfaction.

Psychologists have also shown that the opportunity to use initiative, thought, and independent judgment in one's work is a major predictor of one's general psychological functioning. Job autonomy is also the best predictor in the social sciences of outcomes such as health; stress researchers have demonstrated the negative health consequences of having low discretion at work.[6]

Explaining Changes in Control over Work Activities

There is sharp disagreement about trends in work autonomy. Writers differ in their views of whether workers' control over their jobs has increased or decreased since the 1970s. One broad perspective holds that workers' control over their work tasks has generally increased, while the other viewpoint maintains that such autonomy has declined, or at least has not changed. Consistent with the polarization argument developed in previous chapters, I argue that these conflicting explanations can be reconciled. As discussed in chapters 2 and 4, there is a dichotomy between high-road and low-road firms with regard to their human resource management strategies and policies, and this is likely to lead to increased inequality in autonomy and control. Workers in high-road, high-performance work organizations are apt to receive more training and opportunities to exercise greater autonomy and control, while those in low-road organizations are more liable to be subject to bureaucratic command and control systems, have less training, and have fewer chances to influence the performance of their work activities. Before turning to the evidence for trends suggested by the survey data, I briefly summarize the rationale behind the two main conflicting perspectives.

The first point of view claims that the degree of control that workers have over their work tasks has increased over the past several decades. As I discussed in chapter 4, there has been an increase in the proportion of the labor force (especially for women) in managerial-administrative and professional occupations since the 1970s, and workers in these occupations are likely to have more control over their tasks. Skill levels associated with some of these occupations have also been upgraded. For example, professional occupations' growth has been fueled by technological changes, such as the use of increasingly sophisticated equipment and the general growing complexity of information. Technical workers' skills also grew due to the expansion of professional work, such as paralegals who assist lawyers or nurses who specialize in various categories. Moreover, many low-skill jobs have been either exported to other countries or computerized (I discuss this further later in the chapter).

Theories predicting an upgrading of skills in the workforce generally assume that workers will have greater control over their tasks, since discretion is positively related to skill levels;[7] if employees have higher skills, employers are more apt to give them greater discretion.[8] Moreover, functionalist organization theories generally emphasize task complexity and human capital as sources of job autonomy. Robert Blauner (1964) argued that technological changes would generally increase skill levels; hence the control workers have over their jobs. Michael Piore and Charles Sabel (1984) also painted an optimistic picture about the increase in workers' control, arguing that the rise of flexible specialization and the associated increase in functional flexibility would raise skills (and likely, discretion), replacing mass production with its detailed division of labor.

The increased price competition and rapidity of technological and economic change that characterized the period after the 1970s made bureaucratic organizational forms too inflexible.[9] Consequently, organizations facing increasingly competitive environments sought to elicit the discretionary effort of their employees by providing them with a greater voice in decision-making and autonomy over their work.[10] Giving workers more discretion over their tasks was seen as the key to employee involvement and maximizing the efficacy of high-performance work organization practices, and also as a way to increase organizational performance. Worker discretion also enabled organizations to decrease their administrative component and have less need to supervise workers' activities closely. Such a decline in supervisory intensity might also suggest that there has been an increase in autonomy and control over work tasks even in relatively low-skill, low-wage jobs, like teachers' aides and nursing assistants. In such occupations, workers are able to engage in "job crafting," thereby having input into the way in which work is done. Such autonomy does not necessarily translate into high wages, however.

The penetration of high-performance work practices throughout organizations in the United States increased during the 1990s, which suggests that workers should be more likely to be able to influence decisions in their workplace now than in earlier periods. The use of high-performance work practices is likely to enhance the autonomy of both men and women, as seen in the 1990s, when the tight labor markets increased the urgency of obtaining discretionary effort from all employees.

The second broad perspective argues that the extent to which workers are able to exercise discretion or control over their work tasks has not increased over time and may well have decreased. The literature on the labor process and work alienation inspired by Harry Braverman (1974), for example, predicted that there would be a decline in workers' control due to employers' continuing efforts to de-skill jobs and to separate the conception of work from its execution. Braverman also suggested that there would be a polarization of skills and control, as the detailed division of labor increases the gap between those who conceptualize how the work is to be done and those who execute these directives.

Richard Sennett (1998) illustrates the decline of workers' autonomy using the example of bakers, who are unable to bake when faced with breakdowns in their automated ovens. Other examples include the application of assembly-line and mass-production techniques to white-collar occupations, such as those involved in the health care industry; health maintenance organizations have allowed managers with little or no medical training to dictate the work practices of physicians.

The de-skilling argument is especially applicable to the United States, a country in which managers have traditionally exercised great control (due to Taylorist and Fordist traditions) and union job control strategies have historically resulted in bargaining over job content and rules that have lowered the job autonomy of union members.[11] These forces have led employment systems in the United States to be rule-oriented, a pattern that tends to be associated with lower autonomy for workers.[12]

Critics such as David Gordon (1996, 6) argue that those celebrating the high-performance organization revolution were exaggerating the amount of real change in organizational practices. He maintains that only a small minority of U.S. organizations has experimented with high-performance work practices, and that most organizations adopting innovative practices did so piecemeal and thus are far from being "transformed." Others have argued that an increase in some practices associated with high-performance work organizations may well decrease discretion and autonomy over work tasks: individuals' actions may be constrained by the team ("the tyranny of teamwork"), especially in certain industries, such as apparel.[13] An analysis of organizational ethnographies shows that participative management does not provide workers with the same level of positive and meaningful experiences as the craft organization of work, especially when managerial behaviors are associated with a lack of trust.[14]

Duncan Gallie, Alan Felstead, and Francis Green (2004) find evidence for the second perspective, as they show that measures of task discretion declined in the United Kingdom during the 1990s. They found that there was a significant downward trend in discretion even after controlling for changes in skill requirements, the spread of automated or computer-based technologies, indicators of high-performance work organizations, and measures of occupational and labor force composition. They speculate that this decline in task discretion reflects the consequences of work intensification and the need to adhere to deadlines due to increased competitive pressures, as well as to forces promoting greater accountability and the wider regulative framework of employment. Their study, however, leaves unanswered whether this negative trend in task discretion also characterizes the period between the 1970s and the 1990s.

Changes in Autonomy: Evidence from Survey Data

Three survey items available in national surveys from 1977, 2002, and 2006 provide suggestive evidence about changes in how much control the worker perceives having over the tasks that he or she performs.[15] These are the statements:

"I am given a lot of freedom to decide how to do my own work." (Asked in 1977, 2002, and 2006)

Work freedom: Responses are scored from 1 = "Not at all true" to 3 = "Very true."

"I have the freedom to decide what I do on my job." (Asked in 1977 and 2002)

Freedom to decide: Responses are scored from 1 = "Strongly disagree" to 3 = "Strongly agree."

"It is basically my own responsibility to decide how my job gets done." (Asked in 1977 and 2002)

Responsibility to decide: Responses are scored from 1 = "Strongly disagree" to 3 = "Strongly agree."

Table 7.1 presents changes in both the variance and mean of these items,[16] with and without controls for a set of explanatory variables that are likely to affect the outcome variables.[17] Controlling for these explanatory variables enables us to assess whether the changes in discretion (and in routinization and participation) are due to shifts in supply-side variables (education or gender, for example) or demand-side variables (such as occupational structure). In addition, this analytic model offers a major advantage in that it allows us to estimate changes in both the mean of the dependent variable and the variance, thus enabling an assessment of whether there has been an increase in inequality or polarization. This analysis departs from most studies, which estimate only mean differences and thereby are unable to examine changes in inequality.

The results presented in table 7.1 indicate that between 1977 and 2006 there has generally been an increase in opportunities for workers to exercise autonomy over their work activities: all three measures indicate that there has been a statistically significant increase in workers' mean (average) reported freedom to exercise discretion and autonomy over their work. These mean differences (except for "Freedom

Table 7.1 Changes in Discretion, Routinization, and Participation

	Year Comparison[a]	Year Only		Year with Controls	
		Mean	Variance	Mean	Variance
Discretion					
Work freedom	1977 versus 2002	0.225**	0.025	0.207**	0.121
	1977 versus 2006	0.210**	−0.063	0.169**	0.062
Freedom to decide	1977 versus 2002[b]	0.080**	0.745**	−0.026	0.935**
Responsibility to decide	1977 versus 2002[b]	0.381**	1.193**	0.277**	1.199**
Variety					
Do different things	1977 versus 2002	0.298**	0.139	0.288**	0.138
Participation					
Have a lot of say	1977 versus 2002	0.248**	0.099	0.279**	0.242*
	1977 versus 2006	0.195**	0.164*	0.118*	0.180*

Source: Author's compilation based on data from Families and Work Institute (2002); Davis, Smith, and Marsden (2009); and Quinn and Staines (2000).
**$p < .001$; *$p < .05$.
[a]2002 and 2006 values compared with 1977.
[b]2002 National Study of a Changing Workforce. Other surveys: 2002 and 2006 General Social Surveys; 1977 Quality of Employment Survey.

to decide") persist, despite controlling for relevant explanatory variables.[18]

More striking, perhaps, are the results for changes in the variances of these ordinal variables. For two of the three items ("Freedom to decide" and "Responsibility to decide"), there has also been a statistically significant increase in the variance of the responses, indicating that there has been a growth in inequality in the extent to which respondents report that they are able to exercise discretion or autonomy over their tasks. The variance of the third item ("Work freedom") also shows an increase from 1977 to 2002, though in this case the change in variance is not statistically significant. These results are consistent with the argument developed in chapter 4 and elsewhere: there has been a growing polarization of non-economic as well as economic job rewards since the 1970s.

Less Routinization of Work

One reason workers are better able to exercise discretion and autonomy over their work activities now is that jobs have generally become less routine since the 1970s. Braverman (1974) argued that employers seek to utilize technology (especially computers) to automate production and to replace people by machines whenever possible.[19] The computerization argument has been extended forcefully by Frank Levy and Richard Murnane (2004), who maintain that managers have sought to digitize as many jobs as they can. Some kinds of tasks are more amenable to computerization and automation than others; these have tended to be "middle-level" jobs in manufacturing (automation of blue-collar jobs or computerization of white-collar jobs) as well as repetitive service jobs. Highly complex jobs (such as the work of professionals and technical workers) and relatively low-skill service occupations that involve working with people are less susceptible to computerization, as I noted earlier. As a result, the job structure has become polarized between low-skill jobs and high-skill jobs that cannot be easily routinized because they involve complex pattern recognition, such as identifying business opportunities or repairing complex machines, or because they involve complex communication skills like managing people or devising advertising campaigns.[20]

The computerization hypothesis is supported quantitatively by David Autor, Frank Levy, and Richard Murnane (2003). Figure 7.1 summarizes their evidence.[21] They combine information on job task requirements from the *Dictionary of Occupational Titles* with information on employed workers from the Current Population Surveys to assess changes in industry and occupation task input over a four-decade period from 1960 to 2002. Their study finds that there has been a decline over time in both routine and manual jobs between 1970 and 2002, reversing an

Figure 7.1   Trends in Abstract, Routine, and Manual Tasks, 1960 to 2002

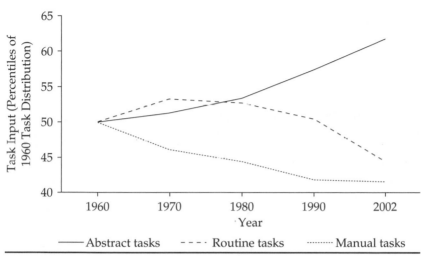

Source: Author's figure based on data from David Autor (personal communication, November 15, 2009).

increase in routine jobs from 1960 to 1970. Manual jobs declined steadily over the four decades. Both routine and manual jobs are amenable to digitization and the replacement of workers by computers. By contrast, there has been an increase in the kinds of jobs that are difficult—if not impossible—to computerize, such as jobs involving abstract tasks.

I should note that not all of the decline in routine jobs is caused by replacing workers with computers, however. Many routine jobs have also been offshored to lower-wage countries. This is especially true for manufacturing jobs, which have been outsourced to areas of the world with lower wage costs, and often lower labor standards. A large number and variety of routine service jobs (such as form processing) have also been offshored, but these generally involve the use of computers that permit employers to exercise high degrees of technical control (such as the case with call centers).

A final piece of evidence of the growth in variety of jobs (and, in turn, the decline in routinization) is shown by responses to the following survey item:

"I get to do a number of different things on my job." (Asked in 1977 and 2002)

Do different things: Responses are scored from 1 = "Strongly disagree" to 4 = "Strongly agree."

The findings for the control variables (not shown in table 7.1) reveal that workers in more highly complex occupations are able to do more varied tasks, as are supervisors and those in managerial and professional occupations. Workers in larger establishments are more apt to have routine jobs.

The results for this item (shown in table 7.1) indicate that there has been a significant increase in the extent to which people report that they are able to do a variety of things on their jobs (that is, a decline in routinization). Moreover, there has been a positive increase in the dispersion or polarization of routine work, but this change in variance is not statistically significant. This too is consistent with the computerization-automation hypothesis, since it predicts there will be a general decline in routine jobs, not a growth in both nonroutine and routine jobs.

Participation in Decision-Making

Participation is a broader concept than autonomy over work activities, since having discretion over one's tasks is but one way that an employee can participate in decisions. Eileen Appelbaum and her colleagues (2000) conceptualize autonomy as one component of employees' opportunity to participate in substantive decisions, the others being the chance to participate in self-directed teams, membership in offline committees, and chances to communicate with others. The desirability of having workers participate in decision-making in order to elicit their discretionary effort and to utilize their commitment and creativity is a fundamental tenet of the literature on high-performance work organizations. The spread of such organizational forms is thus likely to have increased opportunities for workers to participate in decisions. In addition, the decline of the administrative component of organizations has enhanced organizations' reliance on workers to solve problems and make decisions.

The intimate relationship between autonomy and participation suggests that the patterns of changes in these two concepts should be similar. Gallie, Felstead, and Green (2004), however, examined changes in these two closely related aspects of control and found that in Britain, there has been an increase in group forms of participation and consultative involvement but a decline in the ability of workers to exercise discretion over their tasks (see the earlier discussion).

Explaining Changes in Participation

There are good reasons to expect there to have been a rise in opportunities for workers in the United States to participate in decision-making since the 1970s. The strategy of decentralizing decision-making and shifting risks to workers is likely to have provided workers with opportunities across a wide variety of settings to participate in new team-based forms of production involving heightened employee involvement.[22]

In addition, the changes in the occupational structure discussed earlier have led to an increase in occupations that are distinguished by the ability of their incumbents to make decisions (such as professionals) and a decline in occupations that are relatively routine and do not permit workers to have much input into how work is organized and carried out (such as manual, blue-collar jobs). Moreover, the increase in the educational attainment of the labor force (discussed in chapter 3) has created a larger pool of workers who place great importance on making decisions about how work is done and have the capability to contribute positively to the organization of work.

There are also reasons to expect that some workers have had greater opportunities than others to participate in decisions. Robert Reich (1992) pointed to the growing division between those who do work in a routine, repetitive fashion and "symbolic analysts" who use their imagination in work and to engage in problem-solving. In principle, all workers can be problem solvers and make useful contributions to the organization's goals, even assembly-line and clerical employees; Reich estimated that 60 to 70 percent of the labor force had the potential to become "technologically empowered" to solve problems via complex computer software. However, not all workers have this opportunity. One constraint on workers' ability to participate in decisions is a lack of education and training, which supports Reich's argument that education and training are needed to turn workers into problem solvers.

Changes in Participation: Evidence from Survey Data

One item that appears on several surveys sheds some light on changes in participation:

"I have a lot of say about what happens on my job." (Asked in 1977, 2002, and 2006)

Have a lot to say: Responses are scored from 1 = "Strongly disagree" to 4 = "Strongly agree."

The results presented in table 7.1 also indicate that there has been a general mean (average) increase in reported participation from 1977 to 2002 and 2006 (the difference between 2002 and 2006 is not statistically significant). These mean differences persist after controlling for the variables described earlier.[23]

In addition, there has also been an increase in the variance of reported participation, especially between 1977 and 2006, though the difference between 1977 and 2002 is also statistically significant once other variables are controlled (the difference between 2002 and 2006 is, again, not statistically significant). The significant increase in variation is consistent with the scenario presented in chapter 4 that there has been a polarization of corporate responses between high-road and low-road organizations, which has subsequently increased the divergence in workers' opportunities to participate in decisions.

Intrinsic Rewards

Intrinsic rewards are subjective assessments of peoples' task experiences and may differ substantially from one person to another: what is interesting, meaningful, or challenging to one person may not be so to another. One person's challenging job may be another's boring, uninteresting task, depending on these two peoples' skills, interests, abilities, aptitudes, and, quite simply, preferences. Nevertheless, the correlations between measures of intrinsic rewards and autonomy or control tend to be relatively high, suggesting that people do obtain meaning and challenge from being able to decide how to do their own work, especially in a highly individualistic culture like the United States.[24] Intrinsic rewards, then, may be regarded as job rewards that intervene between objective work characteristics (such as control over one's work or participation) and evaluations of job quality (represented by job satisfaction).

Such subjectivity might even be desirable for some purposes, since it is the individual's perception of objective job rewards that really matters for assessments of job quality; as W. I. Thomas noted long ago, "What is perceived as real is real in its consequences" (Thomas and Thomas 1928). And, as J. Richard Hackman and Edward E. Lawler (1971, 264) argued,

> It should be emphasized that it is not their objective state which affects employee attitudes and behavior, but rather how they are experienced by the employees. Regardless of the amount of feedback (or variety, autonomy, or task identity) a worker really has in his work, it is how much he perceives that he has which affects his reactions to the job.

It is not surprising, given the individualistic culture of the United States, that Americans place great importance on jobs that enable them to obtain intrinsic rewards. An analysis of work values from 1973 to 2006 using the General Social Survey found that intrinsic rewards (measured as "work that is important and gives a feeling of accomplishment") was the highest-ranked work value throughout this time period.[25] Americans' tendency to evaluate intrinsic dimensions of jobs as more important than extrinsic dimensions shows in the results of other worker surveys.[26]

Indeed, it is arguably the case that the importance that workers (especially young ones) placed on autonomy, challenging work, and other intrinsic rewards, as well as their concern for individual rights and power, helped to spur the spread of high-performance work organizations and made available greater opportunities for participation in decision-making. This helped to ensure that high-performance work organizations provided a good fit between the growing desires of a significant group of workers and the realities of the workplace.

It is likely that the increases in autonomy over work activities and participation—and declines in routinization—that were observed earlier in this chapter will also be accompanied by a growth in opportunities to obtain intrinsic rewards. However, the subjective nature of intrinsic rewards suggests that this may not necessarily be the case. For example, it is widely accepted that as workers become more educated, they tend to be increasingly disaffected with jobs that do not provide them with intrinsic rewards. Thus, while such jobs might always have constituted a form of objective alienation from work in Marx's sense, they are now likely to be more alienating in a subjective sense as well, and be major sources of dissatisfaction with work.

Changes in Intrinsic Rewards: Evidence from Survey Data

The surveys described earlier in this chapter contain three items that are often used to measure the concept of intrinsic rewards. These items are:

"I have an opportunity to develop my own special abilities." (Asked in 1977 and 2006)

Opportunity to develop skills: Responses are scored from 1 = "Not at all true" to 3 = "Very true."

"My job lets me use my skills and abilities." (Asked in 1977, 2002, and 2006)

Use my skills: Responses are scored from 1 = "Strongly disagree" to 4 = "Strongly agree."

"The work I do on my job is meaningful to me." (Asked in 1977 and 2002)

Work is meaningful: Responses are scored from 1 = "Strongly disagree" to 3 = "Strongly agree."

These items are relatively highly correlated: the pairwise correlations range from .42 ("Opportunity to develop skills" and "Use my skills") to .53 ("Use my skills" and "Work is meaningful"). This is consistent with the notion that these three items are tapping the same concept of "intrinsic rewards." Indeed, a scale formed by summing these items has an internal consistency coefficient (Cronbach's alpha) of .70.[27]

The results in table 7.2 indicate that there has been an average increase in all three intrinsic rewards since the 1970s: the mean levels of the three items show significant increases between 1977 and 2002 and between 1977 and 2006 (the mean difference between 2002 and 2006 for "Use my skills" was not statistically significant). These findings are consistent with those observed earlier in the chapter for discretion, variety, and participation, the objective characteristics of jobs that are the sources of intrinsic rewards.[28]

Table 7.2 further indicates that though the average level of intrinsic rewards has grown since the 1970s, the dispersion of these rewards has, for the most part, not grown. The only intrinsic reward indicator that shows a growing polarization is "Work is meaningful," the responses to which became more divergent after the 1970s. On the other hand, there seems to be less dispersion in the degree to which workers perceive they have opportunities to develop their own special abilities.

Indirect evidence about the increase in intrinsic rewards is provided by research on work values. Workers placed a great deal of importance on intrinsic rewards in the 1970s, as the attainment of such rewards was difficult then due to the dominance of Fordist systems of production. Over time, however, the valuation of intrinsic rewards relative to economic rewards and job security has declined, though these still remain the highest-ranked work value (see also chapter 9, this volume). One way to interpret this decline is to read it as a reflection of the increasing difficulty of obtaining both high-paying jobs and job security (see chapters 5 and 6), coupled with the growing availability of intrinsic rewards (see table 7.2).[29]

Conclusions

The quality of a job can be assessed by its noneconomic job rewards—such as the degree of control that workers have over their work activities, how much they are able to participate in decisions, and whether they are able to find meaningful, challenging work that makes use of their skills. I have examined trends in these noneconomic rewards in this chapter.

The quantitative results in this chapter should be evaluated in light of the limitations of the measures used. While the conclusions are based on data from nationally representative surveys, these are only two or three surveys, conducted twenty-five to twenty-nine years apart. This is

Table 7.2   Changes in Intrinsic Rewards

		Year Only		Year with Controls	
	Year Comparison[a]	Mean	Variance	Mean	Variance
Opportunity to develop skills	1977 versus 2006	0.121**	−0.342**	0.105**	−0.189
Use my skills	1977 versus 2002	0.459**	−0.067	0.443**	−0.015
	1977 versus 2006	0.482**	−0.102	0.401**	0.001
Work is meaningful	1977 versus 2002[b]	0.621**	1.266**	0.475**	1.180

Source: Author's compilation based on data from Families and Work Institute (2002); Davis, Smith, and Marsden (2009); and Quinn and Staines (2000).
**p < .001; *p < .05.
[a]2002 and 2006 values compared with 1977.
[b]2002 National Study of a Changing Workforce. Other surveys: 2002 and 2006 General Social Surveys; 1977 Quality of Employment Survey.

not nearly as preferable as a more complete time series, which could assess the pattern of trends in these measures more precisely. It is also possible that over time, respondents may redefine the meaning of key concepts, such as intrinsic rewards or participation, based on changing societal norms and expectations. Unfortunately, data to evaluate these concepts more precisely are simply not available.

Despite the limitations of these quantitative analyses, the results tell a consistent story. Taken as a whole, these results suggest that there has been an expansion of opportunities for workers to exercise autonomy and discretion in their jobs, to participate in decision-making in their organizations, and to obtain intrinsic rewards from their work. Responses to survey items tapping these three sets of concepts, administered to national samples of workers over a twenty-five- to twenty-nine-year span, provide suggestive evidence that there has been an increase in their overall mean levels.

There has also been an increase in the degree of polarization or inequality in a number of these noneconomic rewards, in particular for opportunities to exercise autonomy over work tasks and to participate in decisions. The significant increases in the variances of measures of these concepts are independent of their mean differences and of a large number of explanatory variables. These increases in variances are consistent with a scenario that there has been a growing polarization in the responses of organizations to the kinds of macro social and economic forces we discussed in chapters 2 and 4.

═ Chapter 8 ═

Time at Work: Hours, Intensity, and Control

Tіме is a central aspect of the employment relationship and a key feature of the quality of jobs. Social scientists have long recognized that control over the use of time underlies the organization of production practices and power relations in the workplace. Questions about how much time workers spend at work and who controls what they do during this time have been fundamental to labor-management struggles concerning the restructuring of time, such as defining the length of the working day.[1]

Both scholars and the general public have raised concerns that Americans are working increasingly hard and suffering from a "time squeeze" between their work and family lives. Attention was first drawn to this issue by Juliet Schor's *The Overworked American* (1991), in which she argued that Americans were working more hours than ever before, based on an analysis of data from the CPS.[2] Many academic and popular writers have since decried the time expectations that tether men and women to the workplace.[3] A number of these writers have called for a reapportionment of time for men and women to achieve balance in their lives, a notion that expresses a particular value (and one that has taken on greater urgency) in contemporary life.

This chapter provides an overview of two main dimensions related to the role of time at work. The first is how hard people work. The commitment to working hard is deeply rooted in the American character and can be traced back to the Protestant work ethic. Americans have traditionally placed great importance on the value of hard work and have tended to regard work as a central life interest. There are two components to how hard people work: how many hours they spend at work and how much effort they expend during that period of time.[4] I explore both of these components of working hard by examining trends in the number of hours or the duration of time that Americans have worked since the 1970s, as well as the intensity of the labor, or how hard or fast people work and how much work they have to do.

A second dimension of time at work is the degree to which workers are able to exert control over their schedules. Workers who are able to control when they work are better able to obtain the flexibility to balance their work lives with their family lives and other activities. Having control or autonomy over one's schedule is conceptually distinct from having autonomy over one's tasks.[5]

I first summarize some of the conclusions of social science research about each of these two dimensions of time at work and their implications for understanding how they have changed since the 1970s. I then present the results of analyses of comparable survey data from the 1970s and the 2000s that address whether and how the average levels and the polarization of these noneconomic rewards have changed over this period.

Hours of Work

The number of hours a person works in a week or year is an indicator of the duration of time that they spend at work. Unions in the United States and elsewhere have long recognized that control over time is key to power in the workplace and the labor process, and one of their objectives has been to avoid exploitation by setting upper limits on how much time employers can legally demand of their employees. The Fair Labor Standards Act of 1938 defined the full-time workweek in the United States as forty hours for workers covered by the act (mainly nonsupervisory employees); working more than forty hours constitutes overtime. The definition of a workweek varies among countries, and some European countries (like France) consider full-time work as less than forty hours a week.

The total number of hours worked by Americans has increased since the 1970s. According to the International Labour Organization, employed Americans worked 1,978 hours annually in 2000, a full 350 hours—nine weeks—more than Western Europeans, and more hours per year than workers in any other industrialized country.[6] The average American actually worked 199 hours more in 2000 than in 1973, a period of three decades during which worker productivity per hour nearly doubled.[7]

This increase in hours is due mainly to a rise in the number of weeks worked per year rather than a rise in the average workweek, which has not changed much in the United States since the early 1970s.[8] There was little change in the overall average (mean) number of hours worked per week by either men or women between 1970 and 2000: the average man worked 43.1 hours per week in 2000, compared with 43.5 in 1970; the average woman worked 37.1 hours per week in 2000, compared with 37.0 hours in 1970.[9] Among employees working 20.0 or more hours per week, however, the average number of all paid and unpaid hours at any location on their primary or only job increased from 43.6 hours per week in 1977 to 47.1 in 1997. When all jobs a person might have are considered (about 13 percent of employees have multiple jobs), the average total hours worked per week in 1997 was 46.0 (49.0 hours for men and 42.0 hours for women).[10]

One reason that workers may be working more hours per year is the stagnation in wages and increases in earnings inequality discussed in chapter 6. Americans needed to work more hours to finance their spending and to pay down their debts. Moreover, a study by Linda Bell and Richard Freeman (1994) suggests that greater economic inequality motivates people to work harder in order to move up in the income distribution. The authors compared data from labor markets in the United States and Germany and found that in both countries, workers in occupations with greater wage inequality worked more hours. However, in the United States, where inequality is greater, a much larger proportion of workers felt that they would be more likely to be promoted and obtain higher economic rewards if they worked harder.

Workers may also have to work more hours due to pressures imposed by corporate restructuring. Downsizing has created short staffs in many companies, as surviving workers have to do more with less. The growth of globalization and competition has encouraged companies to get their workers to work harder, and technological developments make it possible for people to work 24/7.[11]

The increase in female labor force participation—along with greater financial pressures—led to a rise of dual-earner couples during the latter part of the twentieth century, a trend I discussed in chapter 3. Moreover, the combined workweek of dual-career couples increased by ten hours between 1970 and 1997.[12] Middle-class parents in dual-earner households worked a total of 3,932 hours in 2000, equivalent to more than two full-time jobs in most European countries.[13] The increase in hours worked by dual-earner families has made it increasingly difficult to achieve a balance between work and personal life, thereby contributing to the perception of a time squeeze felt by such families. The increase in time pressure can be attributed to dual-earner families, which now typically comprise a husband and wife, both bound by the demands of their jobs—unlike many of the families in which they grew up, where their fathers worked outside the home but their mothers typically stayed at home.

These perceptions of a time squeeze on families have been given voice by a highly articulate and visible segment of the public, leading both scholars and lay persons to question the legitimacy of time demands at work, the sacrifice of other values to the ever faster production of goods and services, and the resulting burden placed on the family and the health of citizens.

Not surprisingly, this increase in work hours has led to stress, work-family conflicts, and other negative consequences, especially for people in high-skill jobs and in dual-career families.[14] In general, it appears that

> even among the groups of employees that have benefited most from the upturn in the economy, reports of stress, overwork, job insecurity, and difficulty in balancing the dual obligations of work and family are common. (Osterman et al. 2001, 1)

The growth in hours worked has also resulted, not surprisingly, in many persons feeling overworked. In the late 1990s, about six out of ten people in the United States wanted to work fewer hours per week than they actually did. For men, the average difference between actual hours worked (47.3 hours per week on average) and ideal number of hours (37.5) was 9.8 hours. For women, the difference was 9.3 hours (41.4 instead of 32.1). Men typically want to work full time, and women typically prefer somewhat less than full-time hours. The vast majority of those who wanted to work fewer hours said that they wanted to work at least five hours less than they actually worked. And about half of the 60 percent of workers who reported wanting to work fewer hours (about three in ten workers in the overall labor force) said they wanted to work at least twenty hours less than they actually did.[15]

The gaps between actual and ideal hours were greatest for highly educated workers, those in managerial and professional occupations, married workers, and middle-age workers (age thirty-six to fifty-five). For women, the biggest gap was for those who were married with an employed spouse, reinforcing the conclusion that dual-earner couples are the ones who are most likely to experience a time squeeze or "leisure pinch."[16]

The number of hours worked differs over time due to fluctuations in the business cycle, however. It is typical during labor market downturns for there to be an increase in involuntary part-time employment—that is, persons who want full-time jobs but worked less than thirty-five hours during the survey reference week because they could not find full-time work or because their hours were cut back due to unfavorable business conditions. The number of persons who were employed part time involuntarily during the Great Recession of 2007 to 2009 was the highest in over half a century.[17]

Polarization in Hours Worked

The coexistence of workers who feel overworked with other workers who feel underworked illustrates the polarization of different sections of the labor force over time. In the late 1990s, about 25 percent of men and almost 20 percent of women in the U.S. labor force were either full-time or part-

Figure 8.1   Polarization in Total Hours Worked per Week, 1970 and 2000

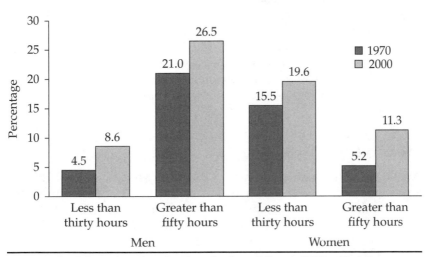

Source: Author's figure based on data from Jacobs and Gerson (2004, table 1.2).

time workers (especially those who worked part time involuntarily) who wanted to work more hours.[18]

The use of average hours worked as an indicator of how much people work masks an important set of diverging trends: there is a growing polarization in hours worked that represents a time divide differentiating people who work very long hours from those who have relatively short schedules.[19] Figure 8.1 shows the growing inequality in hours worked: the percentages of men and women who worked more than fifty hours a week and of men and women who worked less than thirty hours a week were both higher in 2000 than in 1970.

Thus, there has not been a single trend in the United States either in the growth of leisure or in the rising time demands of work. Instead, changes in family life have affected different groups of workers, as well as those living in different family situations, in disparate ways. There has been a growing polarization in hours worked between highly skilled, professional-type workers, on the one hand (who work more hours), and lower-skilled, nonexempt workers on the other (who may work fewer hours). Members of professional and technical occupations, as well as managers, are exempt from the overtime regulations of the Fair Labor Standards Act, and so they can be asked to work more hours without being compensated economically. The standard forty-hour workweek is disappearing in many occupations: professionals regularly put in extra hours to meet deadlines, and many hourly employees are required to work overtime or evening hours.[20] Salaried workers are often expected to spend night and weekend hours answering emails and doing paperwork from home, but these activities are typically not counted by government statistics as hours worked.

Increased polarization in hours worked is consistent with a view of the workforce as "increasingly divided between demanding but potentially enriching jobs held by educated workers—especially at the very top—and short-time, low-paid, low-skill, and often contingent work held by less-educated workers" (Cappelli et al. 1997, 194).

Work Intensity

Another vital temporal dimension of the employment relationship is the amount of work a person does in a given time period, or the intensity of working time. The realization that time is a valuable resource led managers long ago to try to maximize the amount of work they expected of their employees in a given unit of work time by scientifically managing work procedures and designing work organizations so as to elicit as much labor as possible for given units of their employees' labor power.

Explanations of why workers are working harder now than in the recent past generally attribute the greater intensity to workers' either being more fearful of their employers or being more motivated to help their organizations succeed.[21] The Marxian theory of the labor process emphasized that the development of capitalism was associated with a continuing effort by capitalists to use coercion to exploit their workers by extracting surplus value from them in order to increase profits. One strategy to get workers to produce more is to coerce them to work harder and at a faster pace by applying a "stick strategy"—that is, managers may threaten workers with layoffs if they do not work hard and require survivors of downsizing and other forms of organizational restructuring to do additional work to pick up the slack left by those who have been laid off.[22] Capitalists have the upper hand in hegemonic systems that characterize advanced capitalism, and workers have few options but to consent to managers' demands that they work hard, especially when unemployment is high and there is a sizable reserve army of unemployed workers ready to take one's job.[23] Pressures to work harder may result from the imposition of production targets as well as from managers' desires to adapt to customer demands. Both of these time pressures may be tied directly to the short-term approach to management that stems from the capital market changes discussed in chapter 2.

The decline in unions may also help explain why employers are able to use coercive means to make employees work harder, especially in recent years. Unions have historically sought to protect workers from managements' attempts to increase the speed of production, as was the case during the introduction of assembly lines at the beginning of the twentieth century. At the height of union power in the 1950s and 1960s, most collective bargaining contracts, particularly in manufacturing, contained language that regulated workload and pace. The decline of union power since the 1970s has made workers (even those who are union members) more vulnerable to managers' demands for work intensification.

An alternative explanation for an increase in work intensity is that workers are motivated to work hard in high-performance work organizations. Such organizations are designed to elicit the discretionary effort of workers, and those who work within them are more committed to them.[24] Workers may put forth greater effort and engage in organizational citizenship behaviors because they want their organizations to succeed, or to advance their own careers. Such high-performance work organizations may also elicit hard work through coercion. Working in teams, for example, may lead to increases in output not only because workers have more opportunities to participate in decision-making, but also because of the intensified peer pressure and dependence on colleagues' pace of work that is likely to be associated with "the tyranny of teamwork."[25] In addition, the demands made on employees who are asked to make decisions on their own are likely to be much greater than the job requirements associated with more routine and closely supervised work systems.[26]

Organizational restructuring by means of high-performance work organizations may thus be a two-edged sword: it has the potential to increase the degree of control that workers have over their work tasks, but it also may lead to pressures for workers to work more intensely and for more hours. The greater control that workers have over their tasks may have come at a price: making jobs more demanding and time-consuming. Even good jobs require people to work hard.

An increase in work intensification has also been explained on the basis of technological change. New techniques and new ways of organizing work have increased the efficiency with which work can be performed. Machines and equipment have helped quite a bit in settings that once relied on brute human force. In the white-collar setting, computers, cell phones, email, and other tools have made tasks that used to be nearly impossible now almost effortless. These trends provide the potential for great increases in productivity. To take advantage of this potential for productivity growth, however, workers must be persuaded (or coerced) to devote high levels of effort. This hypothesis of effort-biased technological change is supported by evidence of a strong association between reports of increased skill requirements and work intensification.[27]

It is also likely that pressures to work more intensely are experienced by a wide variety of workers.[28] Work intensity thus seems to contradict the argument of greater polarization in the workplace. Highly educated professionals and managers and those in full-time and traditional work situations have seen their hours increase and have had to work harder (see my earlier discussion). Meanwhile, workers at lower strata often have to put together two or more jobs to make a decent living, and those who are not working enough hours likely work just as hard as the high-wage earners, though not necessarily as long, since they get paid by the hour and employers often do not want to pay them overtime.

Perceptions that there has been a general quickening in the pace and hours of work raise concerns about the quality of jobs. The anxiety over an intensification of work has been fueled by corporate restructurings such as downsizing and has been supported by feelings of economic insecurity on the part of those employees who have survived layoffs. Such intensification and insecurity constitute a "dark side" to the booming American economy of the 1990s and are reflected in part in an increase in workloads for formerly privileged white-collar workers; some writers have even used the metaphor of the sweatshop to describe the deterioration of white-collar work that has accompanied the greater time pressures resulting from corporate restructuring.[29] The intensification of white-collar as well as blue-collar work has been facilitated by technological developments that have enabled employers to become increasingly sophisticated in their ability to monitor and control the amount of time that workers spend at work as well as their activities at the workplace.

Changes in Work Intensity: Evidence

Evidence of increases in work intensification is largely anecdotal. Complaints about job speedup and work pressure abound. Increased pressure to work hard is emerging as a top complaint for low-wage employees in sectors as diverse as food processing and tourism. It has also become a pivotal bargaining issue in some union contracts. Some health and safety experts, moreover, consider work pressure to be a major source of injury and illness.[30]

Quantitative studies of work intensification generally rely on measures based on subjective perceptions of intensity of work.[31] Francis Green and Steven McIntosh (2001) use two indicators of effort expended at work and find that there was an intensification of work effort across many European countries between 1991 and 1996.[32] They also showed that Britain experienced a faster increase in average work effort in the early 1990s than did other European Union countries. France and the Netherlands were not far below Britain, though the increases in average work effort in Denmark

Table 8.1   Changes in Work Intensity

	Comparison Year	Year Only		Year with Controls	
		Mean	Variance	Mean	Variance
Too much	1977 versus 2002	0.075**	0.014	0.09**	0.02
work	1977 versus 2006	0.073**	−0.046	0.07**	−0.09
Work fast	1977 versus 2002	0.081**	−0.196**	0.07*	−0.06
	1977 versus 2006	0.098**	−0.250***	0.08*	−0.16
Work hard	1977 versus 2002[a]	0.449***	1.198***	0.43***	1.23***

Source: Author's compilation based on data from Families and Work Institute (2002); Davis, Smith, and Marsden (2009); and Quinn and Staines (2000).
***$p < .001$; **$p < .01$; *$p < .05$.
[a]2002 National Study of a Changing Workforce. Other surveys: 2002 and 2006 General Social Surveys; 1977 Quality of Employment Survey.

and Germany were much smaller. Pierre Boisard and his colleagues (2003) also found that work intensity increased in Europe from 1995 to 2000. The overall level of work intensity in the United States appears to be at least as great as in Europe, with 30 to 40 percent of respondents to the General Social Surveys saying that their work was "often" or "sometimes" stressful over the period between 1989 and 2002.[33]

Analyzing several national survey items illuminates the trends in work intensity in the United States. The results of these items are presented in table 8.1.

"I have too much work to do everything well." (Asked in 1977, 2002, and 2006)

Too much work: Responses are scored from 1 = "Strongly disagree" to 4 = "Strongly agree."

This item can be interpreted as an indicator of a "time famine," which is a feeling of having too much to do and not enough time to do it.[34] Table 8.1 indicates that in 2002 and in 2006, workers were significantly more likely to say that they have too much work to do everything well, compared with 1977 (the difference between 2002 and 2006 is not statistically significant). These findings are consistent with the hypothesis that work intensity has increased overall since the 1970s, and the differences between years persist even after the control variables are added to the equation. There appears to be no significant increase in polarization among workers in the extent to which they perceive that they have too much work to do everything well, however. Rather, it appears that the increase in overwork is a fairly widespread perception.[35]

"My job requires that I work very fast." (Asked in 1977, 2002, and 2006)

Work fast: Responses are scored from 1 = "Strongly disagree" to 4 = "Strongly agree."

This item taps workers' perceptions that there has been a speed up that forces them to work more quickly on their jobs. The results presented in table 8.1 indicate that there has also been an increase in the tendency of respondents to say that their job requires them to work very fast. People were more likely to say this in 2002 and in 2006 than in 1977 (again, the difference between 2002 and 2006 is not statistically significant). Moreover, there has been a significant decrease in the variance of "Work fast," suggesting that workers are much more similar now than they were in the 1977s in feeling that their job requires them to work fast. This reduction in inequality in working fast is explained by the control variables, however, since there is no significant difference in the variance in "Work fast" once the control variables are included in the model.[36]

The final indicator of work intensity is a general question asking people whether or not their job requires them to work very hard:

"My job requires that I work very hard." (Asked in 1977 and 2002)

Work hard: Responses are scored from 1 = "Strongly disagree" to 3 = "Strongly Agree."

Table 8.1 indicates that there has been a general increase in peoples' perception that their jobs require them to work hard. This result is consistent with the pattern observed for the other two indicators of work intensity and supports the overall hypothesis that work intensity is greater now than in the 1970s. Moreover, there also appears to have been a significant increase in polarization in the perceptions that jobs require people to work hard. Furthermore, this increase in the variance of "Work hard" is not explained by the control variables. In addition to divergence in working hours, then, this result suggests that there has also been a growing polarization in how hard people work.[37]

Control over Work Time

Most research on working time has focused on how many hours people work, though a growing number of studies emphasize the importance of also considering the timing of those hours and how much control an employee has over the amount—but especially the scheduling—of working time. An employee's control over working time refers to his or her ability to increase or decrease one's working hours and to alter one's work schedule. Workers who are able to exert control over their work time may be able to choose when they come to work during the course of a day, which days they work during a week, even which weeks they work during a given month. There are a large variety of flexible forms of working time that are, in theory, available: flextime, job sharing, telecommuting, part-time work, and compressed workweeks.

People who have a high degree of control over their schedules are more likely to have flexibility in dealing with their nonwork obligations and activities, such as those related to their family or their communities. For consequences such as health and the quality of family relations, the degree of control that individuals have over their work time is often more salient than how hard or long they work. Workers who are able to decide when they work are less likely to experience stress, regardless of the actual schedule worked.[38] Workers with a high degree of control over their jobs may also be able to schedule work to avoid having "too much to do."[39]

Institutional and cultural arrangements affect the degree of control that people have over their working time.[40] In some countries, there are mandatory minimums on the length of vacation time (and sometimes the timing of vacations), in addition to limits on the number of hours a person can work. These regulatory constraints affect peoples' work intensity, as well as the amount of control they have over their working lives. Recent efforts to restructure working time in many European countries have come largely in response to demands for greater control over work scheduling, especially on the part of dual-career couples. These gains have occurred where employees have increased their power through collective bargaining, government legislation, or labor market conditions. In Sweden and the Netherlands, for example, workers have used their collective bargaining control to negotiate reductions in working time and flexibility over the use of time.

In countries such as the United States, where collective bargaining in the private sector is not widespread and labor institutions are relatively weak, employers tend to have considerable control over the type and structure of working time. The distribution of flexible forms of working time tends to be narrow, reflecting employer interests; this serves to restrict employees' choice of various flexible work schedules and control over their own working time. While other countries around the world have taken steps that increase employee control over working time, in the United States, market forces such as supply and demand for labor affect the nature and control of working time. This has resulted in a relatively low level of employee control, limited flexibility in working time, and an uneven distribution of control over working time across occupations.

In the United States, then, employees must rely largely on their position within the labor market or their value to a particular employer in order to gain bargaining power and control over working time. Workers with more market power—derived from having more valuable skills, unique expertise, more education, and other sources of human and social capital—are more likely to have control over their work time and schedule. Employers who wish to attract and retain valued workers may set up flexible work arrangements (such as flextime or job sharing) that accommodate workers' needs and desires for greater control over the scheduling of work time.

The type of work one does also affects the extent to which one can exercise control over work schedules; thus, worker control is distributed unequally across occupations. Workers are better able to control their schedules if their work is evaluated in terms of their output, such as performing surgery or repairing plumbing. Professionals with valuable skill sets generally have more control over working time and more flexibility than do less-skilled occupational groups. On the other hand, workers who are easily replaceable and whose work is evaluated by means of behavior control are likely to have less control over their schedules. While managers and professionals have experienced an increase in hours worked (see earlier discussion), they may be able to trade off working more hours for greater control over when and where the work takes place; this is reflected in the growth of telecommuting and flexible starting and finishing times for these employees.[41] For many American workers, however, the need for greater flexibility and control over work time means accepting part-time or contingent work arrangements.

Data from the May 2001 Current Population Survey indicate that about 31 percent of employed workers had some sort of flexible work hours that allowed them to vary their starting and ending work times. Access to scheduling flexibility was greater for college graduates, those who were salaried and did not belong to a union, and parents of young children. Managerial and professional occupations were most likely to have access to flexible schedules (especially lawyers and judges, mathematical and computer scientists, sales representatives in commodities besides retail, and college and university teachers), while laborers, assemblers, transport and material movers, machine operators, and K–12 teachers had the least. Those who worked very long hours (more than fifty hours per week) or relatively few (less than twenty) had the most scheduling flexibility, while those who worked forty hours per week had the least. Workers who had access to flexible schedules were more likely to obtain them through informal arrangements with supervisors, managers, or coworkers than by participating in formal flextime programs.[42]

The amount of control that workers in general have over their schedules appears to have increased, at least since the early 1990s (comparable data before the early 1990s are scarce). For example, when asked the question, "Overall, how much control would you say you have in scheduling your work hours?" about 45 percent of the respondents to the 2002 National Study of a Changing Workforce (NSCW) said they either had "a lot" or "complete control," compared with 34 percent responding to the same question in the 1992 NSCW. This increase in perceived control over schedules also occurred between 1992 and 1997. These differences are statistically significant even after controlling for the demographic variables described earlier (results not presented in tabular form). Moreover, the variance in control over schedules is significantly smaller in 1997 and 2002 than in 1992. Men, college graduates, part-time workers, self-employed persons, and managers and supervisors had greater control over their schedules, while workers in larger establishments had less.

Surveys by the Society for Human Resource Management indicate that the proportion of employers offering flextime peaked in 2002, with 64 percent of employers saying they made the practice available. This proportion decreased at the beginning of the 2000s and fell below 50 percent for the first time in 2009, in part due to layoffs associated with the Great Recession of 2007 to 2009 in industries such as financial services.[43] The extent to which employers offer options such as flextime will likely vary depending on business conditions.

These general increases in workers' control over their schedules are consistent with the view that employers have responded to their employees' needs for flexible work options by making this coveted job reward available to them. Doing this is likely to help employers retain valued employees and may well improve workers' performance. Providing schedule flexibility might also substitute for the absence of other job rewards, such as higher earnings and opportunities for advancement, as well as asking workers to work longer or more intense hours. Still, even in 2002, over half of the employees in the United States reported that they had only some, very little, or no control at all over scheduling their work hours, and in 2001, about 70 percent of workers said that they were unable to alter their starting and ending times of work.

Balancing Work and Family

The increase in both work hours and work intensity have made it more important for workers—especially married workers with employed spouses—to have control over their work schedules. As noted earlier, the issue of whether people have enough control over their working time has come to the forefront of public concern due to the change in the structure of the typical family from one dominated by a male bread-winner to one headed by a dual-earner couple or a single working adult. Workers with families, especially those with children, are under more pressure to have greater flexibility in the timing and scheduling of their work. Children's schedules, especially in middle-class families, have become more demanding, and parents today are expected to partici-pate in their kids' school, sports, and social enrichment activities.[44] These changes have made it more imperative for people to have control over their work schedules, so that they may be able to cope with the responsi-bilities associated with family activities and paid employment. Moreover, there exist sharp inequalities in control across the social divides of class, gender, disability, and family structure.[45]

Surveys conducted over a twenty-five-year span contained an item that sheds some light on trends in peoples' perceptions of how difficult it is to balance their work and family lives.

"How hard is it to take time off during your work to take care of personal or family matters?" (Asked in 1977 and 2002)

Responses are scored from 1 = "Very hard" to 4 = "Not at all hard."

Workers perceived that it is generally harder to take time off to take care of personal or family matters in 2002 than it was in 1977 (results not pre-sented in tabular form). This finding is consistent with the scenario pre-sented in this chapter that there has been a growing need for workers to have control over their schedules in order to balance their work and fam-ily needs. Moreover, it is not necessarily inconsistent with the general findings described earlier that workers generally have more control over their schedules now than in the past. Thus, while the amount of control that people have over their schedules appears to have increased (at least since the early 1990s), these increases in control and the structural changes that have taken place in jobs and workplaces have not kept pace with the explosive growth of workers' needs for flexibility and control.

In addition to being generally harder for workers to take time off to take care of personal or family needs, the variance in perceived difficulty appears to have decreased since the 1970s. This reduction in inequality among workers in their ability to balance work and personal life appears to be explained by demographic and work structure variables, however. Women, full-time workers, younger workers, and supervisors say that it is hard for them to take time off to take care of family matters, while those in managerial occupations and in larger establishments say it is relatively easy to take time off.

Conclusions

Time is an essential aspect of job quality. This chapter has examined three important aspects of time at work: how much time workers spend at their jobs, how intensely they work during this time, and how much control they have over their work schedules.

The evidence suggests that there has been a growing polarization in the number of hours that people work. Those who have good jobs as determined by many of the criteria discussed in earlier chapters (earnings, fringe benefits, and control over work activities) are more likely to work more hours than those who have relatively low-skill and poorly paid jobs.

In addition, there has been a general increase in how intensely workers report working during the hours they spend at their jobs. As with the number of hours worked, the evidence suggests that those in better jobs are more likely to also report that they are working more intensely in these jobs. However, the evidence for polarization of work intensity is relatively weak; it is likely that workers in both bad and otherwise good jobs are now working more intensely.

Finally, the degree to which workers report that they have control over the timing of their work and schedules appears to have increased, at least since the 1990s. Nevertheless, the majority of workers still do not have access to flexible schedules. Moreover, it seems that workers are less likely to perceive that they are able to take time off from work to take care of family and personal matters now than in the past. This may reflect a structural mismatch between the growing needs of workers for more flexibility to take care of family and personal matters and the relatively slow changes in jobs and workplaces to meet these needs.

═ Chapter 9 ═

Job Satisfaction

THE ECONOMIC and noneconomic job rewards examined in previous chapters are especially salient to workers and their employers and are useful for summarizing the broad trends in job quality. At the same time, these dimensions of work do not exhaust all the potential rewards and benefits to workers that might be available from their jobs.[1] It is difficult, if not impossible, to measure all aspects of work that might constitute job rewards, so it would be useful to supplement the assessment of specific job facets with an overview of changes in the overall quality of jobs.

The concept of job satisfaction is the most popular solution to measuring overall job quality.[2] There are an enormous number of studies about job satisfaction and its effects. Sociologists and psychologists have often studied job satisfaction in order to understand differences in the quality of jobs and in workers' well-being at work. Economists have been generally more interested in job satisfaction because it has been shown to predict quits and to be positively related to productivity.

Job satisfaction is an overall affective response on the part of individuals to their jobs. It is an evaluative measure based on workers' perceptions of the overall goodness of their jobs and their judgments about the quality of their employment situations. Job satisfaction is thus not a measure of the objective quality of jobs; such a measure is impossible to create for diverse populations because of the large number of possible benefits associated with jobs and the difficulty of combining them in a summary fashion. But more important, as discussed in chapter 1, job quality necessarily includes a subjective component; people weight their various job rewards differently to come up with an overall evaluation. It is well known that workers' evaluations of their jobs reflect comparative judgments rather than straightforward assessments of an objective reality; evaluations are sensitive to the comparison standards that people assume, as well as to the importance they place on various job characteristics.[3]

The concept of job satisfaction thus acknowledges that whether a job is considered good or bad is to some extent in the eye of the beholder. Judgments about whether workers are satisfied with their jobs as a whole must take into account variations in individuals' valuations and other assessments of particular job characteristics. People differ in what they want or value in their jobs (such as income, health insurance, control over work, pleasant social relationships, an easy commute, flexible hours, relatively few demands or duties, and so on), and so the bases of satisfaction are diverse. Jobs may not have the same meaning for individuals or even groups (such as women versus men, blacks versus whites, or members of different types of households). The impacts of particular job rewards on satisfaction are filtered through the subjective lens of one's work values or the importance that people place on various economic and noneconomic job rewards, as well as their expectations.

Since workers differ in their preferences for and evaluations of the quality of particular job characteristics, a theoretically appropriate composite measure of job quality should reflect individual differences in preferences and utilities for economic as well as noneconomic rewards. The weights people assign to various job characteristics are likely to differ among individuals as well as change over time, as the importance that workers attach to different dimensions may vary according to circumstances, such as the state of the economy or the availability of different kinds of job rewards.

Studying job satisfaction is also useful since it has been measured at various points in time and in a large number of populations. Some authors explicitly equate job quality with job satisfaction, arguing that the use of this global concept enables the assessment of overall job quality without identifying and measuring all the job rewards and benefits that the job provides.[4] These analysts generally assume that workers are able to balance the pros and cons associated with their jobs and arrive at an overall assessment of them.[5]

There is considerable evidence that these assessments provide useful information: extensive research has shown that people are capable of consistently evaluating their own states of well-being. Thus, after noting that job rewards are multidimensional and that it may not be possible to measure many of the job characteristics that constitute potential benefits, for example, Andrew Clark (1998, 2) argues that

> the simple response to a question on overall job satisfaction does a good job of summarizing this often missing information and . . . is closely related to other, more complicated measures that can be derived from a battery of questions concerning job quality.

At the same time, it is important to recognize that the concept of job satisfaction is a fairly blunt instrument with which to assess changes in job quality. The fact that job satisfaction is based on both objective job rewards and peoples' subjective assessments of them is both an advantage and a disadvantage: it enables the analyst to take into account individual differences in assessing job quality, but it is unclear whether changes in this concept are due to differences in job characteristics or in peoples' expectations and values.

In this chapter, I first examine how the various kinds of job rewards discussed in chapters 5 through 8 are related to perceptions of overall job satisfaction and how these job rewards' contributions to worker satisfaction have changed since the 1970s. I next assess overall job satisfaction in the United States, drawing on data from nationally representative samples of the U.S. labor force since the 1970s to provide a picture of the changes that have occurred in both average levels and inequality in job satisfaction.[6]

Job Satisfaction and Job Rewards

There are two main ways of measuring job satisfaction. The first asks workers to make a global judgment about their overall satisfaction with the job. A second approach assesses one's satisfaction with various facets of the job and then combines them in some way to create a summary measure of overall satisfaction. I adopt the former approach here since it has the advantage of not requiring information on all the possible aspects of work that might go into an overall assessment.[7] Moreover, this approach permits an appraisal of the impacts of job rewards (that is, the evaluations of particular job facets) and individual differences in the importance of these facets on the overall quality of one's work experience.

The analyses presented in this chapter are based on the commonly used "direct" indicator of job satisfaction, which asks workers some variant of the question, "On the whole, how satisfied are you with your job—would you say you are [1] not at all satisfied, [2] not too satisfied, [3] somewhat satisfied, or [4] very satisfied?" Virtually all the available evidence on changes in job satisfaction for large, diverse populations is based on some version of this direct indicator. Despite the criticisms of this measure,[8] it has many advantages: it implies a commonsense notion of satisfaction and is straightforward and easily understood.[9] It also costs relatively little to include on surveys (which accounts in large part for its popularity) and has been found to correlate highly with more complex scales.

In the United States, workers generally report very high levels of satisfaction with their jobs when asked directly. For example, in the General Social Survey data, six in seven persons report being "moderately" or "very" satisfied with their work. These high levels of satisfaction have been interpreted by some as suggesting that workers may express more satisfaction than they really feel in order to appear competent and successful to the interviewer.[10] On the other hand, the tendency of people to express contentment with their jobs should not be too surprising: people who are very unhappy with their jobs are likely to leave them if they can and search for work that is more to their liking, especially during relatively good economic times. Since respondents are typically asked how satisfied they are with jobs they are currently occupying, there are likely to be substantial selection effects that inflate reports of satisfaction.

In any event, the relatively high levels of satisfaction found in studies in the United States for the direct indicator are not unique: in 1997, for example, workers in Denmark, Switzerland, and Spain all scored higher than Americans on this item, with at least 50 percent of the workers reporting that they feel "very satisfied" or even "completely satisfied" with their jobs.[11]

Table 9.1 presents the results of ordered logistic regression models of overall job satisfaction on the types of job rewards discussed in chapters 5 through 8. Results for 1977 and 2006 are presented for the effects of job rewards alone and then controlling for a set of demographic and work structure variables that past research has shown to be related to job satisfaction. I examine the relationships between overall job satisfaction and job security (chapter 5); earnings and fringe benefits (chapter 6); autonomy, participation, and intrinsic rewards (chapter 7); and work intensity and ability to take time off (chapter 8). Italicized coefficients represent significant differences between the two years in the effects of a job reward on job satisfaction.

The results presented in table 9.1 confirm that many of the job rewards considered in earlier chapters have distinct impacts on overall job satisfaction, underscoring the utility of job satisfaction ratings as a global measure of job quality. In both 1977 and 2006, workers were likely to be more satisfied with their jobs if they regarded their fringe benefits and job security as being good; if they were able to participate in decisions in the workplace; if they received intrinsic rewards, such as having the opportunity to develop their own special abilities; and if they did not feel that they had too much work to do.

Having the freedom to decide how to do one's own work does not seem to affect overall job satisfaction independently of being able to participate in decisions and being able to develop one's abilities, though all of these variables are relatively highly correlated among themselves. In addition, whether a worker perceives that she or he is able to take time off for familial or personal reasons does not appear to have a distinct significant impact on overall job satisfaction.

Table 9.1   **Effects of Job Rewards on Overall Job Satisfaction, 1977 and 2006**

	1977		2006	
Job Rewards	No controls	With Controls[b]	No Controls	With Controls[b]
(log) Income from main job	*-0.26***	-0.14	*-0.03*	0.01
Fringe benefits[a]	0.32***	0.43***	0.21***	0.28***
Promotion opportunities[a]	0.17**	0.33***	0.05	0.12
Job security[a]	*0.31***	0.26***	*0.59***	0.65***
Participation (have a lot of say)	0.31***	0.32***	0.45***	0.50***
Discretion (work freedom)	0.12	0.07	0.14	-0.06
Intrinsic rewards (opportunity to develop skills)	0.50***	0.47***	0.69***	0.57***
Work intensity (too much work)	-0.39***	-0.49***	-0.39***	-0.45***
Can take time off for family matters	0.07	0.09	-0.01	0.00
(pseudo) R^2	0.13	0.20	0.15	0.18
N	1,133	1,063	1,284	802

Source: Author's table based on data from Davis, Smith, and Marsden (2009) and Families and Work Institute (2002).
***$p \leq .001$; **$p \leq .01$; *$p \leq .05$. Italicized coefficients: $p < .05$. The equations were estimated by ordered logistic regression techniques.
[a]Fringe benefits: "My fringe benefits are good" (1 = Not at all true, 4 = Very true); Promotion opportunities: "The chances for promotion are good" (1 = Not at all true, 4 = Very true); Job security: "The job security is good" (1 = Not at all true, 4 = Very true).
[b]Equations control for demographic characteristics (gender, race, age, employer tenure, education, part-time status, and marital status) and work structures (supervisor, establishment size, occupational skill levels, union membership, and occupation and industry categories).

Income was negatively related to job satisfaction in 1977, but this negative effect becomes insignificant once the demographic and work structure variables are controlled. Income was unrelated to job satisfaction in 2006. The weak or even negative effect of income on job satisfaction likely results from people using different frames of reference for evaluating their jobs (I discuss this further later in this chapter). Job security appears to be more strongly related to job satisfaction in 2006 than in 1977, though this difference by year becomes nonsignificant when control variables are added.

By contrast, workers who perceived that their opportunities for promotion were good were more satisfied with their jobs overall in 1977, but perceived promotion opportunities were unrelated to satisfaction in

2006 (although the differences in the effects of perceived promotion opportunities between these two years were not statistically significant).

The greater effects of job security on job satisfaction in 2006 as compared with 1977 are likely due to the availability of jobs that provide security becoming increasingly problematic from 2000 onward compared with the 1970s, as I note in chapter 5. As particular job rewards become more problematic, workers are likely to be relatively more satisfied with jobs that provide them.

Trends in Overall Job Satisfaction

Increases or decreases in job satisfaction over time are often interpreted as indicators of the growth or decline in the quality of jobs. As my earlier discussion has underscored, however, it is not always clear what changes (or lack of changes) in job satisfaction necessarily imply about the growth or decline in good or bad jobs, since assessments of overall job quality are shaped by individual differences, as well as by the multiplicity of job rewards.

In view of the declines in job quality for large groups of American workers—especially the increases in job insecurity and uncertainty, growing inequality in earnings and fringe benefits, and greater work intensification and hours worked—it would be surprising if job satisfaction had not also decreased since the 1970s. For example, it has been well established that job insecurity is a stressor that is frequently linked to poor mental and physical health outcomes, as well as to lower job satisfaction.[12] On the other hand, I have also documented some positive changes in job quality since the 1970s, especially the increasing opportunities for workers to exercise control over their jobs and to obtain intrinsic rewards. These counterbalancing changes in job rewards may be offsetting in their effects on job satisfaction, some increasing it and others decreasing it.

Moreover, changes in labor force composition, such as the growing proportion of women in the labor force, may also affect patterns of job satisfaction. Women tend to be more satisfied with their jobs than men, for example, which reflects both the different reference groups that men and women use when assessing their jobs and that women's expectations are often lower than men's.[13] The increase in female workers in the labor force since the 1970s may thus have produced an upward pressure on average levels of job satisfaction.

Moreover, Richard Easterlin (1980) famously argued that one's economic fortunes are shaped by the size of one's cohort as well as by the experiences of different cohorts with dissimilar slices of history. He presented evidence indicating that happiness (that is, subjective well-being) varied directly with one's own income and inversely with the incomes of others.[14] Andrew Clark and Andrew Oswald (1996) also provide evidence for such a model of interdependent preferences, showing that people with higher incomes within a country are, on average, happier at a given time, though changes in happiness depend on changes in comparison incomes over time.[15]

Such reference groups may also help explain why workers' assessments of the goodness of a job (or of job components, such as job security, earnings, or work intensity) may remain unchanged despite objective changes in jobs. Peoples' standards for judging job quality may change as the idea of what constitutes a good or bad job transforms over time. If reduced job security or lower earnings come to be viewed as typical features of a job, for example, then expectations may decline together with job quality, and levels of satisfaction might remain steady. Workers who have jobs at all during times of growing precarity might consider themselves to be relatively fortunate, and hence satisfied with their jobs. If workers perceive their peers' jobs to be no more secure or well paying than their own, they may also be relatively satisfied with their jobs.

The overall result of these complex processes of evaluating job quality may be that there has been relatively little change in average job satisfaction in the United States since the 1970s. Such constancy in job satisfaction would be consistent with economists' claims that the labor market efficiently sorts individuals into jobs. In addition, psychological theories predict that individuals tend to adjust their expectations to changes in the environment and the economy, as when, for example, workers modify their work values and expectations depending on which job facets are more problematic and thereby adapt to a new world in which there is a marked decrease in job security.

Cross-national studies of trends in job satisfaction have shown that average satisfaction has either remained relatively constant or decreased over the past several decades. In Britain, job satisfaction has declined since the early 1990s; Francis Green attributes this decrease to the effects of rising work intensity and declining task discretion (see my discussion in chapters 7 and 8).[16] In Germany, there was a decline in satisfaction from 1984 to 1997, and then a slight recovery. Green argues that the trends in job satisfaction in both of these countries are due primarily to changes in workers' well-being, not to adjustments in the norms against which job satisfaction is assessed. He also notes that the story in other European Union countries is less clear and not as pessimistic as in Britain and Germany, though he bases this conclusion on data from only the period between 1994 and 2000.

Evidence of Changes in Job Satisfaction in the United States

Given the widespread interest in job satisfaction held by social scientists, managers, and the public, there is surprisingly little systematic evidence on trends in satisfaction for national samples of American workers. This partly reflects the dominance of job-satisfaction research by psychologists, whose studies are mostly based on relatively restricted samples of particular jobs or workplaces. It also reflects the general lack of broadly representative, longitudinal studies of work and workers that I have alluded to at various places throughout this book.

Studies by the Conference Board have documented a decrease in job satisfaction in the United States over the past several decades. The most recent survey of a representative sample of five thousand households, in 2009, found that only 45 percent of all Americans say they are satisfied with their jobs, compared with 61 percent in the first survey that was conducted in 1987. Furthermore, satisfaction levels appear to have decreased among all workers, regardless of age, income, or residence.[17] These analyses did not examine changes in polarization or inequality in job satisfaction, however.

Table 9.2 presents evidence on trends in job satisfaction from two sets of data. Panel A uses the 1977 Quality of Employment Survey and the Quality of Work Life Supplement to the 2006 General Social Survey (which repeats many of the same questions asked in 1977). Panel B uses information from the General Social Surveys for 1972 to 2006. For each data source, I present estimates of changes in the means as well as the variances of job satisfaction.

The results presented in panel A suggest that there has not been an overall change from 1977 to 2006 in either the mean or variance of job satisfaction. The raw comparisons in the means or variances in job satisfaction between these two years are not statistically significant (first row), nor are they different when we control for the demographic characteristics and work structures used in table 9.1 (second row). We only observe a significant decline in the mean (but not the variance) of job satisfaction when measures of job rewards are added to the model (third row). The role of job rewards in explaining changes in job satisfaction is complex, as is also clear in table 9.1: some rewards have increased over time (such as opportunity to develop skills), thus enhancing satisfaction, while others have declined over time (such as greater work intensity), hence lowering satisfaction. The fact that the negative effect of year on job satisfaction is revealed once we control for job rewards

Table 9.2   Changes in Overall Job Satisfaction, 1977 and 2006

| | Unstandardized Coefficient | |
	Mean	Variance
A. Quality of Employment Surveys		
1977 versus 2006	−0.079	−0.089
1977 versus 2006 (controls included)[a]	−0.082	−0.048
1977 versus 2006 (controls included)[b]	−0.342***	−0.153
B. General Social Surveys (1972 to 2006)		
Year	−0.005***	−0.006**
Year	−0.004*	−0.004
Unemployment rate	0.009	0.22
Year	0.025***	0.003
Unemployment rate	0.012	0.016
Cohort	−0.022***	−0.003**
Year	0.022***	0.006*
Unemployment rate	0.017	0.015
Cohort (controls included)[c]	−0.019***	−0.005***

Source: Author's table based on data from Davis, Smith, and Marsden (2009) and Families and Work Institute (2002).
***$p \le .001$; **$p \le .01$; *$p \le .05$.
[a]Control variables are the demographic characteristics and work structures used in table 9.1.
[b]Control variables are the measures of job rewards, demographic characteristics, and work structures used in table 9.1.
[c]Control variables are education, gender, race, full-time employee, occupational categories, and real family income.

suggests that the decline in job satisfaction is driven by changing norms, expectations, and other attitudes—not the measures of job rewards that are included in the model.

The results using the GSS are based on information for twenty-six data points between 1972 and 2006. The sample pools all twenty-six General Social Surveys conducted between 1972 and 2006; the direct indicator of job satisfaction is available on all of these surveys.[18] Most trend studies of the U.S. labor force have relied on the General Social Surveys, which have asked this question in each survey since 1972. When we estimate a model containing only the mean and variance (first row), we find that there has been a statistically significant decline in average satisfaction.[19]

Adding the unemployment rate—so as to control for fluctuations in the business cycle and hence the availability of job opportunities—does not significantly change the negative effect of year on overall job satisfaction (second set of rows in panel B). The coefficient for the unemployment rate is statistically insignificant; its positive sign, however, suggests that workers may view their jobs more optimistically when jobs are relatively scarce. This could be because workers lower their standards and expectations for satisfaction when jobs are in short supply.

The declines in average job satisfaction since the early 1970s are not due only to events associated with the passage of years, however. Social scientists have long recognized that such trends reflect composite patterns involving differences among periods (years), cohorts (persons born in the same year), and age (the consequences of getting older). Given the complexity of the processes underlying changes in job satisfaction—in particular, the consequences of an intricate combination of individual differences and changes in job rewards—I try to disentangle these effects in order to identify better the mechanisms that are producing the decline in job satisfaction since the 1970s. This is a difficult problem: one cannot estimate equations that contain period, cohort, and age effects simultaneously since each of these three variables is a linear combination of the other two.

The linear decomposition technique suggested by Glenn Firebaugh offers a partial solution to this problem by adding a measure of cohort (for example, birth year) to the equation containing year.[20] This allows the trend in job satisfaction to be decomposed into changes attributable to cohort replacement or intercohort change (that is, the coefficient for cohort) and to changes within cohorts (that is, the coefficient for year).[21]

An equation containing both year and cohort (the third set of rows in panel B of table 9.2) reveals countervailing movements in job satisfaction since the early 1970s that are attributable to cohort turnover (intercohort change) and year (intracohort change). There is a significant positive effect of intracohort change (that is, the year variable) and a significant negative effect of intercohort change (that is, the cohort variable). The coefficient for the unemployment rate remains positive but is still not statistically significant.

The negative and significant coefficient for cohort indicates that circulation in the labor force—the departure of older workers in earlier birth cohorts in favor of younger ones from later cohorts—serves to decrease overall satisfaction in the workforce. Workers entering the labor force typically are less satisfied than those they replace. Once people enter the labor force, however, their satisfaction tends to increase as they age and time advances.[22] This pattern is evident in the significant positive coefficient for year, which here estimates the extent of intracohort change.

A likely explanation for the lower satisfaction reported by entering cohorts is that their work values and expectations are different; in particular, they value income and security more than the cohorts they are replacing. One reason they may place greater importance on income and security is that these aspects of work have become more problematic to attain, as discussed in chapters 5 and 6. Evidence for this is provided by an analysis of changes in how Americans rank various aspects of jobs, for which data are available in sixteen GSSs between 1973 and 2006.[23] These surveys asked respondents to rank the relative importance of five work values: high income; no danger of being fired; short working hours and lots of free time; chances for advancement; and work that is important and gives a feeling of accomplishment.[24] These values correspond roughly to the job rewards discussed in previous chapters.[25]

Analyses of these data indicate that while the highest ranked value during this period is consistently "work that is meaningful and gives a feeling of accomplishment," the relative importance workers place on having both a high income and job security has increased relative to the other job facets from the early 1970s to 2006.[26] The average increases in relative valuation of income and security are consistent with the story that has been told in previous chapters: as employment relations have become more precarious and earnings more polarized, workers are becoming less certain that they will be able to obtain jobs that are secure and pay well. Hence, they place greater priority on obtaining jobs that provide substantial security and wages. This is especially true for younger cohorts of workers, who are especially likely to rank the importance of income and job security highly.

An alternative explanation of why younger cohorts are more apt to be dissatisfied is that their expectations that they will obtain economically as well as noneconomically rewarding jobs are higher. Members of Generation Y, or the "Millennial Generation" (those born after 1980), are widely regarded as having a high sense of entitlement (and high expectations), and thus are more likely to be dissatisfied if their jobs do not measure up to these expectations.[27] Moreover, due to the spread and advancement of communication technology such as the Internet, persons (especially younger workers) can obtain comparative information on jobs much more quickly. Hence, their comparison groups are likely to be wider, and so they may be more likely to judge their jobs more critically.

The hypothesis of cohort effects in job satisfaction is not new, though the types of work values associated with younger and older cohorts may have changed. This idea was suggested by social scientists in the 1970s, who predicted that highly educated, younger workers entering the labor force were more likely to value intrinsic rewards, while older workers with less education were more apt to value extrinsic rewards. The widespread concern with dissatisfaction in the 1970s may well have been overstated, however: Charles Saunders, Hugh O'Neill, and Oscar Jensen (1986) analyzed data from the GSS for the 1972 to 1978 period and found little dissatisfaction for any occupational group except for blue-collar workers.[28]

The possibility remains, however, that increased educational attainment could presage greater job dissatisfaction, while other changes in labor force composition that enhance job satisfaction—such as growing numbers of women and professional or managerial workers—may have introduced compensating changes toward higher satisfaction levels. The final set of rows in table 9.2 assesses this explanation by reporting the coefficients of year, unemployment rate, and cohort for models that add sociodemographic and occupational characteristics. The cohort replacement (cohort) and intracohort change (year) coefficients decline only moderately from the previous equation, while the nonsignificant but positive coefficient of the unemployment rate increases slightly.[29] People with higher levels of education express less job satisfaction in this model, presumably because their expectations are higher.[30]

The results in table 9.2 also speak to the question of whether there has been an increase in inequality in job satisfaction, in addition to changes in overall levels. Panel B suggests that there was a decline in inequality in job satisfaction when only the coefficient of year is in the equation (first row). The unemployment rate is positively (though not statistically significantly) related to the variance in job satisfaction, indicating that there is also greater dispersion in workers' evaluations of their jobs when there are fewer alternative jobs available (second set of rows).

Adding a measure for cohort (third set of rows in panel B) implies that this negative effect of year on dispersion in job satisfaction is again due mainly to intercohort replacement; in addition to being generally more dissatisfied with their jobs, new cohorts entering the labor force are more alike in their levels of dissatisfaction than the cohorts they replace—presumably because workers in younger cohorts are more similar to one another than those in older cohorts are in having higher expectations and valuing income and security.[31]

The intercohort effect does not change much when controls for the sociodemographic and occupational characteristics are added to the model (final set of rows in panel B), but the intracohort change variable (year) is now significantly and positively associated with dispersion in job satisfaction. The latter finding is consistent with the interpretation that workers diverge in their job satisfaction as they age, presumably due to their differential experiences and greater inequality in their job rewards.

The occupational differences in particular job rewards found in earlier chapters also suggest that there are likely to be some differences in job satisfaction (and perhaps in its determinants) across different occupations.

There is some evidence to support this hypothesis. Analyses of the GSS data suggest that there has been more change in job satisfaction in some occupational groups than others. Managerial occupations, for example, experienced declines in satisfaction from 1972 to 1991.[32] Cappelli (1999, 122–23) also reported the results of studies that showed that job satisfaction among managers dropped from the early 1980s onward. This is consistent with the argument that managers are the formerly privileged occupational group for whom the violation of the psychological contract was especially sudden and dramatic.

The results for white-collar workers generally are consistent with the patterns of organizational restructuring discussed in previous chapters. There have been relatively steady declines in satisfaction among sales and clerical occupations since the early 1970s. The satisfaction of professional and technical occupations declined during the 1970s but has since appeared to level off and increase slightly in the first decade of the 2000s (results not shown in the table). On the other hand, there is no evidence of much change in the satisfaction of workers in blue-collar occupations since the 1970s.[33]

Conclusions

This chapter has assessed the changes in overall job satisfaction in the United States since the 1970s. The evidence presented here suggests that the job rewards discussed in previous chapters are, in general, positively related to overall job satisfaction. Moreover, there is some indication that earnings and job security have become more salient for job satisfaction. This is consistent with the argument developed in previous chapters that these job rewards have become more problematic for workers since the 1970s.

There is also some evidence that the overall level of job satisfaction in the American labor force has declined since the 1970s. This appears to be due primarily to processes of intercohort replacement, as new cohorts entering the labor force tend to be more dissatisfied than the cohorts they are replacing. I have explained this in terms of the higher expectations and greater emphasis on income and security on the part of these younger cohorts. There is less evidence that there has been a growing polarization in job satisfaction during this period.

= Part III =

Challenges for Policy

= Chapter 10 =

Confronting Polarization and Precarity

T
HE CHANGES in economic and noneconomic dimensions of job quality discussed in this book result from institutional, economic, legal, political, and social transformations in employment systems and relations in the United States since the 1970s. These changes in job quality reflect structural modifications rather than simply fluctuations of the business cycle. During the past several decades, employers have had relatively free rein to implement workplace practices that were designed to increase their flexibility, cut labor costs, and maximize shareholder value in response to greater price competition, technological change, globalization, and other social and economic forces. Changes in financial and capital markets provided incentives to employers to restructure work in order to increase short-term profits. Employers were able to do this essentially without taking into consideration the views of workers, who were unable to act as a countervailing force due to their relatively weak position.[1] Workers were also increasingly vulnerable to market forces due to political decisions to remove institutional protections for workers, such as government regulations and standards in labor markets. These macrostructural changes were supported by ideological shifts toward greater individualism—shifts that have considerably reduced any sense of communalism.

At the same time, changes in the composition of the labor force in the United States since the 1970s have shaped both the rewards available from jobs and how workers evaluate the quality of these rewards. The growth of dual-earner families, for example, has made it more important for workers to have control over their work schedules and the flexibility to attend to nonwork activities, especially those related to the family. The expansion of educational attainment within the labor force has accompanied opportunities for challenging work, while the growth of a low-skilled immigrant population has helped fuel the expansion of low-wage jobs.

In this chapter, I first summarize briefly my main conclusions about reasons for the growth of polarized and precarious employment systems

179

since the 1970s and how these transformations have led to changes in job quality. I then describe other countries' efforts to deal with similar economic and social structural problems, drawing especially on the principles suggested by the general notion of "flexicurity." This discussion helps to identify components of a new social contract that is needed to reduce inequalities in the various components of job quality and to protect workers from the insecurity and uncertainty associated with precarious jobs. This sets the stage for the final chapter, which seeks to identify some strategies for implementing this new social contract in the United States.

Changes in Job Quality in the United States Since the 1970s

The evidence presented in this book suggests the following seven conclusions about changes in job quality in the United States since the mid-1970s.

First, there has been an increasing polarization on a number of dimensions of job quality since the middle of the 1970s. The evidence of growth in inequality in economic rewards, such as wages and fringe benefits, most clearly illustrates this polarization (see chapter 6), although there is also evidence of growing inequality in the degree of control that workers have over their work activities and their ability to participate in decisions, as well as in some types of intrinsic rewards and work intensity (chapters 7 and 8).

Polarized jobs result from institutional, legal, and political forces that encourage or discourage the creation and maintenance of jobs that pay well or poorly, provide workers with more or less control over their activities and schedules, and so on. These forces are not inexorable, however; the actions of government, business, and labor can create well-paying jobs, give workers more control over their jobs and lives, and reduce inequality in job rewards. Inevitably, some bad jobs are bound to occur in a dynamic industrial society like the United States, and some people will always be more vulnerable than others to working in these bad jobs. Nevertheless, labor market and other social institutions—such as labor laws and standards and collective bargaining agreements—can markedly influence the extent of such bad jobs.

Second, there has been a general increase in precarious work and insecurity (see chapter 5). All workers have been made more insecure by the greater precarity of work that has pervaded the occupational structure. The anxiety associated with precarious work constitutes a major concern for current and future generations of workers. Some workers are more vulnerable to the consequences of precarity than others, however: workers with more valuable skills, for example, are better able to take advantage of new opportunities created by the growth of open, market-mediated employment relations.

Third, the past three decades have seen the creation of a large number of low-wage jobs (see chapter 6); many of the good jobs that have been lost have been replaced by jobs of lower quality. The low-wage sectors of the labor force encompass both white-collar and blue-collar jobs that generally provide few benefits, such as health insurance and pension coverage, while often requiring workers to work long hours and providing few opportunities for advancement. Black and Hispanic workers are especially likely to be concentrated in low-wage jobs.

Fourth, the economy has also generated substantial numbers of good jobs. There has been an overall increase in intrinsic rewards and control over work activities, for example. Nevertheless, not as many good jobs have been created as one would have expected, given the increases in productivity and in the educational attainments of the labor force.

Fifth, even these good jobs are more likely to have some bad aspects. For example, relatively well-compensated workers and those with considerable autonomy over their jobs have also experienced greater insecurity. And added workloads and time pressures have forced persons to work harder and often for more hours per week.

Sixth, workers' needs for greater control over their work schedules have grown faster than their jobs have changed to permit them to balance work with their family and personal life. The continued growth of dual-earner and single-parent families, along with more complex family arrangements, such as parents with shared custody of children and responsibility for their own parents, coupled with increases in work intensity (chapter 8), have raised concerns about the paucity of available family-friendly policies, such as flexible work hours and assistance with child and elder care.

Seventh, differences in education and skill levels increasingly separate those workers who have good jobs from those who have bad jobs (see chapters 4 through 8). Transformations in work have underscored the growing importance of skills for labor market success; workers with more human and social capital are better able to take advantage of opportunities created by the greater marketization of employment relations. While more-educated and higher-skilled workers may not necessarily have more job security with a particular employer, their more marketable skills enhance their labor market security, which, in turn, generally provides them with higher earnings, greater control over their jobs, higher intrinsic rewards, and better-quality jobs overall.

The expansion of bad jobs has made things worse for minority group members (such as blacks and Hispanics) in particular, who tend to be concentrated in these jobs. Jobs that pay very low wages are not valued very highly by employers, customers, or employees. When jobs require few skills and workers can be easily substituted and replaced, employers have few incentives to train workers and to develop compensation strategies designed to retain them, a pattern that leads to high turnover. Low wages also leave many Americans at or below the poverty line, even in periods of high employment.

The hollowing out of middle-class jobs has hurt opportunities for upward mobility by decreasing the number of jobs that might provide stepping stones to better jobs. This decline in the middle layer of occupations (see chapter 4) has made it more difficult for people to experience career advancement and upward mobility (see chapter 6). Workers in low-wage jobs, in particular, have few opportunities to advance to better-paying jobs, if any at all. The polarization of work into either good or bad jobs, with little in between, is linked with the growing divergence in other aspects of life, such as the decline of the middle class and the growing polarization of politics.

The dire economic situation precipitated by the Great Recession of 2007 to 2009 has exacerbated these difficulties. This was the longest and most severe recession since the Great Depression. While unemployment rates were equally high during the recessions of the early 1980s, people back then were not out of jobs for as long. Moreover, the effects of the 1980s recessions focused mainly on the Rust Belt of America; in contrast, the extent of job loss and unemployment in the Great Recession of 2007 to 2008 was much greater and more widespread, and characterized virtually all occupations. Consequently, this economic recession and its aftermath will have an imprinting effect on the future: the skills of many workers will deteriorate due to joblessness, a generation of young workers will experience uncertainty and have their careers delayed, families will come under great stress, and communities will face the risk of unraveling.[2]

Given these potential dangers, it is essential that we meet the challenges caused by the growth of polarized and precarious jobs. Government and businesses in the United States have abandoned their obligations to their communities and employees over the past several decades, and workers have lost much of their collective bargaining power, as documented in previous chapters.[3] Fortunately, polarization and the other consequences of globalization and technological change for job quality and employment systems are not inexorable, but instead are shaped by labor market institutions and the choices made by employers, workers, and other social actors. To address these concerns, we need a new social contract that reduces inequality and socializes risk again.

In facing the consequences of the growth of polarized and precarious employment systems, we must be sensitive to the conditions that led to the transformation of employment relations in the first place, as I outline in chapter 2. Employers must continue to have flexibility in order to compete in the global marketplace. They must be able to respond to the rapid pace of technological innovation and adjust to the shifting composition of the labor force, among other changes.

Examining the experiences of other developed countries that face similar challenges as the United States provides insights about ways of developing synchronized strategies to create good jobs and provide workers with security.[4] The economic forces that have led to the creation of polarized and precarious jobs in the United States are global in nature, as I have emphasized throughout this book. All countries are faced with the basic problem of balancing flexibility for employers and security for workers (due to precarious work). Countries have sought to solve this dilemma in different ways, depending on their institutional and cultural traditions. The example of "flexicurity" illustrates how a number of other countries have approached this dilemma.

Flexicurity

The notion of flexicurity—a portmanteau word combining flexibility and security—has attracted a great deal of attention among European labor market reformers looking for a way to give employers and labor markets greater flexibility while still providing protections for workers from the insecurity that results from this flexibility. It is an appealing concept, as it proposes a solution to tensions between employers and workers, suggesting that flexibility for employers and security for workers are mutually supportive. This offers a "win-win" situation that addresses the needs of both groups, in contrast with a "trade-off" thesis, which posits that the requirements of more flexible labor markets inevitably reduce levels of economic security.[5]

Flexicurity is a fairly ambiguous concept (or "meta-policy") that has been used to refer to a variety of policies that have been bundled together in different ways in different countries. It is a policy strategy that requires coordination between employment and social policies that generally socialize risks and help people deal with uncertainty. The vagueness of this multidimensional concept is politically advantageous in that it encourages thinking about principles by which to reconcile the needs of both employers and workers.[6] The concept must be defined more precisely to be useful for analytical purposes, however.

There are a few key design principles that underlie flexicurity programs.[7] First, flexicurity provides employers and labor markets with flexibility to adjust levels of employment (numerical flexibility, which includes both adjusting the number of employees and the number and distribution of working hours) and compensation (wage flexibility). In some cases, flexicurity can also provide employers with functional flexibility to move employees among tasks or to change the content of work.[8]

Second, flexicurity provides economic security, or a safety net, for workers through generous unemployment assistance that gives workers a "soft landing" if they lose their jobs. A key element of a typical safety net is health insurance, which is provided to all citizens, regardless of employment status, in most developed countries of the world.

Third, active labor market policies associated with flexicurity provide workers with greater opportunities for lifelong learning and employability.[9] This reemployment assistance includes job counseling, opportunities for retraining, and help in finding new jobs, thereby giving workers security as they move from one job to another. Moreover, receipt of these benefits requires engagement on the part of individuals, who must take personal responsibility to search for jobs, participate in retraining, and visit job counselors in order to take advantage of the opportunities that active labor market policies offer.

Fourth, flexicurity programs tend to be individualized and can provide a customized—rather than a standardized, one-size-fits-all—set of services. Thus, benefits are often adjusted to the needs of particular individuals, old or young, with families or without, and so on.

A final design feature of flexicurity is that the system takes different forms in different settings and is adaptable to the characteristics of particular countries. A number of countries have adopted—or are in the process of adopting—some version of the flexicurity system. The most prominent examples of this system in action are found in the Netherlands and Denmark.

The term *flexicurity* was coined by Dutch sociologist Hans Adriaansens in the mid-1990s to describe particular pieces of labor market regulation: the Dutch Flexibility and Security Act and the Allocation of Workers by Intermediaries Act.[10] In the Netherlands, employers achieve flexibility through atypical, flexible types of jobs, such as part-time work. Workers in these nonstandard or atypical jobs have similar social security rights as those on standard employment contracts, however. The Dutch system emphasizes employment (as opposed to job) security and social security, especially for weaker groups (such as those in nonstandard employment relations), both inside and outside the labor market.

In Denmark, the famous flexicurity system combines "*flexible* hiring and firing rules for employers and a social *security* system for workers" (Westergaard-Nielsen 2008, 44). The Danish "golden triangle" of flexicurity has three main points; the ability of employers to easily hire and fire workers; a generous safety net for the unemployed; and active labor market policies that socialize the risks of uncertainty by helping people get new jobs once unemployed.[11] Low levels of employment protection are combined with high levels of social protection: security on any one job is relatively low, but employment security is fairly high since unemployed workers are given a great deal of protection and help in the form of income compensation, education, and job training to find new jobs. (Laid-off persons are guaranteed about 80 percent of their wages in benefits, although this amount is capped for high earners.) The idea is to protect individual workers (through mechanisms such as opportunities for retraining) rather than to try to protect existing jobs. Danish employers have a great deal of numerical flexibility under this system, but it does not provide them with much internal, functional flexibility.

By contrast, the Japanese system of flexicurity has traditionally provided employers with high levels of internal, functional flexibility, as broad job classifications have permitted them to move workers among tasks and departments in response to organizational needs. Such flexibility was facilitated by high levels of employment protection for workers, especially males below a certain age who enjoyed "lifetime" employment in large organizations. Once unemployed, however, Japanese workers had relatively low levels of social protection due to a weak welfare system. Recent pressures on this system have resulted in employers' adoption of a variety of nonstandard work arrangements, such as temporary and part-time work, in order to obtain numerical flexibility in the external labor market. The challenge for Japan is to provide more social protections for these atypical workers in order to compensate for their low employment protections.[12]

European countries' experiences with flexicurity in particular illustrate both the content of policies that could be useful in helping to address precarious jobs in the United States and the process by which flexicurity principles might be implemented.[13] Employers in the United States already have a great deal of flexibility in their relations with employees. However, workers in the United States have both low employment protection and low social protections. The challenge for developing "flexicurity with an American face," then, is primarily to provide more security for workers. Moreover, while the flexibility portion of flexicurity generally refers to flexibility for employers, it is also important to provide flexibility to workers in order to help them balance their work and nonwork lives.

Components of a New Social Contract

We need to build an innovative new social contract among the government, business, and labor to replace the postwar social contract that was dismantled during the 1980s and 1990s.[14] The metaphor of a social contract refers to a portfolio of "expectations and obligations that workers, employers, and their communities and societies have for work and employment relationships."[15] Creating a new social contract will enhance both the competitiveness of the American economy and the quality of work experienced by individuals.

Policies seeking to address issues of job quality and inequality should be guided by considerations of efficiency as well as equity. Efficiency includes the ways in which people are allocated to jobs and the extent to which work can be organized in order to enhance productivity and organizational performance. Equity refers mainly to reducing the degree of inequality between good and bad jobs, as well as to raising the floor for low-end, bad jobs.[16] A new social contract needs to restore the link between wages and productivity so that when companies succeed, so do their employees. As I discuss in chapter 2, workers have not shared in employers' productivity gains in the past several decades; this is reflected in the growing gap between investors and employers, on the one hand, and workers, on the other. These gains must be distributed equitably in order to achieve the potential for prosperity of productivity growth associated with the new economy.

The new social contract must take into account the new work realities that have been summarized in previous chapters. Moreover, as we discussed earlier, the central feature of an American version of flexicurity is the provision of security for workers. Security is a multidimensional concept, and there are various types of it; a useful taxonomy of security is provided by a recent cross-national study by the International Labour Organization (ILO).[17]

The ILO's report outlines seven types of security. Of these, the most basic are income, representation, and skill-reproduction security.[18] Income and skill security are fundamental design principles of flexibility programs. Representation security (that is, the right to bargain collectively with employers) is an essential feature of the European flexicurity models, which involve both employers and workers (through unions) in a cooperative effort. These three forms of security arguably are also causally prior to the other types of security. For example, if workers are able to have representational security, they are also likely to be able to enjoy greater occupational health and safety. Moreover, if workers should lose their jobs or if the labor market does not provide job opportunities, economic and skill security will likely help them get new jobs or be retrained.

Policies that seek to provide employment security directly are not likely to be as effective since they may reduce some of the flexibility in labor markets that employers require in order to remain competitive in the global economy. Employment protections have traditionally been low in the United States, which is why this nation is characterized by the notion of "employment at will."[19] Moreover, regulations to inhibit layoffs may have unintended consequences, as the experiences of European countries such as Spain and France have shown: employers may be reluctant to hire workers on standard contracts, thereby spurring the expansion of temporary and other forms of nonstandard work. On the other hand, providing employers with some disincentives for layoffs is likely to be useful in the United States. The case of Germany illustrates the potential for regulations designed to enhance employment protections; employers have complete flexibility on hiring and firing, but they are rewarded with tax advantages and even subsidies for retaining workers, while facing penalties for layoffs.

A new social contract that addresses the consequences of polarized and precarious employment systems should thus try to achieve three main things: providing workers with economic security that can protect them from the consequences of precarious work; guaranteeing workers the rights to collective representation and bargaining power; and retraining and preparing workers for good jobs. Taken together, these forms of security are also likely to encourage employers to create more good jobs and discourage them from creating bad jobs.

Building a Better Safety Net: Enhancing Economic Security

Economic security refers to the assurance workers have of an adequate level of current and future income. In the 1990s, the United States ranked twenty-third out of ninety-six countries on the ILO's index of economic security.

A new social contract should help people deal with the uncertainty and unpredictability of their work—and their resulting confusion and increasingly chaotic and insecure lives—while still preserving some of the flexibility that allows U.S. employers to remain globally competitive. We might best accomplish these goals by building a better safety net outside of the labor market to protect people from the negative consequences of uncertainty and insecurity that will certainly continue to characterize the American (and world) economy for the foreseeable future.

Social insurance is a common solution to problems of high risk.[20] Since people are very loss averse, uncertainty has a big impact on their lives; we therefore need insurance to socialize risks and help them cope with losses and compensate them for bad events.[21] Such insurance is also needed to give people the self-confidence to take entrepreneurial risks. The highest priority should be on providing three types of social insurance: portable health insurance benefits; more generous retirement benefits; and expanded unemployment benefits and other wage supports (including assistance with acquiring new skills and relocation) to help people navigate the increasingly treacherous transitions between jobs and employers.[22] This is consistent with the practice in most developed industrial countries, which provide their citizens with basic protections, including health insurance and retirement benefits.

Health Insurance   The most basic element of a safety net is the provision of affordable health insurance for all. Employment-based health insurance is now the only real source of health coverage for Americans who are not yet eligible for Medicare and not poor enough to qualify for Medicaid; we thus need to protect those who do not receive health insurance from their employers. The 2010 Patient Protection and Affordable Care Act, discussed in chapter 6, attempted to expand health insurance to most U.S. citizens and legal residents. This law was an important step in the direction of universal health care, though a number of its reforms will not be effective for a number of years, and there is considerable uncertainty about how well the various parts will hold together, as a large number of details remain to be worked out.[23]

Retirement and Pension Benefits   We need strategies to help workers save more money so that they may be able to supplement their federal Social Security benefits upon retirement. The amount that Americans have set aside for retirement is shockingly low: a 2001 study found that only half of the households in the United States with retirement accounts and who neared retirement had savings of $55,000, and one-quarter had savings of less than $13,000.[24] The market turbulence of the recession of 2007 to 2009 dramatically exposed the riskiness of the 401(k) system, and demonstrates the necessity for alternative, more reliable, and universal additions to the Social Security system.[25]

In view of the precarious nature of employment relations, sources of retirement funds in addition to Social Security should be portable across employers. Supplementing Social Security will not be cheap, of course: the aging of America and its labor force (see table 3.1) will require massive government commitments to the older population, extending retirement eligibility ages and possibly shifting income from younger workers to older retirees.

Unemployment Insurance   Insurance against job loss is vital due to the high degree of mobility and job changing that characterizes modern labor markets. The Unemployment Insurance system (a product of FDR's New Deal) now covers less than one-half of the unemployed. Less than a third receive benefits; these benefits are lower and last for less time and for fewer people, compared with systems in other industrial countries. The problems with this system were clearly revealed in the Great Recession of 2007 to 2009, when millions of unemployed persons exhausted their unemployment benefits (though Congress extended them temporarily). Moreover, contingent and part-time workers are disadvantaged by the minimum earnings and hours' requirements that most states use to determine eligibility.[26] Extending unemployment insurance supports to part-timers or low-wage workers who have not worked enough hours or earned enough money to qualify would help to give these workers greater security in times of economic adversity.

Beyond unemployment insurance, a minimum severance package would help workers who are laid off or had to take a lower-paying job.[27] It would be especially important to focus financial support on the neediest workers and their families and on those workers who have the greatest potential upside for retraining.

Wage insurance can also help those who are displaced from their jobs for long periods of time to avoid sharp income losses. It might subsidize their retraining costs and incentivize workers to take new jobs that may pay less than their old ones.[28] Income averaging could also help ease the burden of job loss on workers: this would lower taxes for people who had seen their income drop because they lost their jobs. This was an option offered to some American taxpayers until 1986, but thereafter it was only available to people whose incomes spiked up, not down.

This strategy for enhancing economic security is consistent with the vision of the classic American welfare-state model, which lets the labor market operate relatively competitively and then try to clean up its negative consequences afterwards, as opposed to placing constraints on the labor market itself. This model recognizes that it is likely futile to try to guard American jobs through protectionism and other forms of controls on international trade and capital flows, and just as ineffective to try to regulate wages and other job rewards through the labor market.

Unions and Worker Power: Reestablishing Representation Security

Representation security refers to individual rights in laws and collective rights to bargain with employers. As I have discussed, there has been a decline of collective power, especially in the form of unions, in the private sector in the United States since the 1970s. The decline in unions contributed to the decoupling of wages and productivity and the growth of polarized and precarious employment systems. In the 1990s, the United States ranked relatively low (forty-one out of ninety-nine countries) on the ILO's index of representational security.

It took the corrective actions of unions to help pass the legislation that reduced the oppressive employment conditions of the Depression era in the United States. In similar fashion, it is unlikely that the government would enact social and economic policies designed to create good jobs and high-road business strategies unless workers have sufficient power over their employment situations to be able to press for their interests and to provide a countervailing force to government and business. Implementing the new social contract depends on the reconfiguration of political forces within the United States to give workers a real voice in decision-making and to exercise collective agency.[29]

The decline of unions in the past several decades has been fueled by antiunion behavior on the part of employers, who have discouraged workers from organizing as well as taken steps to avoid unionization— for example, moving workplaces to areas of the United States and the world where unions are relatively weak. Labor revitalization hinges to a large extent on our ability to reverse the antiunion climate in America and to build a more hospitable environment for workers to join unions and benefit from their presence. We also need to change the adversarial nature of the National Labor Relations Act, perhaps in the direction of cooperative legislation, like the European Works Councils.

The potential for increased unionization clearly exists: while unions have declined to their lowest point since before the Depression, nearly 50 percent of workers would join a union if given the chance.[30] Moreover, the growth of precarious work, increase in inequality, and deterioration of living standards for the middle class have all provided good reasons for workers to engage in collective action. And pressures from Generation Y and other waves of new workers whose expectations are not being met by the jobs that are available in the labor market are likely to turn up the volume on demands for change, as I discuss in the next chapter.

Enhancing the collective power of workers depends on the reaffirmation of the right of workers to organize and bargain collectively. We need legislative programs, as well as regulatory initiatives, to reaffirm workers' rights to organize.[31] We also need stronger enforcement of existing rights to organize by watchdog agencies like the National Labor Relations Board. Existing labor laws severely constrain workers' abilities to organize, thus weakening pressure on employers to raise wages and improve job quality. Many key labor laws grew out of the New Deal and were based on an institutional structure of work that assumed that employment relations were organized at the employer's fixed site, workers were supervised by employers and managers, and the work was generally done full-time. This has now changed, as my discussions in chapters 2 and 5 have shown.

Traditional industrial unions in the United States were based on a firm or workplace model of organization. These unions engaged in collective bargaining with employers (either single employers or coordinated groups), and the main focus was on bread-and-butter issues such as earnings and job security. However, the changes in work, workers, and workplace that have arisen since the 1970s raise the broader question of whether this traditional form of workplace unionism is the most viable form of worker power in the United States in the twenty-first century. People are no longer tied to specific firms and industries with the same level of stability that characterized the postwar period. The growth of precarious employment relations has reduced workers' attachments to their employers and increased the salience of labor market intermediaries that help to create channels for mobility between firms. An appropriate new social contract should foreground the role of work in virtually everyone's life, thereby making sensible employment policy an issue for everyone.

Education and Training: Achieving Skill-Reproduction Security

Skill-reproduction security refers to access to basic education and vocational training. The United States does relatively well on this dimension, ranking twelfth out of 138 countries on the ILO index. Nevertheless, a great deal more needs to be done. We must intercede on the supply side of the labor market and provide people with better and more extensive education and training in order to prepare them for good jobs. For four decades of both Republican and Democratic administrations, the dominant approach to improving job quality and reducing inequality has been a supply-side strategy of enhancing peoples' human capital through job training and education.[32] While a higher level of education cannot by itself reverse the growth of earnings inequality—most of which has been due to the expansion of incomes at the very top of the distribution, as I discussed in chapter 6—it is an essential component of a new social contract for most Americans.

A new social contract must help workers and employers cope with job insecurity and the likelihood that workers will not spend large portions of their careers with a single employer. Because it is increasingly likely that all workers will have to move among jobs relatively frequently, social and economic protections must be portable and transferable from one employer to another. Employment policies and regulations are needed to help workers cope with this increased variability and uncertainty, especially for more vulnerable workers, who do not have the marketable skills that can enable them to find new jobs after job loss.

Supply-side policies that prepare workers for high-quality jobs should expand the pool of qualified job seekers by augmenting workers' skills and by inducing more people to look for work. These policies need to supplement peoples' own efforts to develop their human and social capital, both of which are needed to help workers function well in the knowledge and service economy of the future.[33]

The importance of education and job-related training for improving workers' career prospects cannot be overemphasized. The explosive growth of information technology and the escalating importance of knowledge in the economy have underscored the significance of human capital, skills, and education for obtaining and performing well in high-quality jobs and for avoiding confinement to bad jobs. Life-long learning is becoming more essential than ever, due to the need for people to adjust to the technological changes that help to create job insecurity and uncertainty. Capitalizing on the skills and knowledge of American workers also enhances the competitiveness of American firms, which cannot otherwise compete with developing countries on their low labor costs. Rather than considering income redistribution, Americans prefer to expand education spending (as a means of ensuring greater equality of opportunity) in response to increasing concerns about inequality.[34]

Educational policies should be supplemented by job training strategies that provide workers with the skills they actually need to perform jobs. These include both technical skills—such as cognitive and motor skills—and soft skills—such as work motivations, workplace communication, and teamwork skills.

The Need for a Coordinated Strategy

Enhancing economic, representation, and skill-reproduction security is likely to result in the creation of better jobs. If we make workers more economically secure, provide them with more effective representation and institutional protections, and facilitate their acquisition of human capital throughout their careers, then employers are likely to be encouraged to be more innovative in creating more skilled jobs, and thereby would be more likely to adopt high-road employment relations. More economic security is also likely to spur entrepreneurial activity and make people more willing to invest in their human capital. Greater representation security will facilitate collective bargaining, which, in turn, will create good jobs. And a greater number of skilled workers will incentivize employers to create better jobs to take advantage of a higher-skilled workforce.

We must address all of these components of a new social contract simultaneously through a coordinated strategy, however. Piecemeal efforts that focus on either job creation or providing workers with more training opportunities are not sufficient by themselves. It is pointless to try to generate jobs if workers do not have the skills to perform them. By the same token, education and training policies must be embedded in more-comprehensive demand-side labor market policies; giving workers more education and training is wasted unless there are jobs available in which they can utilize these skills. It is not helpful to train people for occupations that are declining or for which opportunities do not exist.[35] Failures to link education and training policies to demand-side job creation strategies have resulted in skill shortages in some sectors of the economy (as many workers are often under-qualified for some of the jobs that are available) while workers are over-qualified for jobs in other sectors.[36] On the other hand, quality skills create their own employment pull, as can be seen in countries that place high value on education and training, such as India, Singapore, and the Republic of Korea.

Nevertheless, it is also necessary to focus directly on job creation and intervene on the demand side of the labor market. We need labor market institutions (such as unions, active labor market policies, or minimum wages) that upgrade the quality of bad jobs, forestall the deterioration of good jobs, and create additional high-quality jobs, thereby increasing the availability of high-end work while discouraging low-end jobs. As I have argued throughout this book, good jobs should pay at least a living wage, enable workers to exercise control over their work activities and participate in decisions, and permit workers to influence their work schedules so they can better balance their work and family lives.

Moreover, we need to create more job structures, not just jobs. Creating job ladders is easier in some occupations than in others, naturally, since some do not allow much room for advancement; this makes it even more essential that all jobs pay at least a living wage.[37] Career-ladder programs are more apt to be effective if they are part of a broader strategy to provide enhanced compensation and advancement opportunities for workers.[38] If they are to succeed in more than a token fashion, career-ladder programs should have a combination of public policy support (regulatory policies, in some cases mandatory), employer commitment to career ladders, and tight labor markets. They need to assist in providing training and education to help people move from one rung to the next, as well as the financial and other support to enable them to undergo the training. Establishing career ladders also requires that there be higher-level jobs to move to (for example, from nursing aides to licensed practical nurses, bank tellers to loan officers, clerical workers to information technology workers, and so on).[39]

Conclusions

The growth of polarized and precarious employment systems in the United States presents challenges for governments, businesses, and workers. To address the concerns raised by the impacts of these employment systems on job quality, we need a new social contract that takes into account today's realities of the world of work. This chapter has outlined such a contract, the elements of which can be found in other countries with differing institutional structures. The general idea of flexicurity is a useful way of thinking about the kinds of policies that are needed, as this provides employers with the flexibility they need to compete while also providing employees with the security they need to construct career narratives. Implementing a new social contract inspired by the flexicurity models is possible, depending on the construction of the appropriate labor market institutions.

Chapter 11

Implementing the New Social Contract

W E FACE vast challenges in implementing the components of the social contract described in the last chapter. The pendulum representing the second part of Polanyi's "double movement" does not automatically swing back to create social protections and regulations that remedy the negative consequences of polarized and precarious employment systems. Nor did Polanyi provide a theory of power that would help account for the mechanisms by which countermovements would emerge in response to unregulated markets. Indeed, we now have what amounts to an ideological vacuum in which we do not have anything close to a consensus theory about how to deal with the consequences of polarization and precarity.[1]

All public policies are based on value sets that identify what ought to be changed and how best to implement these changes. I have argued that the rise of polarized and precarious employment systems has had profound consequences not only for individuals' experiences of work, but also for their families and communities, as well as businesses and society in general. Putting into practice a new social contract to address these problems requires the coordinated actions of government, business, and labor. This is a difficult task due to a variety of obstacles: ideological disagreements about the appropriate role of the government in the economy and in labor markets; a lack of trust in the government and institutions in general; the current weakness of the labor movement, which prevents workers from exercising voice and being a countervailing force; businesses seeking to cut costs and lobbyists trying to obtain favorable regulations for their clients; and all the economic challenges imposed by concerns over budget deficits, slow growth, and unemployment.

In this chapter, I first outline the roles that the government, business, and labor should play in order to address the growth of polarized and precarious employment systems and to realize the social contract described in the last chapter. I then summarize some of the obstacles that hinder these efforts. Finally, I outline some possible strategies to overcome these barriers in order to implement a new social contract.

The Role of the Government

The experience of other countries underscores the importance of a commitment to the government as a vehicle of the good society and as an instrument to be used in the public interest. Looking after the common good is the job of the government; the state exists not only to preserve freedom, but also to protect the weak and the vulnerable and to manage uncertainty and risk.[2] The government also needs to provide economic security, a strong infrastructure for job creation, and greater opportunities for people to succeed.

The government is not a unitary actor, of course, and its activities are dispersed at local, state, and federal levels. Government intervention at the federal level needs to be supported by initiatives at community, local, and state levels:

> The New Deal established the federal government as the main regulator of the labor market and of employment relations in the United States. . . . Today a different starting assumption for the role of government is needed [due to globalization, which has undermined many of the federal government's powers]. . . . Paradoxically, the importance of regional, state, and local governments has increased. . . . We envision the federal government as supporting and complementing . . . innovations. . . . Its role is less one of direct action than one of providing financial support, strategic direction, and leadership for other governmental actors. (Osterman et al. 2001, 149, 151).

Creating Economic Security and a Safety Net

The government is ultimately responsible for creating a safety net that provides all of its country's citizens with basic protections such as health insurance and retirement benefits. Basic social protections should not be dependent on a private welfare system that relies on the benevolence and economic success of particular employers; workers should have access to a safety net regardless of whether they work a minimum number of hours for an employer who is willing and able to pay for various benefits. Regrettably, components of the existing public welfare system, such as Social Security, food stamps, Medicare, and Medicaid, are fraying under pressures imposed by debt, tax cuts, an aging population, and rising health care costs.[3]

All the types of social insurance discussed in the last chapter can be provided primarily by the government, but they do not have to be: models of financial markets can be adapted to provide companies and workers with ways of sharing the risks and expenses with the government.[4] The government could mandate a minimum employer payment for employees' health care costs, for example.

Setting Labor Market Standards

The government should set standards in the labor market, thereby helping to slow the creation of bad jobs by removing the conditions that allow and encourage employers to create low-wage jobs. The increase in the federal minimum wage to $7.25 an hour in July 2009 was a step, albeit a small one, in the right direction.[5] The government can also enforce overtime laws that govern the number of hours worked and that do not exempt more workers from the Fair Labor Standards Act, thereby regulating work intensity, health and safety regulations, and pay-equity laws. In addition, the government could require that employers provide a minimum number of paid sick days and even paid family medical leave.

The government can also direct employers to compensate part-time workers similarly to full-time workers in terms of their hourly wages and benefits.[6] Legislation created to enhance the rights of part-time workers would help to remove the incentives that employers now have for creating low-quality, part-time jobs. Expanding the rights of part-time workers could also be coupled with legislation that provides a minimum amount of vacation time for all workers, as well as time for personal and sick leaves.

Immigration Reform

Immigration reform is an essential component of efforts to set standards in the labor market and to upgrade the quality of jobs. We should look at immigration reform through the lens of jobs and labor markets and make it both possible and required for immigrants working in the United States to have legal status and be legally integrated into the labor force. Immigration can address labor market shortages (as well as reunify families and other goals), but any immigration must be legal and uphold high labor standards. Penalties for hiring undocumented aliens should be increased for employers. These changes would reduce the supply of undocumented immigrants who have little choice but to take bad jobs; in turn, employers would be forced to seek alternatives to low-wage jobs that cannot be offshored.

Creating Good Jobs

The government creates jobs directly by funding positions (either in the public or private sectors) and by providing incentives for private-sector companies to create jobs. Both of these job creation strategies are needed to create good jobs and upgrade bad jobs. Direct job creation by the government is necessary because the private sector is not capable of generating enough good, well-paying jobs in the United States to meet the needs of all those who are qualified and want them. The idea that we can depend mainly on the private sector to create good jobs is an illusion, albeit a widely held one.[7]

The government's investments in creating good jobs could help sustain a broad middle class and at the same time address important public needs. The list of pressing needs is long; it includes rebuilding our nation's decaying infrastructure of roads, bridges, schools, sewers, airports, trains, and mass transit. Public investments can also create new private sector industries around as yet unproven technologies—such as wind turbines, solar-collection farms, ethanol production, and electric cars—that can help drive the economy toward green jobs in the renewable energy industry.[8] Creating green jobs and meeting the nation's infrastructure needs can help support U.S.-based manufacturing of the equipment needed for them. Building infrastructure like transportation and bridges also requires more high-skill jobs. There are also tremendous opportunities to create good jobs for women by investing in the infrastructure of human capital through augmenting professional occupations such as teachers, library workers, nurses, and social workers.[9]

The federal government could also require the large number of jobs it creates directly through federal and state contracts to meet certain standards; for example, they could require that all government-subsidized jobs must be high-wage, career-track jobs. This is illustrated by President Obama's decision in 2010 to use federal contracts to encourage businesses to take the high road, an idea long advocated by some unions and communities.[10] The federal government could also give money to state and municipal governments with the restriction that they use it to hire public-sector workers (police officers, teachers, engineers, and others) who might otherwise be laid off.

Government policies also create the environmental contexts that help shape the behavior of private-sector employers. The extent to which employers are incentivized to retain or lay off workers depends on the structure of accounting rules, for example. Employers react mainly to tax and accounting regulations due to the investor-centered nature of employers' employment models. The less the tax benefits of a particular practice, the less incentive the employers have to adopt it. For example, current accounting rules allow companies to take layoff-related costs as "investments" below the line, but to treat hiring, training, and development-related costs as operating expenses. This is counterintuitive; changing these rules would create incentives for employers to retain employees, as in the case of Germany discussed in the last chapter.

To supplement the direct public creation of jobs, the government could support private-sector employment indirectly by incentivizing employers through targeted tax credits and other economic subsidies. The government can structure the incentive system so as to encourage companies to adopt certain high-road policies or practices. For example, the government can provide economic incentives to companies that implement comprehensive day-care programs for children (preferably at the work site) or provide creative flextime work schedules to accommodate workers' family needs.[11] Moreover, the government could provide job tax credits to businesses and nonprofits for adopting job-sharing practices that would reduce working hours rather than laying off workers, or for agreeing to manufacture products in the United States. Government support of high-wage businesses through its investments in research and development and in innovative, high-skill production technologies would enhance economic development while sending a strong signal about the importance of a high-wage economy.

Education and Training

The government also plays a big role in providing support for education and training. I have argued throughout this book that differences in education and skills are increasingly important for differentiating workers who have good jobs from those with bad jobs. Most directly, government policies are needed to remedy deficiencies in the basic public education system and to ensure that all Americans have the opportunity to obtain a high-quality education, both in K–12 and at the college level. Educational inequalities that are tied to differences in the ability of local school systems to fund schools must be eliminated.

The government also provides support for training initiatives through the U.S. Department of Labor, called by some the "Department of Training." The government has an important role to play in developing job skills since there has been a vacuum created by the decline in employee training offered by employers.[12] The amount of money that companies spend on training has not increased very much in recent years,[13] which is not surprising given the changing employment relationship (see chapter 5): in the absence of employer-based institutions that guard against free-rider problems, employers will be reluctant to invest in training workers who might then move on to other companies. Moreover, short-term horizons reflected in concerns about quarterly financial reports are often too brief to justify employers' investments in training.

Public investment in training should also be targeted at jobs based on potential returns: for example, programs to help certified nursing assistants (CNAs) move up a nursing career ladder might be good investments, given the strong anticipated demand for nurses and the fact that CNAs have already demonstrated the ability to work closely with patients.

How Will the Government Pay for These Initiatives?

Public spending on new, good jobs needs to be substantial. This is likely to require a return to a more progressive tax system in order to generate the revenue needed to make the public investments required.[14] The capacity of the government for creating jobs is presently underutilized: for example, government spending on research and investment, such as highways, software, medical research, and other things that have societal but not necessarily big financial returns, has dropped from about 7 percent of GDP in the 1950s to about 4 percent today.[15] Moreover, taxation as a proportion of GDP is lower in the United States than in most other industrial countries: it is 27 percent in the United States, compared with nearly 40 percent on average in the European Union, for example.[16] We can create more high-quality jobs in the public sector if we have the political and ideological will to do so.

Strategies to raise revenue to increase wages of low-paid workers would also be facilitated by a revision of tax laws. Despite the Supreme Court's recent affirmation that corporations are persons (in *Citizens United v. Federal Election Commission*), corporations pay relatively few taxes compared with human persons.[17] Corporations are exempt from paying billions of dollars' worth of taxes through tax incentives, for example. We need to reexamine our tax laws to see where we need to rethink tax subsidies and tax expenditures. We should also explore the wide variety of options in what we tax: perhaps too much taxation is now targeted at work rather than on consumption (as in Europe) or on things we want to get rid of (like carbon). Alternative taxes might produce advantages for employers as well as workers.

The Role of Business

Employers are key actors in any efforts to reestablish high-quality jobs and employment relationships. A new social contract requires models of corporate governance that increase managerial accountability and empower employees. Businesses must be encouraged to add social factors to their prevailing economic logic in designing jobs. While the government can help to create an economic environment that stimulates job creation, however, the norms that govern business behavior are shaped more by societal and community values, often originating in pressures from consumers and workers.

Firms have considerable discretion in which kinds of employment and wage policies they choose to adopt in responding to similar market pressures, as I have argued throughout this book. A minority of companies in the United States have boosted their competitiveness through workplace practices that enable workers to participate in decisions, integrate them into workplace communities, and provide good pay for performing skilled jobs. While such high-road strategies are relatively expensive, they can result in higher-quality products, faster response times, and reductions in labor turnover.[18] Moreover, while changes in the business environment toward greater insecurity have made it unfeasible for companies to guarantee their employees long-term jobs, managers can compensate workers for the lack of security by providing them training to enhance their employability. This might also enhance competitiveness, since companies that provide their workers with security and training during hard times are often at an advantage during economic recoveries. Adopting some of the features of active labor-market policies (as in the Danish example of flexicurity, discussed in the last chapter) would help to create a larger labor pool of skilled workers, which would attract capital and incentives to organize work so as to take advantage of these workers' greater human capital.

Business must have a stake in creating good jobs: employers must believe that creating high-quality jobs is a viable business strategy that is likely to result in higher productivity. They must believe that it is in their interests to enhance their employees' development, retention, and commitment. Unfortunately, the business case for job quality is often difficult to prove conclusively, especially during periods of economic crisis and high unemployment. For example, companies that are often held up as creating good-quality jobs (such as the SAS Institute or Southwest Airlines) might be hiring much younger, healthier workers compared with its competitors.

Agreements among groups of employers in an industry who could share the risks of providing job-related training might help to avoid concerns about free riding and ensure that nobody gains a competitive advantage by not participating in these activities. There are a number of examples of how employers can use new labor market institutions to help them do this, such as companies that band together to train workers (in industries as diverse as hospitals, hotels, and hosiery) and set industry skill standards.[19] Comprehensive retraining programs that require mandatory contributions from employers help to ensure that all employers have a financial stake in retraining and will have a real interest in making sure that they get their money's worth by providing high-end jobs. Firms could also work closely with public schools, providing apprenticeships as a way to hire graduates.[20]

The adoption of a new social contract is likely to spur entrepreneurial activity, as people will be more secure and willing to take risks and the pool of highly skilled workers will be larger. This is crucial because small, entrepreneurial businesses are particularly important sources of innovation and, hence, are generators of good jobs. It is relatively easy to start businesses in the United States, and so the stage is being set for an upsurge in entrepreneurs' identifying services and products that are marketable and that attract people with skills, as suggested by Schumpeter's model of creative destruction. In contrast, the high stability of the post–World War II period may have decreased innovation and produced complacency in American companies, compared with, say, Japan and Germany, where less stability was associated with more innovation. Robert Shiller, in the *New York Times*, has described the reticence of American managers to take risks as the "survival of the safest."[21]

The Role of Labor

Worker power is necessary to get governments and businesses to act on the new social contract and to ensure that employees can share in the very gains in productivity and business profits to which they contribute. Employers are more likely to adopt high-road strategies if they are prodded into doing this by strong, progressive unions or other forms of worker organization that encourage collaborative efforts between managers and workers and that make abusing workers costly. A number of the organizations that have adopted training programs, for example, did so as a result of prodding from unions, who often acted as partners with management in implementing these programs. A study of call centers found that a unionized call center had invested more than twice as much in training, pay, and benefits than had a similar call center that was not unionized.[22] Union participation in the efforts to provide career advancement in the San Francisco and Las Vegas hotel campaigns (chapter 10, note 39) was essential; their absence creates strong disincentives to employer participation.

The key question is: What kinds of worker power are best suited to meet the challenges created by the transformations in the nature of work? The next generation of worker organizations needs to experiment with a variety of new forms in order to meet the challenges posed by the changing nature of employment relations.[23] To be successful, unions must adapt to and match up with changes in the structure of the economy and the organization of work.[24] A variety of new institutional forms offer the promise of enhancing workers' power and providing some of the essential things (such as career security) that workers need to be able to deal with the new employment relations.[25] The New York City–based Freelancers

Union, for example, organizes independent contractors and helps to provide them with health insurance and other elements of a safety net, as well as help in navigating job changes between employers.[26]

These new approaches have in common the recognition that unions, collective occupational groups, and other worker associations must provide ways of helping workers cope with interfirm mobility. They could do this, for example, by facilitating lifetime learning, linking workers in networks, and otherwise providing them with information on job opportunities in the external labor market.[27] Forms of occupational unionism are likely to be especially important in white-collar and professional occupations whose members (many of whom were formerly from the middle class) also need to organize to obtain a collective voice.

Unions are not the only vehicle for employee voice, however. The specific mechanisms by which the collective actions of workers are exercised are less important than the ability of workers to exert countervailing power in order to influence government policymakers and businesses. The introduction of works-council type legislation and the encouragement of cooperative efforts between workers and employers (and not just in the private sector) are both important. Unions have also collaborated with other kinds of social movements in order to better position themselves to help these groups—and all workers—enhance the quality of jobs.[28] Nonunion social movements include worker advocacy groups (such as immigrant groups, women's groups, racial and ethnic movements, social movements concerned with global justice, and movements to provide more support for working families), living wage campaigns, and worker centers.[29] These movements represent the efforts of the most vulnerable people in the labor market to enhance their own market power.

In the manufacturing economy, there was often a split between consumers and producers, and the key social relations were primarily defined as those among workers (labor solidarity) or between labor and management (class conflict). By contrast, the growth of the service sector changes the standard management-labor story and brings into focus the autonomous consumer. It thus enhances the potential for consumer-worker coalitions, often in local communities, to influence work and its consequences.

Obstacles to Implementing the New Social Contract

Flexicurity has been successful in Denmark and the Netherlands in large part because these countries are relatively small and homogeneous. In Denmark, organizations tend to be relatively small, so there are lots of opportunities for new employers to start businesses. There is also a high level of trust in the government and in institutions in general, as well as a history of a strong union presence. Moreover, there is weak integration of immigrants into labor markets in Denmark, where immigrants are generally excluded from the flexicurity system. Significantly, government spending accounts for about half of GDP in Denmark, and top tax rates are 50 percent; this provides funds to finance unemployment, pensions, health care, and other public goods.[30]

The United States differs in a number of important respects from countries that have successfully adopted flexicurity policies; hence, implementing a new social contract in the United States requires overcoming a number of major obstacles. I have discussed the obstacles created by a weak labor movement. In addition, the United States is much bigger geographically, and so housing and transportation are more problematic issues when seeking to relocate people from areas of job decline to locations where jobs are growing. This has been particularly true in recent years, when workers found it very hard to move geographically because of upheavals in housing markets that made it difficult for them to sell their houses, especially in areas of high unemployment.

The United States also has a much more diverse and heterogeneous population than the European countries. Substantial racial differences in unemployment in the United States (for example, unemployment rates are typically twice as high for blacks and run high for Hispanics as well, compared with whites) make it difficult to build consensus for active labor market policies across labor force groups, as well as between skilled and unskilled workers. In addition, immigrants are much more integrated into the labor force in the United States, which has a less dualistic insider-outsider labor market than countries like Denmark. This creates additional challenges for social solidarity and financing active labor market policies.

There are a number of additional ideological, social, political, and economic obstacles to the implementation of a new social contract, which I consider briefly next.

Reliance on Markets

Economists, legislators, journalists, and political pundits generally contend that economic efficiency (and, hopefully, social welfare) will be maximized if labor markets are allowed to function without interference from the constraints imposed by institutions, such as the government, employment and labor laws, unions, and other sources of market "imperfections." Many Americans are often more skeptical about the ability of government than of labor markets to enhance job quality, and they share a preference for letting private markets make economic decisions.[31]

The market-based view suggests that polarized and precarious jobs are crucial market signals to which individuals must respond: to the extent that polarization in earnings and other indicators of job quality reflect the increasing returns to skills, for example, this becomes an important signal to individuals that they should be investing more in their human capital. The key problem for public policy is, then, to lower the barriers that prevent people from investing in their human capital.[32] Moreover, this perspective maintains that precarious work is simply the by-product of flexible labor markets, as it reflects the ability of employers to shed labor (or inefficient workers) in order to keep the company going in the face of demand or other shocks.

There is little reason to assume that unfettered labor market mechanisms will operate efficiently to produce good jobs, however. Approaches that free the labor market are likely only to exacerbate the trend toward greater inequality and the continued expansion of the low-wage sector, and not to eliminate the mismatches between persons and jobs. The evidence reviewed in this book indicates that reliance on deregulated and unconstrained markets has led to downsizing, falling living standards, and rising insecurity regarding employment. Moreover, markets do not operate freely: they are social constructs, not powerful independent forces. They are created by social actors according to a set of rules. Markets work best when we develop social institutions and policies that systematically remedy their weaknesses. In these cases, markets are able to do what they do best: increase productivity.

Individualism Versus the Need for Collective Action

The political debate over the role of unconstrained markets in the United States is linked to broader ideological disagreements about values. A central American value is that of individualism and the belief that individuals should be free to make their own bargains with one another and with employers without outside interference. This view generally disapproves of institutions that may get in the way of individual-employer negotiations—unions or government intervention in the labor market, for example.[33]

The will to implement the components of the new social contract is constrained by the embeddedness of individualism as a cultural idea in the American psyche. The Reagan administration grasped some cultural crosswinds that redefined America again as individualist, putting the emphasis on the rhetoric of the market in the 1980s. During the past three decades, the ideology of individualism has been dominant, holding that individuals are responsible for managing their own risks and solving their own problems. As a response to the growth in precarious work, for example, individual workers have been encouraged to focus on becoming "employable," and employers on making their employees' skills useful in other companies.[34] These are individual, not structural, responses. Many see Obama's administration as attempting to redefine things in a collective sense under the belief that "we're all in this together," a swing back to relatively rare times in U.S. history.[35] The New Deal and World War II were among the few moments in the twentieth century that the government was able to get people to sacrifice their individual interests to address a collective problem.

Trust, Confidence, and Other Concerns About the Government

For many years now, public opinion analysts have observed Americans' ambivalence toward government: Americans like the particular services that government provides but tend to dislike big government in the abstract; there has thus always been some distrust of an activist government in the United States. This skepticism reached a high point during the Reagan revolution in the 1980s, which ushered in a period where there was little enthusiasm for government intervention in the economy. In 1996, the Democratic president Bill Clinton declared, "The era of big government is over."[36] (This was accomplished by accelerating the trend of privatizing government functions through subcontracting and other means, however, so the ideology of small government has not always been accompanied by small government in practice.)

The federal government started growing again under George W. Bush, partly in response to the crisis of the September 11th terrorist attacks.[37] Between December 2007 and June 2009, the Great Recession—combined with the ambitious public policy agenda of the Obama administration—led to a renewal of interest in (and debate about) the nature of government involvement in the economy. Americans have grown increasingly receptive to this; a recent poll by the *National Journal* found the most desire for government activism to be in the area of health care. Americans also seem to be open to rethinking the safety net in the twenty-first century, as long as they believe that the government is competent.[38] As a number of pundits have recently proclaimed, the "era of the end of big government is over."

Support for sustained public investment requires that people perceive that the government is equitable and "works."[39] The confidence that Americans have in the integrity and competence of their government has been eroded by recent government failures to cope with natural disasters, foreign policy challenges, and domestic economic turmoil. Furthermore, taxpayers have grown increasingly angry over what they perceive as unfair spending on public employees. The informal bargain that public employees should receive lower wages than private sector employees in return for earlier retirement and more generous pensions has eroded, and BLS figures show that state and local government employees now earn on average 34 percent more than those in the private sector.[40] One reason for this is the growth of unionization in the public sector, as shown in figure 2.2. There may well be a "taxpayer revolt" brewing, as people increasingly object to paying public employees high salaries and pensions, especially when these rewards are stagnant and declining in the private sector.

We need to reestablish trust in government and in our economic institutions in order to adopt the kind of new social contract implied by the flexicurity model. This is challenging, as big government, big business, and big labor have all been fairly discredited in the public eye over the first decade of the twenty-first century.[41] In addition, the power of lobbyists has put great pressure on politicians to raise money (and to do the bidding of their clients), further destroying trust in the sanctity of the political process. Money increasingly drives politics and is virtually certain to do so even more, in view of the recent Supreme Court decision allowing corporations to support candidates from their general treasuries (in *Citizens United v. Federal Election Commission*).[42]

Distrust and concerns about the government are fueled by the media, the principal source of information for most people. Most of the media, especially radio, is controlled by interests that extol the virtue of free markets and disparage the role of government in addressing their negative consequences. People often hear much more about the failings of the government than about its successes, due to these interests' powerful manipulation of media to further their own agendas; for example, we hear more about the Tea Party and tax protests than about the tragedies avoided by regulating industries.

Economic Crises

In periods of high unemployment and recessions, questions about the quantity of jobs generally take precedence over the quality of jobs. The assumption that any job is better than no job was the basis for creating a lot of bad jobs by the Works Progress Administration during the Great Depression.[43] The assumption that paid employment in any kind of job is preferable to not having paid work also inspired the "workfare" approach to welfare in the United States; the Temporary Assistance to Needy Families (TANF) regulations enacted in 1996 generally required people to have paid jobs in order to obtain welfare payments. These requirements moved people out of welfare (and often unemployment) and into the labor market. Since many of these persons had low skills, their jobs tended to pay low wages and were relatively bad in other dimensions (such as opportunities for upward mobility, autonomy, or control over schedule) as well. The Great Recession of 2007 to 2009 underscored again the question of whether having a bad job is preferable to having no job at all and revived the question of whether some people (for example, unmarried women with young children) might be better off not working for pay so that they can focus on unpaid care work for their children, as opposed to having a bad job.

Economic downturns represent an impediment to the adoption of flexicurity practices.[44] Indeed, the Great Recession has raised questions about the sustainability of flexicurity, even in Denmark. In June of 2010, for example, the Danish government limited unemployment payments to two years instead of four and tightened up on requirements that unemployed persons must increase their efforts to seek another job by submitting weekly job applications and attending more frequent meetings with job counselors and training programs.[45]

Nevertheless, as I have argued throughout the book, the growth of polarized and precarious employment systems and the resulting changes in job quality are not simply functions of a normal business cycle that will be ameliorated with a stronger economy. While public policymakers are unlikely to jettison the unemployment rate as a key marker of economic stability, especially given its linkage to voting behaviors, we cannot focus only on employment numbers. Indeed, economic crises may be more of an enabler than a barrier, permitting a move from incrementalism to a period in which there is punctuated equilibrium or a massive amount of reform.[46] Solving major crises requires a far-reaching rethinking of economic and social policies, ranging from the reregulation of the financial sector to new fiscal strategies, trade policies, home ownership solutions, deficit reduction strategies, and many more. These kinds of far-reaching policies are perhaps only possible in disruptive times. Economic crises and high levels of unemployment are opportunities to consider carefully the kinds of jobs we ought to be creating as our country transitions toward a new institutional structure of work and labor markets. If we are going to create jobs, let's create good jobs.

Strategies for Implementing a New Social Contract

There is no shortage of sources of ferment that will likely lead to pressures on the government, business, and labor to address the rise of polarized and precarious employment systems and their consequences. Compared with previous generations, young workers are starting out at lower wages, will have flatter wage trajectories, and are more likely to feel the strain of having dual-earner families. The retirement of baby boomers in the next several decades will create lots of job opportunities for younger workers—most of whom are nonwhite and many of whom will be well educated—increasing the urgency of creating jobs that will both challenge them and provide chances for them and their families to enter the middle class. There is also widespread outrage at the consequences of the financialization of the economy, such as the government bailouts of Wall Street firms and the outsized bonuses to their CEOs.

Such sources of discontent need to be channeled through institutional venues in order to fashion a framework that would permit the implementation of a new social contract. Creating functioning institutions that could lead toward deliberation and consensus on a new social contract is likely to be a more promising approach than thinking about this simply in terms of social movements—an approach that might lead to the adoption of some flexicurity principles through punctuated equilibrium that will only last until political and economic conditions change.

A major challenge is to get the government, business, and labor to take employment policy and the creation of good jobs seriously. The United States does not really have a job creation policy, but rather, an economic policy that stimulates spending to make the GDP grow faster, assuming this will incentivize companies to hire people. However, this presumes that increases in economic growth will translate into jobs (not necessarily even good jobs), which it did not appear to do during the Great Recession of 2007 to 2009. Okun's law—which specifies a rough but empirically regular relationship between increases in GDP and decreases in unemployment—is broken. Given the rise of polarized employment systems, we can no longer assume that growth in productivity will translate into better jobs. The lack of consensus about the major obstacles to job creation exacerbates the difficulties that this country faces. The government tends to see barriers to job creation as political problems; business often sees the impediments as labor obstacles; and labor sees these obstructions as business problems.

The idea of flexicurity offers a counternarrative to a reliance on either markets or the government to address the negative consequences of polarized and precarious employment systems. The three components of the new social contract (economic, representation, and skill-reproduction security) are intimately related to many broader policy goals that are designed to get the economy working again. A sensible and equitable system of health care provision is likely to reduce labor costs to businesses, for example, and creating good jobs is integral to the success of any economic stimulus package. Education and training policy is a top issue for business groups—as well as for government and labor—since better-educated workers are more productive. The adoption of flexicurity principles will benefit virtually everyone: creating an expanded safety net, good jobs, and better training opportunities would help average

Americans in addition to benefiting particular groups, such as low-wage workers.

A combination of strategies that emanate from the bottom up as well as from the top down is likely to be most effective in addressing the consequences of polarized and precarious employment systems.

Local Experiments and Initiatives

Local and regional solutions provide opportunities for experimentation with adopting alternative flexicurity principles and demonstrating their feasibility. Based on the Danish flexicurity system, the United States can learn a lesson about the importance of local-level interventions in the promotion of training and employment opportunities.[47] In Denmark, the local-level initiatives have offered tailored individual retraining plans, which have been successful in reemploying workers. Community and local-level experimentation conforms to the principle of subsidiarity, which holds that those closest to the problem have the best information as well as the best ideas for solutions.[48]

There are a number of examples of local and state experiments that approximate some pieces of the flexicurity model.[49] Various states have already tested a range of programs related to the quality of work in a scenario that is reminiscent of the early twentieth century, when a number of states (such as Wisconsin and New York) experimented with unemployment insurance and various protections that eventually ended up in the federal New Deal legislation.[50] In recent years, for example, Washington and New Jersey joined California in adopting the first paid family-leave programs in the United States. MomsRising, an advocacy group focused on family-friendly practices, played a key role in securing paid family leave in New Jersey and Washington.[51] Massachusetts has experimented with universal health coverage, enacting a plan that has many similarities to the federal health insurance legislation adopted in 2010.

The Industrial Areas Foundation (IAF) model is a community-based local initiative that includes activities (such as Project QUEST in San Antonio) that establish labor-market intermediaries to help design training programs and bargain with employers on behalf of their constituencies. These are networks of community organizations that have grown substantially—albeit slowly—around the country. While they do not yet have a national footprint, they do have a substantial presence in about a dozen states. They also have relationships with unions but are not part of the union movement.

Jobs for Life (JfL) is another local, nonunion organization that links individual churches and employers, and provides persons with job training and job-finding assistance. JfL also connects individuals to networks of community members who provide emotional and other forms of help in addition to job opportunities and resources. Founded in 1996 in Raleigh, North Carolina, JfL spread to forty cities and twenty-two states by December 2006.[52]

Various levels of government also provide support for local networks of employers and educational institutions in specific regions or industries.[53] The Hosiery Technology Center (HTC) at Catawba Valley Community College in North Carolina illustrates a cooperative effort between employers' groups, local governments, and community colleges. The HTC—in partnership with individual firms, industry suppliers, and the regional industry trade association—has helped the hosiery industry survive in North Carolina. The HTC provides industry-specific training and is geared toward the largely immigrant labor force in the local area, a group that does not have much formal education. It has also focused on retraining machine technicians with skills to repair and maintain new, highly computerized knitting machines.[54]

Local networks can access existing resources for worker training, partner with community colleges, develop voluntary quality standards for members, benchmark technology, and seek out new niche and export markets. The Wisconsin Regional Training Partnership (WRTP) illustrates how unions, businesses, and colleges can act together to promote training. The WRTP is a consortium of about forty employers in the metalworking, electronics, plastics, and related manufacturing industries, along with another sixty companies participating in some way, representing a total of about 40,000 workers—along with unions and technical colleges—in the Milwaukee metropolitan area. The partnership facilitates communication among these groups and seeks to develop high-quality jobs and skill standards that help workers transfer their skills across employers. The members of the partnership have also developed a youth apprenticeship program and a training program for inner-city residents that facilitates access to entry-level jobs.[55]

Community colleges, important institutional venues for training programs, offer great potential for preparing workers in local areas for the kinds of jobs that are created there. In the biotechnology industry, for example, community colleges are trying to meet the demand for skilled workers. Biotechnology is a particularly important manufacturing industry because it is likely to be the core enabling technology of the twenty-first century, similar to the microprocessor's role in the late twentieth century.[56] Government policies should also be targeted at training particular groups of people who are especially powerless in the labor market, such as workers in factory towns that have lost their sustaining industry or workers injured on the job who need significant reskilling to change fields.

A drawback to such local solutions is that they create incentives for employers to "venue shop" by moving to other local areas that have more lax standards or policies, as has been the case historically when businesses relocated to the American South (or to other countries) to take advantage of the lack of unions and other features of an area's "good business climate." Local initiatives, therefore, need to be supplemented by national approaches.

National Strategies

National elites and other institutional centers of power need to be convinced of the importance and desirability of adopting the new social contract. State and local governments are at a disadvantage when dealing with global corporations, whose executives increasingly think in national and international terms. The federal government needs to take action to counterbalance the activities of such entities. Assistance from the federal government is also vital for state and local governments on a wide range of matters related to the new social contract, such as unemployment insurance, funding of education and training initiatives, assistance with medical payments, and so on.

Linking together local initiatives and institutions such as the IAF and other community-based groups across the nation requires coalescing forces that persuade parties with different goals and interests to join in common efforts. The spread of the Internet and various social networking media helps to generate these coalescing forces, making it possible to bring people together on issues in a short time. Strategies to get around the political blockages that persist in the United States, however, are still needed.

The experience of European countries with flexicurity provides insights into possible processes by which these policies could be enacted here in the United States. In Germany, for example, which is a federated system like the United States, reform occurred by a process of institutional layering, where new features were added onto old policies, creating a dynamic that eventually led to compromises in which the new policies gradually replaced the old.[57] This approach avoids direct confrontation with entrenched interests and helps to circumvent political blockages. A version of this strategy was used in New Jersey, where paid family leave was added to an existing law (the Temporary Disability Benefits law).

A potentially promising widespread application of this strategy of institutional layering might build on the Trade Adjustment Assistance (TAA) legislation to facilitate the transition of displaced workers to new jobs. The TAA legislation originated in the early 1960s and was designed to protect workers in manufacturing industries from job displacement produced by import competition. The TAA recognizes that most people who lose their job are not likely to get their old job back; it underscores the importance of establishing a reemployment system to help workers transition from unemployment to employment by providing support for retraining, among other benefits. The transition mechanism within the TAA could be replicated and expanded beyond manufacturing to service industries. It could also be extended to cover other reasons for job displacement in addition to import competition; this would acknowledge that it is often difficult to distinguish job losses due to import competition from those due to other forms of competition that reduce the prices of goods, or other reasons that might cause displacement.

Another national strategy to break the political gridlock is to identify bridging issues, or win-win topics, within labor market policies that might provide common ground and thus get buy-in from business, labor, and perhaps different parties in the government at both local and national levels. A few key issues serve to illustrate the potential of bringing together people with different interests into coalitions in order to help achieve various pieces of the new social contract.

Energy Policy and Green Jobs   The environment and green jobs might provide a basis for a political coalition between the Right and the Left: entrepreneurs seek to create new jobs in the energy sector; labor tries to make the jobs created high-quality ones; student organizations are mobilizing for the environment all over the United States; and developing alternative sources of energy enhances our national security. A focus on the environment and green jobs might link business processes and government funding to institutions related to job creation.

The potential of linking energy policy to economic development and new job creation is illustrated by the success of Pennsylvania in attracting Gamesa, the second largest wind energy company in the world, to build plants in that state.[58] Instead of requiring the typical tax subsidies, Gamesa asked Pennsylvania to become a major purchaser of alternative energy, leading the state legislature to require that 10 percent of the state's electricity must come from renewable sources by 2020.

Another example of a business that has a targeted solution to environmental problems and is characterized by labor-management cooperation is McGough Construction, which built the first office building in Minnesota to be certified LEED Platinum. Yet another example is Flambeau River Papers, soon to be the first pulp and paper mill in North America to be free from fossil fuels.[59]

Work-Family Balance   The family is important to both the Right and the Left. We must equate good jobs with family-friendly jobs that enable working families to better balance their work and family lives. The contradictions between the demands of homemaking and paid employment—and the unrealistic expectations, especially for women who have shouldered a greater share of that double burden—have not been adequately addressed in the public discourse. Work and family issues are intertwined and must be reframed as tightly coupled; linking together family and work policies requires us to think about families, not individuals, as the basic economic units.[60]

The United States lags behind other countries in the adoption of federal laws to help working families. It stands alone among high-wage countries as having no paid maternity leave, for example.[61] It also has no provision for paternity leave and no federal law providing for paid sick days. Working-time legislation modeled after some European countries would help provide working parents with some of the flexibility that they need to take care of their families. In particular, we need a national paid family-leave program like the Family Leave Insurance Act.[62] We must also provide greater financial and flexible schedule supports to those who are charged with elder care, better access to flexible and affordable day care, and general help to dual-earner families. The United States also needs a world-class program of parental leave to help children get off to a good start in the first two years of life.

Investments in the Health and Well-Being of People   Health benefits provide another opportunity for an alliance among government, business, and labor. Health benefits should be viewed as an investment—not an expenditure—that will lead to both greater productivity and a higher-capability labor force. Removing health care expenditures from employers' labor costs would also help them to create good jobs. The burden imposed on employers by health insurance premiums constrains their ability to compete on price and creates incentives for them not to fund health insurance plans and to keep wages down to compensate for the expenses of paying for health insurance.[63] The establishment of a social safety net that provides essential benefits such as health insurance would also go a long way toward alleviating the negative impacts of low-wage jobs on employees. The 2010 Patient Protection and Affordable Care Act that I discussed earlier is an important step in this direction.

A Need for Global Solutions

Addressing some of the consequences of the growth of polarized and precarious employment systems requires global—in addition to national—solutions. The downward pressure on wages exerted by the existence of unregulated low-wage production in some countries highlights the need for local solutions to be linked to transnational unions, international labor standards, and other global efforts.[64] We need greater international cooperation among governments and multinational agencies for setting standards in order to avoid a "race to the bottom." Professional organizations and unions must also cooperate more fully across borders rather than being divided by them. Implementing the new social contract is necessarily incomplete without a fuller elaboration of a global agenda to supplement national and local initiatives.

Conclusions

This book has described and sought to explain the rise of polarized and precarious employment systems in the United States since the 1970s. The transformation of employment relations results from changes in the structure of work and political economy, as well as shifts in the composition of the labor force. This has led to a growing gap between good and bad jobs and greater precarity for all.

We are in dire need of a new social contract to address the consequences of the growth of polarized and precarious employment systems. This social contract requires the coordinated efforts of government, business, and labor. The example of flexicurity suggests that labor market institutions matter; some countries are better able than others to address the challenges and consequences posed by the global division of labor and the tendencies toward polarized and precarious work. Tackling the sources and consequences of the polarization in job quality will enhance both the competitiveness of the American economy and the quality of work experienced by Americans themselves.

= Notes =

Chapter 1

1. I concentrate here on employment, work that produces earnings (or profit, if one is self-employed). Equating work with pay or profit is, of course, a limited view, as there are many activities that create value but are unpaid, such as those that take place in the household.

2. By contrast, there have been recent studies of changes in job quality in the United Kingdom (see, for example, Green 2006; Gallie 2007a; and McGovern et al. 2008) and Canada (see, for example, Lowe 2000).

3. Jacoby (1985).

4. Edwards (1979).

5. Dobbin et al. (1988).

6. Edwards (1979); Jacoby (1985).

7. Goldin and Margo (1992).

8. Harrison (1994); Morse (1969); Szymanski (1976).

9. Whyte (1956).

10. For example, see Sheppard and Herrick (1972).

11. Tilly (1997).

12. This is a "worker-centered" definition of job quality, since it is based on what is good for the worker (as opposed to the employer or customer) (Green 2006, 9).

13. The International Labour Organization's notion of job quality (that is, "decent work"), for example, takes into account varied aspects of work such as social protection and income security, quality of participation in the labor market, and inclusion in society. The Commission of the European Communities (2001, 4) also takes a broad view of job quality by asserting that it is both a relative and multidimensional concept. It defines "better jobs" as including. ". . . equal opportunities for the disabled, gender equality, good and flexible work organization permitting better reconciliation of working and personal life, lifelong learning, health and safety at work, employee involvement and diversity in working life." Social science researchers have also incorporated assorted job characteristics in their definitions of job quality. The labor economist Eli Ginzberg (1979, 36) argued that most specialists would include as indicators of job quality characteristics such as wages, fringe benefits, regularity (or intermittence)

of employment, working conditions, job security, and opportunities for advancement. Chris Tilly's (1997) key indicators of job quality included wages, fringe benefits, flexibility in hours worked, permanence, mobility, control over the work process, and due process (or protection from arbitrary disciplinary action, particularly being fired). Larry Hunter (2000, 463) contended that better jobs are those offering more compensation, benefits, training on the job, and opportunities for advancement. Neal Rosenthal's (1989, 4) list of factors that constitute job quality consisted of earnings, autonomy, job security, and good working conditions, such as the absence of hazardous environment and the lack of stress. The principal investigators of the *National Study of a Changing Workforce* (1997) identified high-quality jobs as those that offer autonomy, learning opportunities, meaning, and a chance to get ahead. Joseph Meisenheimer II (1998) stressed the central role played by occupational safety in determining job quality, in addition to wages, benefits, and job security. Graham Lowe and Grant Schellenberg (2001) contended that good employment relationships—represented by high trust, commitment, influence, and communication—were the key ingredients of job quality and are more important to overall job satisfaction than pay or benefits. One might also include as components of job quality the following: a safe and healthy workplace free from harassment and intimidation; a mentor or supervisor who takes an active interest in the individual needs and well-being of the worker; and a workplace that values and embraces diversity and individual differences. Finally, Maury Gittleman and David Howell (1995) based their classification of job quality on working conditions, employment, status (that is, unemployment, involuntary part-time employment), and institutional setting (public sector employment, union coverage), in addition to earnings, benefits, and skill requirements.

14. A possible definition of a good job that is consistent with this neoclassical view is one that provides economic incentives that exceed those prevailing at a given skill level.

15. See, for example, Acemoglu (2001).

16. Ginzberg (1979, 36).

17. For example, see Farber (1997).

18. Rosenthal (1989, 8).

19. Braverman (1974).

20. For example, see Kohn and Schooler (1973).

21. Maslow (1954); Hackman and Lawler (1971).

22. This is consistent with Amartya Sen's "capability approach" (see Green 2006).

23. Williams (1968).

24. A job or occupation takes on a different character depending on the person who has it; even a job with "bad" characteristics such as low wages or lack of autonomy can be considered "good" by some people, depending

on their family responsibilities, age, or position in the life course (for example, teenagers may think any job that provides them with spending money is good). Moreover, low-wage jobs without fringe benefits such as health insurance and retirement benefits may not be so bad if you are twenty-two years old and do not have any dependents; such jobs would be worse if you are older and are responsible for supporting a family.

25. Kochan, Katz, and McKersie (1986, 206–25).

26. Work values are shaped by social contexts as well as by basic individual needs (see Salancik and Pfeffer 1977). Hence, the relative importance that workers place on particular job rewards—as well as changes in these assessments of desirability—are influenced by the social, cultural, religious, and economic contexts.

27. This recession, the longest of the post–World War II period, officially lasted eighteen months, beginning in December 2007 and ending in June 2009.

28. Goodman, Peter S. 2010. "Despite Signs of Recovery, Chronic Joblessness Rises." *New York Times*, 21 February: A1, A20.

29. In general, unsafe jobs are bad jobs, though some workers may consider them to be good if they provide compensating differentials such as sufficient economic benefits.

30. See Bluestone (1970); Doeringer and Piore (1971); Piore (1971); Harrison (1972); Kalleberg and Sørensen (1979). The primary labor market was further subdivided into an "independent" primary market, consisting of good jobs that also provided workers with autonomy and control over their work, and a "subordinate" primary market, in which jobs were relatively well compensated economically but not always high skill.

31. Tilly (1997, 270).

32. There have been some attempts to measure the overall goodness or badness of jobs by examining the incidence and trends in combinations of economic rewards; see Kalleberg, Reskin, and Hudson (2000); McGovern, Smeaton, and Hill (2004); Schmitt (2007).

33. In reference to these contexts, John Dunlop (1958) used the term "industrial relations system," by which he meant the premises, values, laws, institutions, and practices that govern employment relationships. This system consists of tangible institutions as well as the patterns, norms, and shared "web of rules" reinforced by custom or agreement that describe how work is organized and how labor market outcomes are generated (Kochan, Katz, and McKersie 1986, 7; see also Kalleberg and Berg 1987; Osterman 1999).

34. The debate between those who argue that work structures are central to job quality and those who maintain that quality results from market forces has been a major source of contention in the intellectual history of theorizing and research about the labor market (Osterman 1999, 21). Neoclassical economists, for example, generally assume that job quality is determined

by market forces, and their models leave little room for the independent roles played by institutions, laws, and regulations (however, see Levy and Temin 2007).

35. Gonos (1997).

36. Bernstein (2006).

37. Gray (1998, 111).

38. Mandel (1996); Kalleberg (2009).

39. The percentages in figure 1.1 underestimate the degree of joblessness, as they do not take into account the discouraged workers who have dropped out of the labor force and thus are not counted as unemployed, and those who involuntarily work part-time because they cannot find full-time employment.

40. A recession is defined by the National Bureau of Economic Research (a private, nonprofit, nonpartisan economic research organization) as a broad-based and lasting decline in economic activity. Such a decline is usually (but not always) considered to be two consecutive quarters in which the gross domestic product declines.

41. See the case studies in Gautié and Schmitt (2010).

42. See Gautié and Schmitt (2010).

Chapter 2

1. Bluestone and Harrison (1982).

2. Mandel (1996).

3. Osterman (1999, 31).

4. See, for example, Kochan (2000).

5. Bowles and Gintis (1982); Rubin (1996).

6. Galbraith (1967).

7. The period of government intervention to address labor problems began during the Great Depression. Before this period, the U.S. government was generally involved more in the affairs of business than in the lives of most ordinary citizens (Rubin 1996).

8. However, the power of unions was weakened by the Taft-Hartley Act in 1947, which amended some of the earlier legislation that protected workers during the New Deal, such as the Wagner Act in 1935. Among other things, it opened the way to right-to-work laws.

9. Cappelli et al. (1997).

10. Althauser and Kalleberg (1981).

11. Osterman (1999).

12. See Doeringer and Piore (1971).

13. Osterman (1999, 67).

14. Jacoby (1985).

15. See, for example, Bluestone (1995); Osterman (1999); Cappelli et al. (1997); Cappelli (1999); Osterman et al. (2001); Bernhardt et al. (2008).

16. Wessel, David. 2004. "The Future of Jobs: New Ones Arise, Wage Gap Widens." *Wall Street Journal,* 2 April: A1, A5.

17. Cappelli (1999).

18. Scott, Lee, and Schmitt (1997).

19. Peck (1996).

20. Wallace and Brady (2001).

21. See Silver (2003).

22. Freeman (2007b).

23. Cappelli (1999).

24. Cappelli et al. (1997).

25. Osterman (1999, 65–66).

26. Fligstein and Shin (2004); Useem (1996).

27. Mandel (1996).

28. Cappelli et al. (1997).

29. Osterman (1999).

30. See Bernhardt et al. (2008).

31. Cappelli et al. (1997, 24–26).

32. These statistics come from the Bureau of Labor Statistics' Current Employment Statistics, Table B-1, Employees on Nonfarm Payrolls by Major Industry Sector, Historical. Available at: ftp://ftp.bls.gov/pub/suppl/empsit.ceseeb1.txt (accessed February 7, 2011). The definition of service industries used here is a broad one and includes all non-goods-producing industries (where goods are defined as agriculture, forestry and fishing, mining, manufacturing, and construction). Service industries include finance, insurance, and real estate; wholesale and retail trade; transportation and public utilities; and business, professional, and personal services.

33. Cappelli et al. (1997, 44).

34. The American version of the service economy consists mainly of personal, professional, and business services, while in Europe, welfare services provided by the public sector make up the most important category of services.

35. The latest edition of *Merriam-Webster's Collegiate Dictionary* defines *McJob* as a "low-paying job that requires little skill and provides little opportunity for

advancement." The *Oxford English Dictionary* also includes the descriptor "unstimulating" (Baron 2003).

36. Bluestone and Harrison (1982); Harrison and Bluestone (1988).

37. Bluestone and Harrison (1986).

38. Bernstein (2006).

39. Uchitelle (2006).

40. Hacker (2006).

41. See Parkin (1971); Giddens (1973); Kalleberg, Wallace, and Althauser (1981).

42. See Lukes (1977).

43. See, for example, Wright (2000).

44. The percentage of wage and salary workers who belong to unions has been fairly constant since the middle of the first decade of the 2000s (with slight increases between 2007 and 2009).

45. See also Burawoy (2008).

46. Gordon (1996); Rubin (1996).

47. Smith (2003).

48. Bronfenbrenner (2009).

49. Freeman (2007a).

50. Bronfenbrenner (2009).

51. Bosch, Mayhew, and Gautié (2010).

52. Bosch, Mayhew, and Gautié (2010).

53. Mishel, Bernstein, and Allegretto (2007).

54. See chapter 6, this volume; Levy and Temin (2007).

55. Gray (1998, 114).

56. Vallas (1999).

57. Green (2006).

58. The "production regime" perspective in the "varieties of capitalism" literature privileges the role of employers in shaping institutional structure and has been used to explain differences among countries in the quality of employment (Soskice 1999; Gallie 2007a, 2007b). By contrast, "corporatist" or "coordinated market" countries such as those in Scandinavia rely more on nonmarket arrangements (see Gallie 2007a, 2007b).

59. See Appelbaum and Batt (1994).

60. For more about the "stick strategy," see (Gordon 1996).

61. Gordon (1996); Appelbaum, Bernhardt, and Murnane (2003).

62. See the case studies in Gautié and Schmitt (2010).

63. *New York Times* (1996).

64.   Cappelli (1999, 115–16)

65.   William Baumol, Alan Blinder, and Edward Wolff (2003) argue that downsizing of both firms and establishments in manufacturing has been the norm since the 1980s.

66.   Baumol, Blinder, and Wolff's (2003) extensive analysis of the Panel Study of Income Dynamics led them to conclude that what appears to be downsizing instead reflects the "churning" of the labor market resulting from the decline of some industries and the expansion of others. This churning increased in the 1980s and early 1990s compared to previous years, especially among younger workers. They find that companies often reduced their workforces temporarily due to bad business conditions, but then expanded them again when business conditions improved. In addition, they point out that downsizing dominated only in the manufacturing sector (which constitutes less than 20 percent of the labor force), but not in the service or retail industries.

67.   Baumol, Blinder, and Wolff (2003).

68.   Uchitelle (2006, ix).

69.   Uchitelle (2006, 152).

70.   Uchitelle (2006).

Chapter 3

1.   McCall (2001).

2.   Fischer and Hout (2006).

3.   The expansion of skilled jobs has not kept pace with the growth of educational attainments in many cases over the past three decades, resulting in overqualification and overeducation (see Kalleberg 2007, chapter 3).

4.   Hesse-Biber and Carter (2000).

5.   Rampbell, Catherine. 2009. "U.S. Women Set to Surpass Men in Labor Force." *New York Times,* 6 February: A1, A15.

6.   Mishel, Bernstein, and Allegretto (2007).

7.   Uchitelle, Louis. 2008. "Women Are Now Equal as Victims of a Poor Economy." *New York Times,* 22 July: A1, A17.

8.   Engemann and Owyang (2006).

9.   Cohany and Sok (2007).

10.   Padavic and Reskin (2002).

11.   Coontz (2005).

12.   Families and Work Institute (1997).

13.   Kochan (2005).

14.   Appelbaum et al. (2002).

15. Gomory, Ralph, and Kathleen Christensen. 1999. "Three Jobs–Two People." *Washington Post,* 2 June.

16. Jacobs and Gerson (2004).

17. Bean, Gonzalez-Baker, and Capps (2001).

18. Figures reported at http://web.mit.edu/cis/fpi_immigration.html (accessed February 8, 2011). In addition, an estimated 11.6 million unauthorized immigrants lived in the United States in January of 2008 (Hoefer, Rytina, and Baker 2009).

19. Mosisa (2002).

20. Many of these were political refugees: 2.3 million refugees have entered the United States legally since 1970 (Fischer and Hout 2006).

21. Mosisa (2002).

22. Mosisa (2002).

23. Preston, Julia. 2010. "Work Force Fueled by Highly Skilled Immigrants." *New York Times,* 15 April. Available at: http://www.nytimes.com/2010/04/16/us/16skilled.html (accessed February 1, 2011).

24. Mishel, Bernstein, and Shierholz (2009).

25. These data come from the Pew Hispanic Center's tabulations of the 2008 American Community Survey (1 percent PUMS), available at: http://pewhispanic.org/files/factsheets/foreignborn2008/Table%2023. pdf (accessed July 17, 2010).

26. Uchitelle (2006, 145).

27. Waldinger and Lichter (2003).

28. The assignment of low-skilled jobs to immigrants is, of course, not new. In the early twentieth century, for example, immigrants also held a large proportion of the unskilled and semiskilled jobs. When asked who will work in the low-skilled kinds of jobs he created, Frederick Taylor was reported to have answered, "These jobs can be done by the Poles and Hungarians." Such jobs fit well with the expectations of these workers, since they came to America to escape poor conditions in their homeland, and thus were happy with any kind of work that they could get.

29. See, for example, Borjas (1990).

30. Fix and Passel (1994); Card (2005).

31. Bean, Gonzalez-Baker, and Capps (2001).

32. Massey (1995).

33. Massey (2007).

34. Those classified as being of Hispanic origin can be of any race, white or black.

35. Toossi (2002).

36. Tomaskovic-Devey (1993).

37. Tomaskovic-Devey et al. (2006).

38. See Fischer and Hout (2006, 130). The statistics on labor force participation presented in table 3.1 mask the fact that the labor force consists of both employed and unemployed persons.

39. Western and Pettit (2002).

40. Fischer and Hout (2006).

41. The NLSY is a panel sample of young men and women who were fourteen to twenty-two years old in 1979. Interviews were conducted with these respondents annually through 1994 and then in 1996 and 1998. These data allow analysts to track the early career of these young Americans through age thirty-three to forty-one.

42. Kalleberg (2007, chapter 5).

43. Fischer and Hout (2006, 97).

44. Kalleberg (2007).

45. McArdle (2008).

46. Gautié et al. (2010).

47. Kalleberg (2007).

Chapter 4

1. Bluestone and Harrison (1982).

2. Meisenheimer II (1998).

3. See Appelbaum and Albin (1990).

4. Sassen (1998).

5. The Economic Council of Canada titled its study of the service sector *Good Jobs, Bad Jobs: Employment in the Service Economy* (1990).

6. Sassen (1998, 47–48).

7. See, for example, Blau and Duncan (1967); Treiman (1977); Featherman and Hauser (1978); Bielby and Kalleberg (1981).

8. See, for example, Grusky and Sørensen (1998); see also Weeden et al. (2007).

9. The Duncan SEI measure is derived from the evaluations of respondents in nationally representative samples who are asked to rate an occupation's "general standing" or "prestige." Respondents rank a group of occupations (not only their own occupation) on a scale from poor to excellent. The resulting aggregate prestige scores of the ranked occupations are then compared to their incumbents' average earnings and educational attainments, and the statistical relationships between them are used to predict the general standing of all occupations.

10. Wyatt and Hecker (2006).

11. See Keller (2009).

12. Cappelli et al. (1997, 187) also report that "during the 1980s . . . there is evidence that for men (although not for women), the number of middle-class jobs—that is, those providing earnings in the middle of the income distribution—seems to have diminished."

13. See also Goos and Manning (2007) for a similar analysis of the United Kingdom, and Goos, Manning, and Salomons (2009), who show that there has been an increase in occupational polarization in many European countries.

14. We should view with some caution the exact magnitude of the growth of managers shown in figure 4.1. On the one hand, the percentage of managers probably underestimates the number of persons in authority positions within organizations, since supervisors are included in a number of other occupational categories (for example, "supervisors and proprietors of sales" are included under "sales" occupations). On the other hand, the growth of managers reflects, in part, title inflation, or the proliferation of jobs that include the word *manager* in the title but do not have any real authority. Designating an employee as a manager is a way of increasing the proportion of employees that are exempt from the National Labor Relations Act's regulations for paying overtime premiums, for example.

15. Stainback and Tomaskovic-Devey (2009).

16. Meyer (2001).

17. Cappelli (1999, 5); Osterman (1999, 33).

18. Service occupations differ from service industries. Service occupations include private household workers, police, firefighters, and food service workers. Service industries classify firms that are engaged in non-goods-producing activities, including health, education, and finance, insurance, and real estate.

19. See Autor, Katz, and Krueger (1998); Autor, Katz, and Kearney (2006).

20. Cobble (1991).

21. Licensing, the strongest form of occupational regulation in the United States, refers to the right to practice. The most minimal form of regulation is registration, which generally requires the individual only to file his or her name and qualifications with a government agency before practicing the occupation (Kleiner 2006). In between these two ends is certification; for example, in the informational technology sector, software vendors offer credentials like the Microsoft Certified Systems Administrator (MCSA) certificate.

22. Kleiner (2006).

23. Althauser and Kalleberg (1981).

24. See Vallas (1999); Kalleberg (2001).

25. Gordon (1996).

26. See Cappelli (1999, 49–62).

27. Harrison (1994).

28. Appelbaum et al. (2000).

29. See the review of evidence in Kruse and Blasi (2000).

30. See Frenkel et al. (1999).

31. Osterman (1999, 60–63).

32. Cappelli (1999) reminds us that these kinds of market-based mechanisms for determining wages were also widespread in American industry over a hundred years ago.

33. The term *core-periphery* model is used by Atkinson (1984); Osterman (1988); Harrison (1994); and Drago (1998). *Core/ring* configuration is used by Olmsted and Smith (1989). *Shamrock* organization is used by Handy (1990, 87–115). *Two-tier organization* is used by Christensen (cited in Doeringer et al. 1991). And the *attachment-detachment* model is used by Mangum, Mayall, and Nelson (1985).

34. Despotic regimes are employment systems in which coercion is the dominant form of control, as in the early factory regimes of capitalism when workers were highly dependent on employers and subject to the "economic whip of the market" (Burawoy 1983, 590). Hegemonic regimes, by contrast, are systems of control in which employers must provide employees with "carrots" in order to persuade them to cooperate and to give their consent to the organization of employment.

35. Kalleberg, Knoke, Marsden (1995).

36. Kalleberg (2003).

37. For example, teams, offline committees, multitasking, or performance incentives; see Kalleberg et al. (2006).

38. Harrison (1994); Kalleberg (2000).

39. See Kalleberg (2000) for a review.

40. Cappelli et al. (1997, 182).

41. See Kalleberg, Reskin, and Hudson (2000); McGovern, Smeaton, and Hill (2004).

42. Barley and Kunda (2006).

43. Kalleberg, Reskin, and Hudson (2000).

44. Kalleberg, Reskin, and Hudson (2000); Kalleberg et al. (1997).

45. See Gautié and Schmitt (2010).

46. There was another directive in 2008 for temporary-help agency workers, but not all member states have yet agreed on this.

47. Gautié and Schmitt (2010).

48. Reich (1992).

49. Osterman (1999, 15, 19).

50. Sørensen (2000).

51. See chapter 7, this volume; see also Braverman (1974); Autor, Levy, and Murnane (2003); Levy and Murnane (2004).

52. Mishel, Bernstein, and Allegretto (2007); Goldin and Katz (2008).

53. See Farber (2005).

54. Leicht and Fitzgerald (2007).

55. Mandel (1996).

56. Adler and Kwon (2002); Leana and van Buren (1999); Nahapiet and Ghoshal (1998).

57. For a review of the concept of social capital, see Portes (1998).

58. Coleman (1990); Leana and van Buren (1999).

59. For example, see Granovetter (2005); Mouw (2003).

Chapter 5

1. See Baron (1988).

2. About 90 percent of people in the United States work for someone else. Even self-employed people can be considered to have "employment relations" with customers, suppliers, and other market actors.

3. Cappelli et al. (1997, 11).

4. Sørensen and Kalleberg (1981).

5. See Bridges (1994); Cappelli (1999).

6. Cappelli (1999, 49); Smith (2010).

7. Sørensen and Kalleberg (1981).

8. Cappelli (1995).

9. Bernstein (1997).

10. Krugman, Paul. 2005. "The Age of Anxiety." *New York Times*, 28 November: A23. See also Krugman (1997).

11. Sennett (1998).

12. Gray (1998).

13. Dore (1997).

14. See also Cappelli et al. (1997, 173–207).

15. For a review, see Kalleberg and Sørensen (1979).

16. See Burchell et al. (1999).

17. Greenhalgh and Rosenblatt (1984).

18. Breen (1997); Beck (2000); Jacoby (2001).

19. Cappelli (1999).

20. The kind of information that is collected by government statisticians depends on what is considered important to study; in many cases this reflects political motivations. For example, occupational censuses in the 1700s and 1800s were used mainly to identify possible sources of group action (Anderson 1994).

21. The Current Population Survey (CPS) is a monthly survey of about 60,000 households conducted by the Bureau of the Census for the Bureau of Labor Statistics. The survey has been conducted for more than fifty years and is the primary source of information on the labor force characteristics of the civilian noninstitutional population in the United States. (For more information on the CPS, see: http://www.bls.gov/cps.)

22. The Current Population Survey (CPS) conducts displaced worker surveys in even years (for example, 1984, 1986) and contingent worker surveys in odd years (for example, 1995, 1997).

23. In 1998, the Census Bureau established the Longitudinal Employer Household Dynamics (LEHD) program in response to the need for more information on the dynamics of employer-employee relations. These data offer great promise in understanding the nature of changes in employment relations (see Holzer et al. 2011).

24. Nardone, Veum, and Yates (1997).

25. Uchitelle (2006).

26. Kalleberg and Marsden (2005).

27. A recent review concludes that offshore outsourcing to developing countries accounts for about one quarter of the jobs lost in manufacturing industries in the United States between 1977 and 1999 (Harrison and McMillan 2006).

28. See Blinder (2006).

29. Wessel (2004).

30. Kalleberg (2000).

31. Mishel, Bernstein, and Allegretto (2007, table 4T).

32. See Barley and Kunda (2006).

33. Kalleberg (2009).

34. We should also keep in mind that the Contingent Work Supplement to the CPS is a household survey of workers and thus almost certainly undercounts nonstandard work because it does not count a worker's second or third job (Mishel, Bernstein, and Allegretto 2007, 239).

35. U.S. Department of Labor (2005).

36. Neumark (2000, 1).

37. For example, Farber (1998a); Diebold, Neumark, and Polsky (1997); Swinnerton and Wial (1996).

38. Before 1983, respondents were asked how long they held their current job. After 1983, they were asked how long they worked for their current employer. Since people could change jobs and remain with their current employer, these two ways of asking the question are not really the same.

39. Uchitelle (2006, 212).

40. See the review in Osterman (1999, 41–43).

41. See also Farber (1998b).

42. See the review in Fligstein and Shin (2004); Schultze (1999).

43. Samuelson (2006).

44. Cappelli (2008); Farber (2008).

45. Auer (2005).

46. Interview cited in Uchitelle (2006, 213).

47. Althauser and Kalleberg (1981).

48. Cappelli (1999).

49. See, for example, Jacoby (1999).

50. Cappelli (1999, 67).

51. Cappelli (2008).

52. Bidwell (2010).

53. Cappelli (2008).

54. Cited in Wessel (2004).

55. See Hirsch and De Soucey (2006) for a discussion of changes in the language of organizational restructuring.

56. See, for example, Uchitelle (2006).

57. Uchitelle, Louis. 2002. "Data Show Growing Trend Toward Permanent Layoffs." *New York Times,* 22 August: C9.

58. Ellwood et al. (2000, 45).

59. See also Baumol, Blinder, and Wolff (2003).

60. Uchitelle (2006, 211–12).

61. Uchitelle (2006, 212).

62. Uchitelle (2006).

63. An exception is a study by Peter Gottschalk and Robert Moffitt (1999), who examine changes in short-term job instability and insecurity using the Survey of Income and Program Participation (SIPP) and the Panel Study of Income Dynamics (PSID). They did not find evidence of an upward trend in the 1980s and 1990s in various indicators of insecurity (for example, involuntary job-loss, spells of unemployment after displacement, or lower wage in a subsequent job).

64. Cited in Koretz (1996).

65. Commonly used measures of joblessness and unemployment fail to capture the full extent of precarious work since they neglect to consider workers who have become discouraged (perhaps because work is so precarious) and have given up looking for a job. In addition, the number of people who work part-time but would prefer to work more hours is at record levels in the United States (Goodman, Peter S. 2008. "A Hidden Toll on Employment: Cut to Part Time." *New York Times*, 31 July: C1, C12).

66. Mishel, Bernstein, and Shierholz (2009, figure 4J).

67. Mishel, Bernstein, and Shierholz (2009).

68. Greenhalgh and Rosenblatt (1984).

69. See Kalleberg and Marsden (2011).

70. See also Fullerton and Wallace (2005).

71. See also Anderson and Pontusson (2007).

72. Job and skill security are undoubtedly related since people with high employability and skill security may also have more security with their employer, who may be more apt to try to retain workers that are also valued by other employers. High-skill, high-wage jobs may be insecure as far as the relationship with a given employer is concerned, though incumbents of such jobs may have considerable labor market power and may be employable in other organizations. The changes in the nature of employment relations discussed earlier suggest that there may be greater inequality in skill insecurity or employability since some workers are better able than others to obtain new jobs.

73. Kalleberg and Marsden (2011); see also Schmidt (1999); Fischer and Hout (2006); Valletta (1999); Fullerton and Wallace (2005).

74. Kalleberg and Marsden (2011).

75. Similarly, Green and McIntosh (2001) find that subjective measures of insecurity in the United Kingdom are positively related to objective indicators such as unemployment experiences; they argue that these subjective measures are thus useful indicators of labor market workings.

76. See also Fullerton and Wallace (2005). Stephanie Schmidt (1999) also found that anxiety about job loss has risen among workers as a whole. Workers were more pessimistic about keeping their jobs and about obtaining comparable new jobs during the economic recovery of 1993 to 1996 than during the comparable business cycle recovery periods of the late 1970s and late 1980s. In addition, workers appeared to be just as worried about losing their jobs in the economic recession of 1990 to 1991 as they were in the much more severe recession from 1982 to 1983.

77. Schmidt also found that more-educated workers became more pessimistic about losing their jobs in the 1990s, but that less-educated workers did not experience much change.

78. Kalleberg and Marsden (2011).

79.   Kalleberg and Marsden (2011) defined white-collar occupations to include professional, managerial, sales, service, farm, and clerical categories. Blue-collar occupations include craftspeople, operatives, and laborers. Predicted percentages of workers at risk of costly job loss were plotted separately for blue- and white-collar occupations, assuming an average unemployment rate and average levels of labor force characteristics other than occupations. Kalleberg and Marsden (2011) found a slight growth in predicted insecurity for blue-collar workers, from about 7 percent in 1977 to 8 percent as of 2006. Though predicted insecurity for white-collar workers is always lower than that in the blue-collar group, the growth in their predicted insecurity is much more rapid, so that the blue-collar–white-collar difference is appreciably smaller at the end of the studied period than at the beginning. The predicted risk of costly job loss among white-collar workers was only about 2 percent in 1977, but it tripled to about 6 percent by 2006.

80.   The results presented in figure 5.2 show an increase in perceived insecurity; this differs from the United Kingdom, which shows little change in overall levels of insecurity from the mid-1980s to the mid-1990s, though there was a big change from the early 1970s to the mid-1980s, corresponding to the oil shocks and increased unemployment (Wichert, Nolan, and Burchell 2000).

81.   Samuelson (2006).

82.   Cappelli (1999, 122–23).

83.   *New York Times* (1996, 294).

84.   See Mishel, Bernstein, and Allegretto (2007).

Chapter 6

1.   Leonhardt, David. 2008. "The Return of Larry Summers." *New York Times*, 26 November: B4.

2.   Of course, some relatively low-paying jobs might also provide intrinsic rewards (and other benefits, such as flexible hours or congenial coworkers) and so may still be relatively satisfying.

3.   A person's earnings reflect both the wage rate and the number of hours worked. This is especially true for people who are paid by the hour. The time-money exchange is not as transparent for salaried workers. I use wages and earnings relatively interchangeably when discussing the monetary aspects of job rewards.

4.   Mishel, Bernstein, and Shierholz (2009). These figures are based on analyses of the Current Population Surveys, a common source of information on wages.

5.   Schmitt (2001).

6. Uchitelle (2006, 37).

7. McMurrer and Sawhill (1996b).

8. Bernhardt et al. (2001).

9. Freeman (1997).

10. Maury Gittleman and David Howell (1995) used cluster analysis to group 621 jobs (derived from a scheme with 1,710 potential jobs within 90 occupations and 19 industries, of which 621 had sufficient cases for statistical analysis) covering 94 percent of the work force into 6 job categories. Gittelman and Howell derived "labor market" contours, or clusters, based on five types of indicators: earnings and benefits, skill requirements (based on the *Dictionary of Occupational Titles'* measures of General Educational Development and Specific Vocational Preparation associated with jobs), working conditions (such as physical demands), employment status (whether people were unemployed or involuntarily employed part-time, plus hours worked per week), and institutional setting (public sector employment, union coverage).

11. Leonhardt, David. 2006. "Gender Pay Gap, Once Narrowing, Is Stuck in Place." *New York Times,* 24 December. Available at: http://www.nytimes.com/2006/12/24/business/24gap.html (accessed February 1, 2011).

12. The black-white gap declined from the mid-1970s to the mid-1980s and then increased again, according to data from the PSID.

13. Leicht (2008).

14. Osterman (1999, 11).

15. Wright and Dwyer (2003).

16. Gittleman and Howell (1995).

17. Mishel, Bernstein, and Shierholz (2009).

18. These patterns of wage inequality are paralleled by configurations of household income inequality. The average after-tax income of the top 1 percent of households more than doubled between 1979 and 2003, while the incomes of those in the middle fifth of the income distribution increased by only about 15 percent after adjusting for inflation (Friedman, Shapiro, and Greenstein 2006).

19. Mishel, Bernstein, and Shierholz (2009, table 3.14).

20. Mishel, Bernstein, and Shierholz (2009, figure 3AE).

21. Katz and Murphy (1992); Levy and Murnane (1992); Acemoglu (2002); see Lemieux (2008) for a recent review.

22. See, for example, Levy and Murnane (1992). It is well known—and well grounded in human capital theory—that more-educated and more-experienced workers tend to have higher variances in wages (see Mincer 1974). As a result, an increase in the average educational level and experience (that is, the age) of the labor force will tend to increase wage inequality (Lemieux 2006).

23. Bell (1973).

24. Ellwood et al. (2000, 31).

25. The pattern of growth in the college wage premium in the 1990s differed for men and women. Among men, there was only modest growth in the early 1990s (year-by-year trends show it to be relatively flat between 1987 and 1996), but it increased strongly thereafter. Thus, the 1990s growth in the male education premium occurred in the last few years. Among women, the college wage premium grew steadily but modestly in the early 1990s and then evened out starting around 1995. The college wage premium among both men and women remained fairly flat in the late 1990s and declined a bit in the early 2000s.

26. See Lemieux (2008).

27. Lemieux (2008).

28. Juhn, Murphy, and Pierce (1993); Katz and Autor (1999); Acemoglu (2002); Card and DiNardo (2002); Lemieux (2006).

29. Lemieux (2006); Juhn, Murphy, and Pierce (1993); Acemoglu (2002).

30. Card and DiNardo (2002).

31. Weeden et al. (2007).

32. See, for example, Lemieux (2006).

33. See Autor, Katz, and Kearney (2006).

34. Mouw and Kalleberg (2010b).

35. David Howell and Edward Wolff (1991) find that skills did not correlate very highly with wages, especially for production jobs: high-wage, low-skill jobs in the goods industries declined from 1960 to 1985; meanwhile, low-wage jobs requiring at least moderate skill levels grew rapidly in the services.

36. Gautié et al. (2010, 149).

37. Weeden (2002).

38. Thus, doctors earn high salaries because in addition to their relatively high skills, the American Medical Association artificially restricts the supply of people it certifies to practice medicine.

39. The effect of licensing on earnings is smaller in European countries like the United Kingdom, Germany, and France since there are more constraints on the work of regulated occupations, including restrictions on prices that they can charge and prohibitions on advertising to consumers that they provide better quality because they are regulated (Kleiner 2006).

40. Mouw and Kalleberg (2010b).

41. The CPS data are not really all that sensitive to very high salaries, however, as they were top-coded at $150,000 a year until 2002, when this figure was revised to $200,000. These amounts are below the 99th percentile of earnings (see Lemieux 2008).

42. See Piketty and Saez (2006).

43. There are a number of alternate measures of low-wage jobs. For example, the cross-national study referred to in this section measured low-wage jobs as those paying less than two-thirds of the gross hourly median wage. Alternatively, Marlene Kim (2000, 26) defines low-wage workers as those "who could not support a family of four above the Government's official poverty level while working 52 weeks per year, 40 hours per week, or a total of 2,080 hours per year . . . [at] $7.91 per hour." She finds that nearly two out of five women work in jobs that pay low wages. One could also define low-wage jobs as those that pay the minimum hourly wage—currently, $7.25 per hour—or less, though most people agree that this is too low for a worker to support him or herself, let alone a family. There have also been attempts to define a "living wage," which differs depending on geographical location as well as one's family circumstances.

44. Mason and Salverda (2010, 36–39).

45. Gordon (1996).

46. Mishel, Bernstein, and Shierholz (2009).

47. See Blinder (2006).

48. Thirty years ago, for example, a car cost about the same as a college education; today, a college education costs much more. This is because there was greater productivity growth in autos, which allowed car companies to produce cars more cheaply while paying auto workers more. College educations cost a lot now in part because of highly paid professors, among other things.

49. While the overall share of low-wage work is high in the United States, the probability of being poorly paid is distributed more evenly across sociodemographic groups in this country than in other high-income European countries. For example, in Denmark, low-wage work is concentrated among young workers (Gautié et al. 2010). This underscores the importance of labor supply institutions in shaping the social meaning of low-wage work.

50. These ten occupations account for about one-quarter of the total projected 17.4 million openings. The average increase for all occupations is about 10 percent. These occupations are the biggest in absolute numbers, but not all are among the fastest-growing occupations in percentage terms. They have the largest absolute numbers of projected increases in part because there are already large numbers of them. The story for home health aides (who have extremely rapid percentage growth) is quite different from the story for janitors, food preparation and serving workers, and nursing aides, occupations that have much slower percentage growth because of their overall larger size.

51. Blinder (2006).

52. I refer here mainly to earnings related to the job, not to family or household income, which often results from the combination of job wages from more than one family member.

53. See, for example, Uchitelle (2006, 120).

54. The studies that Bernhardt and her colleagues use are the National Longitudinal Survey of Young Men (NLSYM) (1966 to 1981) and the National Longitudinal Survey of Youth (NLSY) (1979 to 1994).

55. Brooks, David. 2005. "The Sticky Ladder." *New York Times,* 25 January. Available at: http://www.nytimes.com/2005/01/25/opinion/25brooks.html (accessed February 1, 2011).

56. Bernstein (2007).

57. DiPrete and Nonnemaker (1997).

58. Gittleman and Howell (1995); Gittleman and Joyce (1996).

59. McMurrer and Sawhill (1996b).

60. Hacker (2006, 27–29).

61. Saying that rising wage inequality is within-firm is an expansive definition of "within," however, since an important part of the story is that there has been a changing mix of high-inequality and low-inequality firms.

62. Fredrik Andersson, Harry Holzer, and Julia Lane (2005) also look at quarterly earnings—which reflect wage rates as well as hours worked—rather than hourly wages.

63. Uchitelle (2006, 31–33).

64. Kochan (2005, 129).

65. Bosch, Mayhew, and Gautié (2010, 129–30).

66. For a review, see Shuey and O'Rand (2004).

67. Mishel, Bernstein, and Shierholz (2009).

68. Abelson, Reed. 2010. "Employers Pushed Cost for Health on Workers." *New York Times,* 3 September 3: B1, B4.

69. A number of reforms associated with this act will be phased in over the coming decade. A summary of the new health reform law is available at: http://www.kff.org/healthreform/upload/8061.pdf. See also Oberlander and Marmor (2010).

70. Mishel, Bernstein, and Shierholz 2009, 148–50)

71. Ellwood et al. (2000, 14).

72. Mishel, Bernstein, and Shierholz (2009, 149).

73. Fuhrmans, Vanessa. 2003. "Even at Giant Companies, Many Lack Health Benefits." *Wall Street Journal,* 22 October: B1, B4.

74. Mishel, Bernstein, and Shierholz (2009, 150).

75. See the review by Fligstein and Shin (2004).

76. John Schmitt defined business cycles as the low points of the annual unemployment rates: 1979, 1989, and 2000. The years 1985, 1995, and 2006 occur six years after these low points.

77. Schmitt (2007).

Chapter 7

1. Spenner (1990).

2. These labels have been used by the following authors: "self-direction" (Kohn and Schooler 1973), "conceptual autonomy" (Breaugh 1985), and "task discretion" (Gallie, Felstead, and Green 2004, 244). See also Cappelli et al. (1997, 99–102).

3. Braverman (1974).

4. Blauner (1964).

5. Goldthorpe (2000).

6. For stress researchers, see Karasek and Theorell (1990). Of course, not all workers care about or even want to exercise autonomy and control in the workplace, just as many people do not care enough to participate in selecting their political representatives. The importance people place on having autonomy will differ by variables such as education, race, age, and gender.

7. Kerr et al. (1973).

8. Gallie, Felstead, and Green (2004).

9. Osterman (2000); see also chapter 2, this volume.

10. Appelbaum et al. (2000).

11. Slichter, Healy, and Livernash (1960).

12. Dobbin and Boychuk (1999).

13. See Appelbaum et al. (2000); see also Kalleberg, Nesheim, and Olsen (2009).

14. Hodson (2001).

15. The analyses presented in this chapter, chapter 8, and parts of chapter 9 are based on data from the 1977 Quality of Employment Survey (University of Michigan), the 2002 and 2006 General Social Surveys (National Opinion Research Center), and the 2002 National Study of the Changing Workforce (conducted by the Families and Work Institute). I am grateful to Jeffrey Rosenthal, who created a pooled data set to facilitate comparative analyses of these surveys.

16. The ordinal variables presented in this chapter as well as in chapters 8 and 9 were estimated using a cumulative probit model with heteroscedasticity and variable cutpoints developed by Ted Mouw and Michael Sobel (2001). I am grateful to Stefanie Knauer and Ted Mouw for their help in estimating these models.

17. The results presented in tables 7.1, 7.2, and 8.1 control for the following explanatory variables: gender, race, age, tenure with the employer, education, marital status, part-time versus full-time status, self-employment, occupational complexity and skill, and dummy variables for occupations and industries.

18. The results for the control variables (not shown in table 7.1) are generally consistent with previous research: workers in more highly skilled occupations have greater opportunities to exercise autonomy over the work activities, as are workers with more education (on some measures), men (on some measures, though the gender gap in discretion appears to be closing over time), the self-employed, and supervisors and managers. Workers in large organizations were less likely to have decision-making power over how their work was done in 1977 and were even less able to make those decisions in 2002.

19. Computerization is not the same thing as automation. Sometimes computers are used to automate. In other cases, they completely change the nature of the job. Other times they create jobs that did not exist before.

20. As discussed in chapter 6, the use of computers to routinize work is a partial—but by no means complete—explanation of the growth in economic inequality.

21. I am grateful to David Autor for providing me with a condensed and updated (to 2002) version of these data.

22. Appelbaum et al. (2000).

23. Results for the control variables (not shown in table 7.1) indicate that workers in more-skilled occupations have greater opportunities to participate in decisions, as do workers with more education, the self-employed, and supervisors and managers. Workers in larger establishments have fewer opportunities to participate in decisions.

24. Lincoln and Kalleberg (1990). The pairwise correlations between the measures of discretion presented in table 7.1 and the three indicators of intrinsic rewards presented in table 7.2 range from .24 to .48; between variety and intrinsic rewards, from .34 to .38; and between participation and intrinsic rewards, from .34 and .45.

25. Kalleberg and Marsden (2010); see also chapter 9, this volume.

26. See the summary in Committee on Techniques for the Enhancement of Human Performance (1999).

27. Cronbach's alpha is a measure of the internal consistency reliability of a scale that combines individual items. It ranges from 0 to 1.0, with 1.0 indicating that the items are perfectly correlated with one another.

28. Results for the control variables (not shown in table 7.2) indicate that workers in higher-skilled occupations have greater opportunities to develop their own special abilities, are better able to utilize their skills, and perceive their work to be more meaningful. So, too, are supervisors and those in managerial and professional occupations. Self-employed persons have greater opportunities to develop their abilities and use their skills, but not to perceive their work as more meaningful. Those working in larger establishments report fewer opportunities to use their skills, but not greater chances to develop their abilities or to have meaningful work. Men and

women do not differ in their perceived intrinsic rewards, nor do workers with different amounts of education. The latter finding underscores the subjective nature of intrinsic rewards, as those with more education are more apt to exercise autonomy over their tasks as well as participate in decisions, but are also likely to have higher expectations of being able to do so (and thus are more prone to being harsher critics of their opportunities for intrinsic rewards).

29. Kalleberg and Marsden's (2010) analysis of changes in work values in the United States since the 1970s provides evidence that people tend to place greater value on aspects of jobs that they believe are more problematic to attain at a particular time.

Chapter 8

1. See Epstein and Kalleberg (2004).

2. Some writers have argued that instead of being more overworked, Americans have experienced an increase in leisure time (Robinson and Godbey 1999). The disagreement can be attributed, in part, to alternative ways of measuring time spent working—that is, total hours spent at work—as opposed to the actual activities engaged in while at work, including personal errands, as reported in time diaries (see Jacobs and Gerson 2001).

3. See Florida (2002); Fraser (2001); Hochschild (1997).

4. Green and McIntosh (2001, 292).

5. James Breaugh (1985) distinguished the ability to determine one's own work methods from two other facets of autonomy: work scheduling ("control over work schedules" and "control over work pace") and work criteria ("control over the criteria used for evaluating their performance"). He argues that there is no necessary relationship between the control one has over work methods and over work pace. Also see Dobbin and Boychuk (1999).

6. In 2004, the average number of annual hours worked (for people who were employed or self-employed) was about 9 percent higher in the United States than in the United Kingdom and 25 to 34 percent higher than in the Netherlands, Germany, Denmark, and France. The gap between the United States and the United Kingdom versus the other four countries has widened since the mid-1970s, partly due to union pressure in the latter countries, reflected in the European Union's 1993 Working Time Directive—which created a maximum of forty-nine hours per week over a seventeen-week reference period—from which the United Kingdom has opted out (Mason and Salverda 2010).

7. De Graaf, John. 2003. "Workweek Woes." *New York Times,* 12 April. Available at: http://www.nytimes.com/2003/04/12/opinion/workweek-woes.html (accessed February 1, 2011).

8. The number of weeks worked per year as measured by the CPS indicates continuous as opposed to discontinuous employment, as well as occasional or seasonal work. So, the increase in weeks worked is due more to the

changes in the demography of the labor force discussed in chapter 3 (such as the continued increase in women's labor force participation) than to changes in the organization of work (Jacobs and Gerson 2001).

9. See Jacobs and Gerson (2004, table 1.2). Some men experienced an increase in hours worked, however. For example, Peter Kuhn and Fernando Lozano (2005) report that the share of American men who regularly worked more than forty-eight hours per week increased from 16.6 to 24.3 percent between 1980 and 2005. They use CPS data to show that this trend was concentrated among highly educated, highly paid, older men who were paid on a salaried basis and was strongest in the 1980s, slowing in the 1990s and then declining in the 2000s.

10. Families and Work Institute (1997).

11. Presser (2003).

12. Jacobs and Gerson (2004).

13. Mishel, Bernstein, and Boushey (2003, table 1.27).

14. See Cappelli et al. (1997, 195–98). The percentage of employees who would like to work fewer hours increased by seventeen points between 1992 and 1997 (National Study of a Changing Workforce 1997). However, this effect is likely to be at least partly cyclical, as we would expect this to increase as the economy expands, as it did in the mid- to late-1990s.

15. See Kalleberg (2007).

16. Jacobs and Gerson (2004, table 3.2).

17. U.S. Department of Labor (2008); Rosenberg (2008).

18. Kalleberg (2007, 177).

19. Jacobs and Gerson (2004); see also Figart and Golden (1998); Rosenberg (2008).

20. Golden (2001); Golden and Figart (2000).

21. See McGovern et al. (2008).

22. Gordon (1996); Hodson (2001, 36).

23. Burawoy (1985).

24. Appelbaum et al. (2000).

25. Barker (1999).

26. Cappelli et al. (1997, 9).

27. See Green (2006, 69–77).

28. Jacobs and Gerson (2004).

29. See, for example, Fraser (2001).

30. Cleeland, Nancy. 2002. "Workers Might Be Going Too Fast." *Raleigh News and Observer*, 7 July: E1.

31. For example, see Arai (1994).

32.   The questions Francis Green and Steven McIntosh asked were, "How often does your job involve working at very high speed?" and "How often does your main job involve working to very tight deadlines?" The answers to both questions were coded on the same seven-point scale, ranging from $1 =$ Never to $7 =$ All of the time.

33.   Mason and Salverda (2010, 53–57).

34.   Perlow (1999).

35.   Full-time workers are more likely than part-timers to feel that they are overworked, as are supervisors, those with long tenures with their employers, and people with less than a high school education (the results for these variables are not shown in table 8.1).

36.   Workers with higher levels of education are more likely to perceive that they have jobs that require them to work fast, as are self-employed persons, supervisors and managers, professionals and other white-collar workers, younger workers, and whites (relative to blacks). (The results for these control variables are not presented in table 8.1.) This pattern of results suggests that workers in better jobs are more likely to perceive that they have to work fast.

37.   College graduates, full-time workers, self-employed persons, and supervisors are more likely to say that their job requires them to work hard. This pattern of results again suggests that those with better jobs are more likely to experience high work intensity. In addition, younger workers and women are more likely to say their jobs require them to work hard than older workers and men (results for these control variables are not shown in table 8.1).

38.   Rudy Fenwick and Mark Tausig (2001) measured this by means of several questions that asked workers whether they can decide the number of hours they work and how much control they have over their time schedule.

39.   Rosenthal (1989, 4).

40.   See Berg et al. (2004).

41.   Appelbaum and Golden (2003).

42.   Golden (2009).

43.   Shellenbarger, Sue. 2010. "Is Flextime a Casualty of the Recession?" *Wall Street Journal*, 28 June. Available at: http://blogs.wsj.com/juggle/2010/06/28/is-flextime-a-casualty-of-the-recession (accessed September 29, 2010).

44.   See, for example, Lareau (2003).

45.   For example, see Heymann (2000).

Chapter 9

1.   Peter Warr (1999), for example, identifies ten characteristics that affect job satisfaction: *opportunity for personal control; opportunity for skill use;* the impact of externally generated goals (such as *work intensity*); *variety;* environmental

clarity (such as task feedback and lack of role ambiguity); *money;* physical security (the absence of danger); supportive supervision; opportunity for interpersonal contact; and valued social position (prestige). The job rewards on this list that I have examined in previous chapters are set in italics.

2. Perhaps the most innovative approach to measuring the overall goodness of jobs was set forth by Christopher Jencks, Lauri Perman, and Lee Rainwater (1988), who asked workers to rate the overall desirability of their own jobs as well as a variety of characteristics associated with these jobs (see also Kalleberg and Vaisey 2005). Jencks, Perman, and Rainwater then assessed the average value of these job characteristics to workers by means of a regression analysis of the job-quality index on the various job characteristics. They showed that workers value noneconomic rewards as well as economic aspects of work. In addition, "neither a job's occupational standing nor its pay provides a satisfactory measure of how good the average worker judges the job to be" (the job quality index correlated .72 with pay and .53 with prestige) (Jencks, Perman, and Rainwater 1988, 1354).

   While this measurement approach is very elegant and theoretically satisfying, it has not been widely adopted. One reason is that it is cognitively very demanding of the respondent; it is also costly and time-consuming to administer. It is thus not surprising that is has not been included on general surveys that are not focused specifically on the topic of job quality. Moreover, the relative weights assigned to the various job characteristics are specific to a particular study and so must be collected anew for each survey (unlike Duncan's SEI measure). Since data on this kind of job desirability index have not been collected systematically over time, it cannot be used to examine changes in job quality.

   Duncan's SEI measure, discussed in chapter 4, also has drawbacks as a measure of overall job quality. The ratings of occupations tap economic rewards more than noneconomic aspects of work. In addition, the SEI measure is assigned to occupational categories and so cannot be used to assess differences in quality among jobs within particular occupations (for example, lawyers in Wall Street firms compared with self-employed lawyers). Moreover, the SEI does not take into account individual differences in the preferences for various job characteristics, since it is an aggregate measure assigned to an occupational category.

3. Jasso (1990).

4. For example, see Clark (1998); Clark and Oswald (1996); Green (2006).

5. See Kalleberg (1977). It is generally agreed that the best indicators of satisfaction and other measures of subjective well-being (such as happiness) are derived from self-reports, as opposed to alternative indicators obtained from physiological and neurobiological indicators, observed social behavior, or nonverbal behavior (Frey and Stutzer, 2002, 26).

6. Research on job satisfaction illustrates that different conclusions may be reached on the basis of aggregated as opposed to disaggregated studies. Jon Ebeling, Michael King, and Marshall Rogers (1979), for example, show

how conclusions regarding differences in job satisfaction compared by position within an organization differ when using nationally representative samples as compared with a single work organization. One reason for this is that variables such as age, income, prestige, and supervisory status are less highly correlated in national samples.

7.   Kalleberg (1977); Clark (1998).

8.   For example, Kalleberg (1974).

9.   Despite possible response biases and other sources of invalidity of the direct indicator, there is no reason to think that this measure is worse in one time period than another.

10. See Caplow (1982). Alternative measures are likely to yield greater levels of dissatisfaction: for example, people tend to express more dissatisfaction when asked if they would want their children to have the same job as they have.

11. Frey and Stutzer (2002, 103).

12. De Witte (1999); Uchitelle (2006).

13. Hodson (1989); Clark (1997).

14. Easterlin (1995).

15. See also Clark, Frijters, and Shields (2008); Firebaugh and Tach (2011).

16. See Green (2006, 153–60).

17. See Aversa, Jeannine. 2010. "Survey Finds Mostly Grumps: Discontent at Work Hits a High." *Raleigh News and Observer*, 5 January: 3B. While this was a fairly large survey, no information was provided on sampling procedures or on margins of error.

18. The GSS direct indicator asks about the *work* one does rather than the specific *job*. Our analytic models, however, exclude persons who stay at home or are retired, unemployed, or in school.

19. The decrease in average job satisfaction is consistent with previous analyses of the GSS data (for shorter periods) that have found a slight decline in the percentage of workers saying they are "very satisfied" with their work (Ellwood et al. 2000, 63); this decline is due to an increase in people saying that they are "moderately satisfied" rather than an increase in expressed dissatisfaction (which has been fairly constant since 1972).

20. Firebaugh (1997); Firebaugh and Harley (1995).

21. The cohort coefficient combines—but does not distinguish—effects of birth cohorts and aging. Likewise, the year coefficient for intracohort change combines effects of period differences and aging. The linear decomposition does not separate age, period, and cohort effects.

To illustrate the decomposition, start with a simple underlying linear age-period-cohort regression of job satisfaction on age, cohort, and year:

$$Y = A + B_1 Age + B_2 Cohort + B_3 Year$$

Let us also assume the following values for the coefficients of this equation (which are consistent with previous research):

$B_1>0$, satisfaction increases with age

$B_2<0$, more recent cohorts are less satisfied

$B_3<0$, satisfaction is decreasing for everyone in time

The linear decomposition presented in panel B of table 9.2 does not estimate the preceding equation; rather, we leave out age and estimate the reduced form regression:

$Y = A + C_2 Cohort + C_3 Year$

where C_3 is the intracohort change coefficient and C_2 is the cohort replacement coefficient. In these data, C_3 is positive, but C_2 is negative. We can look at how the C coefficients are related to the B coefficients by substituting the definition

$Age = Year - Cohort$

into the first equation:

$$Y = A + B_1 (Year - Cohort) + B_2 Cohort + B_3 Year$$
$$A + (B_2 - B_1) Cohort + (B_3 + B_1) Year$$

This means that

$$C_2 = B_2 - B_1$$
$$C_3 = B_1 + B_3$$

The negative cohort replacement coefficient C_2 observed in table 9.2 reflects the reinforcing effects of the negative cohort effect B_2 and the positive age effect B_1 (which contributes negatively to the cohort replacement coefficient). The positive intracohort change coefficient C_3 observed in table 9.2 suggests that the negative period effect B_3 has a smaller magnitude than the positive age effect B_1. I am grateful to Peter V. Marsden for clarifying this decomposition.

22. See Kalleberg and Loscocco (1983).

23. See Kalleberg and Marsden (2010).

24. By asking workers to rank the relative importance of job characteristics, this approach forces workers to make choices about various job rewards and decide which are more or less important to them. To the extent that workers cannot maximize all job rewards at the same time and need to make trade-offs among them, this approach provides a more realistic view of workers' conceptions of what is more or less desirable in their work activities than approaches that ask workers to rate the importance of each type of job reward.

25. The correspondences between these work values and the job rewards are as follows: high income (earnings, chapter 6); no danger of being fired (job security, chapter 5); short working hours, lots of free time (work hours, chapter 8); chances for advancement (upward mobility, chapter 6); and work that is important and gives a feeling of accomplishment (control over work tasks and intrinsic rewards, chapter 7).

26. Kalleberg and Marsden (2010).

27. See Twenge (2006). This explanation based on expectations is not inconsistent with that based on work values. Workers may be relatively satisfied if they attain something (like security) that is more difficult to obtain and thus that they value highly; they may also be comparatively dissatisfied if their job does not measure up to their expectations for security and other job rewards.

28. See also Wright and Hamilton (1978).

29. Estimated coefficients for the sociodemographic control variables are broadly consistent with those reported by previous studies of job satisfaction. Women tend to be more satisfied with their jobs than men (Bokemeier and Lacy 1986). Blacks and members of other minority races tend to be less satisfied than whites—undoubtedly a result of the lower job quality of their jobs. Differences in satisfaction by occupation generally follow a socioeconomic status (SES) gradient: those in all occupational groups tend to be more satisfied than laborers (the reference category), though the difference between operatives and laborers is not statistically significant. Satisfaction is especially high among professionals and those in farming. Both family income and full-time employment status are positively associated with job satisfaction. In addition, union members are less satisfied with their jobs.

30. Gruenberg (1980).

31. This result conflicts with one of the few studies of cohorts and job satisfaction: Daniel Hamermesh (1999) found some evidence that there has been an increase in inequality in job satisfaction in the United States across cohorts of young men (based on the National Longitudinal Study of Youth [NLSY] between 1978 and 1988, and between 1978 and 1996). The distribution of job satisfaction widened across cohorts of young men in ways that were correlated with changing wage inequality; it rose among workers in upper-earnings quantiles relative to satisfaction of workers in lower quantiles. Hamermesh observed an identical phenomenon among men in West Germany in response to the sharp increase in the relative earnings of high-wage men in the mid-1990s. The differences between his analyses and those reported here may be due to his focus on cohorts of young men rather than on national samples of workers; or they could reflect variations in the analysis of age, period, and cohort effects.

32. Firebaugh and Harley (1995).

33. See also Saunders, O'Neill, and Jensen (1986); Wright and Hamilton (1978).

Chapter 10

1. See Galbraith (1952). There are, of course, some constraints on employers' freedom of action due to requirements of the various Civil Rights Acts and required extensive compliance with nondiscrimination laws (this is especially

true for large firms). We should also remember that during the postwar period of strong labor unions, large portions of the female and minority labor force were excluded from the protections they secured.

2. Peck (2010).

3. Jacob Hacker and Paul Pierson (2010) provide a compelling analysis of how the government has aided the rich at the expense of the middle class, leading to a "winner-take-all" economy that is the result of "winner-take-all" politics.

4. The countries of Western Europe are most similar to the United States in terms of culture and industrial development, and so how they have reacted to the challenges of the 1980s, 1990s, and 2000s are most likely to be instructive for identifying the range of strategies that might be used.

5. Muffels and Luijkx (2006).

6. For a recent review of this concept, see Viebrock and Clasen (2009).

7. Cohen and Sabel (2009).

8. Wilthagen and Tros (2004).

9. Viebrock and Clasen (2009).

10. Viebrock and Clasen (2009).

11. The Danes' total expenditure on active labor market policies in 2005 was 1.85 percent of GDP, compared with 0.14 percent in the United States and 0.45 percent in the United Kingdom (Gautié, Westergaard-Nielsen, and Schmitt 2010, 171).

12. Chatani (2008).

13. Schulze-Cleven and Farrell (2010).

14. Kuttner (1995); Kochan (2000); Aronowitz (2001); Osterman et al. (2001); Reich (2002).

15. See Kochan (2000, 3). This concept has its roots in the philosophies of Hobbes, Locke, Rousseau, and Rawls.

16. Osterman (2008).

17. ILO (2004).

18. The other four types of security summarized in the ILO's 2004 report are: labor market security (opportunities for jobs); employment security (adequate protection against job loss and arbitrary dismissal); job security (ability to continue a particular occupational activity due to enforcement of craft boundaries and job qualifications); and safety and health security (good occupational safety and health conditions).

19. The United States is an exception among major industrial countries in its lack of laws specifically directed at job security. There are a number of ways to create disincentives for employers to lay off workers; for example, by enacting laws to protect job security, the government could try to slow

down some of the corporate restructuring that has increased precarious work. See www.westlaw.com for a description of the Model Employment Termination Act (Uchitelle 2006, 224).

20. See Mandel (1996); Hacker (2006); Kochan (2006). Using social insurance to address unforeseen risks is not a new idea in the United States; it was developed and implemented in the 1930s at the University of Wisconsin by John R. Commons and his students (including Edwin Witte, who would later be known as the father of Social Security).

21. Mandel (1996, 171).

22. Robert Samuelson (2009, 26) suggests that "the sensible thing to do would be to decide which forms of public welfare are needed to protect the vulnerable and to begin paring others." The three types of social insurance discussed here are the most critical ones.

23. Oberlander and Marmor (2010).

24. Kochan (2005, 138).

25. For example, see Ghilarducci (2008).

26. Osterman et al. (2001, 160).

27. Uchitelle (2006, 221).

28. Reich (2010, 133–34).

29. The importance of having "voice" is underscored by the fact that workers who lose union coverage also lose the right to speak up about problems on the job without fear of retaliation.

30. Kochan, Thomas A. 2003. "A New Deal for Labor Day." *Boston Globe*, 1 September. Available at: http://www.boston.com/news/globe/editorial_opinion/oped/articles/2003/09/01/a_new_deal_for_labor_day (accessed February 1, 2011).

31. Legislation like the Employee Free Choice Act would facilitate labor organizing (see http://www.aflcio.org/joinaunion/voiceatwork/efca [accessed February 5, 2011].)

32. The government's support for education and training is needed not only for reasons of social justice, but also for purposes of social efficiency. It is society's (and hence the government's) responsibility to deal with the many varied consequences of having a low-skilled, poorly educated population. For example, the government needs to provide assistance so that disadvantaged children can learn at a pace equal to their peers. Those who never catch up due to inadequate education will be less likely to find jobs that pay living wages, and may be more likely to become criminals. Their crimes would cost the government even more money, and so on the cycle would continue.

33. We do have some reinforcement of individual investments in human capital, such as the Lifetime Learning Tax Credit and training provisions of the Workforce Investment Act. But we need better reinforcement of individual

efforts to invest in one's own training and development, such as through direct reimbursement for these initiatives at some percentage up to 100 percent, or at least a tax advantage for people investing in human capital development, similar to the tax benefits offered to homebuyers.

34. McCall and Kenworthy (2009).

35. Champlin (1995).

36. Kalleberg (2007).

37. Career ladders can exist both internally within firms and externally between firms. Internal career ladders are more likely to be found in relatively large and stable firms and in situations in which the government and public can use their leverage (in part because they may pay the bills) to construct these ladders. Encouraging the creation of career ladders within an industry might be more advantageous than within firms, since companies themselves may desire the ability to change direction (and therefore staffing needs) relatively easily.

38. Fitzgerald (2006b).

39. An example of a venture that has created opportunities for career advancement is the San Francisco Hotels Partnership Project, created in 1994 by twelve first-class hotels and two unions, the Hotel and Restaurant Employees International Union (HERE) and the Service Employees International Union (SEIU). Similarly, in Las Vegas, a campaign by HERE organized 48,000 unionized workers representing 90 percent of the city's hotel jobs and was able to turn low-end jobs (such as room cleaners) into better jobs that paid living wages, with opportunities for career advancement. Additional examples of these kinds of job ladder programs are provided by Bernhardt and Bailey (1998); Appelbaum, Bernhardt, and Murnane (2003); and Osterman (2008).

Chapter 11

1. See Piore (2009). This contrasts to earlier periods of polarized and precarious work, when there were strong ideologies (like Marxism) that conceptualized what a world would look like in which the market was not dominant. These older theories are now largely discredited.

2. Quigley (2003); Shipler (2004).

3. Samuelson (2009, 26).

4. See Mandel (1996).

5. While relatively few people earn the federal minimum wage, this yardstick puts pressure on private sector employers to also raise wages. Raising minimum wages also encourages employers to increase training and develop more inventive competitive strategies than simply low-wage production.

6. One of the few remaining ways in which employers in the United States are legally allowed to discriminate among workers is on the basis of hours

worked; as a result, those who work part-time earn less per hour on average than full-time workers. Some progress has been made in this regard based on case law (for example, *Vizcaino v. Microsoft*), but this needs to be worked into an amendment to the Fair Labor Standards Act or some other legislation. Moreover, under the Employment Retirement Income Security Act (ERISA), employers can exempt from pension plans those workers who are employed fewer than one thousand hours a year.

7. Uchitelle (2006, 64).

8. Dickey and McNicoll (2008).

9. See Hirschman, Linda R. 2008. "Where are the New Jobs for Women?" *New York Times*, 9 December: A31. There are a number of differences today that would make it difficult to replicate the government job creation programs of the New Deal: political resistance to such policies is greater today (in part because we now have unemployment insurance and food stamps); there are more regulations (such as environmental safeguards and requirements for competitive bidding) that create delays in the time that government expenditures can be translated into jobs; and technological advances have reduced the amount of labor (and thus jobs) needed for construction and manufacturing work (the two industries that lost the most jobs in the 2007 to 2009 recession) (Meyerson 2010).

10. For example, the living-wage ordinance passed in Los Angeles in 1997 required firms with city contracts to provide health coverage and pay an hourly wage that was several dollars higher than the federal minimum (and the California minimum) wage. Los Angeles also adopted a variety of community-benefit agreements that required developers to seek retailers that pay living wages (Meyerson 2006).

11. The Families and Work Institute's National Study of the Changing Workforce provides information on family-friendly benefits by job title and income (cited in Kochan 2005, 25).

12. The so-called skills shortage in many occupations, for example, results from the fact that employers are not providing as much training to their workers as in the past. The fact that employers are concerned about skill shortages may lead to opportunities to encourage them to engage in behaviors that might lead to the creation of better jobs.

13. See Cappelli (2008).

14. Kuttner (2008, 17).

15. Leonhardt (2009).

16. Wright (2008).

17. For example, two-thirds of the 1.3 million corporations active in the United States in 2008 paid no income taxes between 1998 and 2005 (Hodge 2010, 213).

18. See the case studies in Appelbaum, Bernhardt, and Murnane (2003).

19. See the case studies in Appelbaum, Bernhardt, and Murnane (2003).

20. Reich (2002).

21. Shiller, Robert J. 2010. "The Survival of the Safest." *New York Times*, 2 October. Available at: http://www.nytimes.com/2010/10/03/business/economy/03view.html (accessed February 1, 2011).

22. Batt, Hunter, and Wilk (2003).

23. For example, Clawson (2003).

24. Osterman et al. (2001, 96).

25. Heckscher (1996); Osterman et al. (2001).

26. More information about the union is available at http://www.freelancers union.org.

27. Kochan (2006, 380–81).

28. Clawson (2003).

29. Worker centers are nonprofit organizations that organize immigrant and low-wage workers who are not union members, among others (see Fine 2006).

30. Alderman, Liz. 2010. "Turning of the Tide: Denmark Starts Trimming its Admired Social Safety Net." *New York Times*, 17 August: B1, B4.

31. See Jencks (2004, 37). The market is not a doer but a place (a store, barnyard, lawn, or auction house); markets are people doing transactions of different sorts. Moreover, markets do not fail, people do: for example, designers of goods that did not suit people, or inventors whose ideas were ahead of (or behind) their time.

32. As I discuss in chapter 6, this "skill-biased technological change" explanation for the growing gap between wage returns and education is only an incomplete accounting. When a person rises to the top of a division of a major company but the organization sheds the entire division, for example, this can hardly be attributed to an individual worker's failure to read market signals correctly.

33. Bernstein (2006).

34. Smith (2010).

35. Bernstein (2006).

36. Clinton (1996).

37. See *The Economist* 2009. Historically, crises have tended to make Americans want more government intervention. This was illustrated vividly during the Great Depression, a time that resulted in the creation of a variety of regulatory agencies (for example, the Securities and Exchange Commission, the Federal Deposit Insurance Corporation), as well as key elements of the federal government's safety net (for instance, Social Security and Unemployment Insurance), among other changes.

38. Brooks, David. 2009. "Yanks in Crisis." *New York Times*, 24 April: A23.

39. Borosage and Lotke (2009, 12).

40. Shiller, Robert J. 2010. "The Survival of the Safest." *New York Times*, 2 October. Available at http://www.nytimes.com/2010/10/03/business/economy/03view.html (accessed February 1, 2011).

41. A survey of 2,505 adults conducted in March 2010 by the Pew Research Center found that only 24 percent felt that Congress positively affected society. Trust in corporations was equally low, with only 25 percent approval. By contrast, 71 percent said small businesses positively affected society.

42. Hacker and Pierson (2010).

43. The negative consequences of unemployment on psychological well-being and stress—as well as family and community disruptions—are well established (Sullivan 1978; Jahoda 1982; Sullivan, Warren, and Westbrook 2001). Richard Layard (2004) argues that human happiness is enhanced more by having any job at all, regardless of the quality of the job.

44. Viebrock and Clasen (2009).

45. Alderman, Liz. 2010. "Turning of the Tide: Denmark Starts Trimming its Admired Social Safety Net." *New York Times*, 17 August: B1, B4.

46. As Rahm Emanuel famously said, "Never let a good crisis go to waste."

47. Ilsøe (2007).

48. Osterman et al. (2001, 13).

49. See Osterman et al. (2001); Dean and Reynolds (2009).

50. Kochan (2005).

51. More information on Momsrising can be found on the organization's website at www.momsrising.org.

52. More information on JfL can be found on their website, at www.jobsforlife.org, and in Spickard (2007).

53. See the examples of these networks in the case studies in Appelbaum, Bernhardt, and Murnane (2003).

54. Willis, Connelly, and DeGraff (2003).

55. Osterman (1999).

56. Fitzgerald (2006b).

57. Streeck and Thelen (2005); Schulze-Cleven and Farrell (2010).

58. Fitzgerald (2006a).

59. Additional examples can be found in the American Rights at Work 2010 Labor Day list (available at: http://www.americanrightsatwork.org/labor-day-list/updates [accessed February 1, 2011]).

60. Kochan (2006).

61. Gautié, Westergaard-Nielsen, and Schmitt (2010).

62. See Boushey (2009). Existing policies to help working families such as the 1993 Family Medical Leave Act (FMLA) illustrate how woefully inadequate our federal laws are in this regard. The fact that the FMLA provides only for unpaid leave makes it difficult for many families to afford to take advantage of it. Even so, many workers are not even eligible to take it; to qualify, an employee must have spent at least a year working at a company that has more than fifty employees within seventy-five miles, for at least 1,250 hours per year. This leaves out many part-time workers, as well as those working for smaller companies. At a minimum, we need to extend the FMLA to cover all workers.

63. A vivid example of the burden of health care costs on employers is found in the automobile industry, where General Motors' bankruptcy was due in part to its huge overhead costs resulting from its long tradition of providing very high-quality health care to its employees and retirees. As a result of these commitments, the costs of health care exceeded the costs of raw materials, such as steel, for producing a car.

64. Silver (2003); Webster, Lambert, and Bezuidenhout (2008).

References

Abraham, Katherine G. 1990. "Restructuring the Employment Relationship: The Growth of Market-Mediated Work Arrangements." In *New Developments in the Labor Market: Toward a New Institutional Paradigm*, edited by Katherine G. Abraham and Robert B. McKersie. Cambridge, Mass.: MIT Press.

Acemoglu, Daron. 2001. "Good Jobs Versus Bad Jobs." *Journal of Labor Economics* 19(1): 1–21.

———. 2002. "Technical Change, Inequality, and the Labor Market." *Journal of Economic Literature* 40(1): 7–72.

Adler, Paul, and Seok-Woo Kwon. 2002. "Social Capital: Prospects for a New Concept." *Academy of Management Review* 27(1): 17–40.

Althauser, Robert P., and Arne L. Kalleberg. 1981. "Firms, Occupations, and the Structure of Labor Markets: A Conceptual Analysis." In *Sociological Perspectives on Labor Markets*, edited by Ivar Berg. New York: Academic Press.

Anderson, Christopher J., and Jonas Pontusson. 2007. "Workers, Worries and Welfare States: Social Protection and Job Insecurity in 15 OECD Countries." *European Journal of Political Research* 46(2): 211–35.

Anderson, Margo. 1994. "(Only) White Men Have Class: Reflections on Early 19th Century Occupational Classification Systems." *Work and Occupations* 21(1): 5–32.

Andersson, Fredrik, Harry J. Holzer, and Julia I. Lane. 2005. *Moving Up or Moving On: Who Advances in the Low-Wage Labor Market?* New York: Russell Sage Foundation.

Appelbaum, Eileen. 2010. "Institutions, Firms, and the Quality of Jobs in Low-Wage Labor Markets." In *Low-Wage Work in the Wealthy World*, edited by Jérôme Gautié and John Schmitt. New York: Russell Sage Foundation.

Appelbaum, Eileen, and Peter Albin. 1990. "Shifts in Employment, Occupational Structure, and Educational Attainment." In *Skills, Wages, and Productivity in the Service Sector*, edited by Thierry Noyelle. Boulder, Colo.: Westview Press.

Appelbaum, Eileen, Thomas Bailey, Peter Berg, and Arne L. Kalleberg. 2000. *Manufacturing Advantage: Why High-Performance Work Systems Pay Off*. Ithaca, N.Y.: Cornell University Press.

———. 2002. *Shared Work, Valued Care: New Norms for Organizing Market Work and Unpaid Care Work*. Washington, D.C.: Economic Policy Institute.

Appelbaum, Eileen, and Rosemary Batt. 1994. *The New American Workplace: Transforming Work Systems in the United States*. Ithaca, N.Y.: Cornell University Press.

Appelbaum, Eileen, Annette Bernhardt, and Richard J. Murnane, eds. 2003. *Low-Wage America: How Employers Are Reshaping Opportunity in the Workplace*. New York: Russell Sage Foundation.

Appelbaum, Eileen, and Lonnie Golden. 2003. "The Failure to Reform the Workday: Employers Fail to Offer Employees Flexible Arrangements That Help Relieve the Time Squeeze." *Challenge* 46(1): 79–92.

Arai, Mahmood. 1994. "Compensating Wage Differentials Versus Efficiency Wages: An Empirical Study of Job Autonomy and Wages." *Industrial Relations* 33(2): 249–62.

Aronowitz, Stanley. 2001. *The Last Good Job in America: Work and Education in the New Global Technoculture.* Lanham, Md.: Rowman and Littlefield.

Atkinson, John. 1984. "Manpower Strategies for Flexible Organizations." *Personnel Management* 16(8): 28–31.

Auer, Peter. 2005. "Protected Mobility for Employment and Decent Work: Labour Market Security in a Globalised World." Employment Analysis and Research Unit paper 2005/1. Geneva: International Labour Organization.

Auer, Peter, and Sandrine Cazes, eds. 2003. *Employment Stability in an Age of Flexibility.* Geneva: International Labour Organization.

Autor, David H., Lawrence F. Katz, and Melissa S. Kearney. 2006. "The Polarization of the U.S. Labor Market." *American Economic Review* 96(2): 189–94.

Autor, David H., Lawrence F. Katz, and Alan Krueger. 1998. "Computing Inequality: How Have Computers Changed the Labor Market?" *Quarterly Journal of Economics* 113(4): 1169–1214.

Autor, David H., Frank Levy, and Richard J. Murnane. 2003. "The Skill Content of Recent Technological Change: An Empirical Exploration." *Quarterly Journal of Economics* 118(4): 1279–1333.

Averitt, Robert T. 1968. *The Dual Economy: The Dynamics of American Industry Structure.* New York: Norton.

Barker, James R. 1999. *The Discipline of Teamwork: Participation and Concertive Control.* Thousand Oaks, Calif.: Sage.

Barker, Kathleen, and Kathleen Christensen, eds. 1998. *Contingent Work: American Employment Relations in Transition.* Ithaca, N.Y.: Cornell University Press.

Barley, Stephen R. 1996. *The New World of Work.* London: British–North American Research Committee.

Barley, Stephen R., and Gideon Kunda. 2006. *Gurus, Hired Guns and Warm Bodies: Itinerant Experts in a Knowledge Economy.* Princeton, N.J.: Princeton University Press.

Baron, David. 2003. "McLanguage Meets the Dictionary." *The Chronicle of Higher Education,* 19 December: B14.

Baron, James N. 1988. "The Employment Relation as a Social Relation." *Journal of the Japanese and International Economies* 2(4): 492–525.

Batt, Rosemary, Larry Hunter, and Steffanie Wilk. 2003. "How and When Does Management Matter? Job Quality and Career Opportunities for Call Center Workers." In *Low-Wage America: How Employers Are Reshaping Opportunity in the Workplace,* edited by Eileen Appelbaum, Annette Bernhardt, and Richard J. Murnane. New York: Russell Sage Foundation.

Baumol, William, Alan S. Blinder, and Edward N. Wolff. 2003. *Downsizing in America: Reality, Causes, Consequences.* New York: Russell Sage Foundation.

Bean, Frank D., Susan Gonzalez-Baker, and Randy Capps. 2001. "Immigration and Labor Markets in the United States." In *Sourcebook of Labor Markets: Evolving*

Structures and Processes, edited by Ivar Berg and Arne L. Kalleberg. New York: Kluwer Academic/Plenum Publishers.

Beck, Ulrich. 2000. *The Brave New World of Work.* Cambridge: Polity Press.

Bell, Daniel. 1973. *The Coming of Post-Industrial Society: A Venture in Social Forecasting.* New York: Basic Books.

Bell, Linda A., and Richard B. Freeman. 1994. "Why Do Americans and Germans Work Different Hours?" Working Paper 4808. Cambridge, Mass.: National Bureau of Economic Research.

Berg, Peter, Eileen Appelbaum, Tom Bailey, and Arne L. Kalleberg. 2004. "Contesting Time: International Comparisons of Employee Control of Working Time." *Industrial and Labor Relations Review* 57(3): 331–49.

Berle, Adolph A., and Gardiner C. Means. 1932. *The Modern Corporation and Private Property.* New York: Macmillan.

Bernhardt, Annette, and Thomas R. Bailey. 1998. *Making Careers Out of Jobs: Policies to Address the New Employment Relationship.* New York: Columbia University, Teachers College, Institute on Education and the Economy.

Bernhardt, Annette, Heather Boushey, Laura Dresser, and Chris Tilly, eds. 2008. *The Gloves-Off Economy: Workplace Standards at the Bottom of the Labor Market.* Champaign: University of Illinois, Labor and Employment Relations Association.

Bernhardt, Annette, Martina Morris, Mark S. Handcock, and Marc A. Scott. 2001. *Divergent Paths: Economic Mobility in the New American Labor Market.* New York: Russell Sage Foundation.

Bernstein, Jared. 2006. *All Together Now: Common Sense for a Fair Economy.* San Francisco: Berrett-Koehler Publishers.

———. 2007. "Economic Mobility in the US: How Much Is There and Why Does It Matter?" In *Ending Poverty in America: How to Restore the American Dream,* edited by John Edwards, Marion Crain, and Arne L. Kalleberg. New York: New Press.

Bernstein, Paul. 1997. *American Work Values: Their Origin and Development.* Albany: State University of New York Press.

Bidwell, Matthew. 2010. "Why Has Inter-Organizational Worker Mobility Increased? Firm Size, Unions and the Growth of External Hiring." Unpublished paper. University of Pennsylvania, Wharton School.

Bielby, William T., and Arne L. Kalleberg. 1981. "The Structure of Occupational Inequality." *Quality and Quantity* 15(2): 125–50.

Blank, Rebecca M. 1998. "Contingent Work in a Changing Labor Market." In *Generating Jobs: How to Increase Demand for Less-Skilled Workers,* edited by Richard B. Freeman and Peter Gottschalk. New York: Russell Sage Foundation.

Blau, Peter M., and Otis Dudley Duncan. 1967. *The American Occupational Structure.* New York: Wiley.

Blauner, Robert. 1964. *Alienation and Freedom: The Factory Worker and His Industry.* Chicago: University of Chicago Press.

Blinder, Alan S. 2006. "Offshoring: The Next Industrial Revolution?" *Foreign Affairs* 85(2): 113–28.

Bluestone, Barry. 1970. "The Tripartite Economy: Labor Markets and the Working Poor." *Poverty and Human Resources Abstracts* 5(4): 15–35.

———. 1995. *The Polarization of American Society: Victims, Suspects, and Mysteries to Unravel*. New York: Twentieth Century Fund Press.

Bluestone, Barry, and Bennett Harrison. 1982. *The Deindustrialization of America*. New York: Basic Books.

———. 1986. "The Great American Job Machine: The Proliferation of Low Wage Employment in the U.S. Economy." Study prepared for the Joint Economic Committee.

Boisard, Pierre, Damien Cartron, Michel Gollac, and Antoine Valeyre. 2003. *Time and Work: Work Intensity*. Luxembourg: Office for Official Publications of the European Communities.

Boisjoly, Johanne, Greg J. Duncan, and Timothy Smeeding. 1998. "The Shifting Incidence of Involuntary Job Losses from 1968–1992." *Industrial Relations* 37(2): 207–31.

Bokemeier, Janet L., and William B. Lacy. 1986. "Job Values, Rewards, and Work Conditions as Factors in Job Satisfaction Among Men and Women." *The Sociological Quarterly* 28(2): 189–204.

Borjas, George J. 1990. *Friends or Strangers: The Impacts of Immigrants on the U.S. Economy*. New York: Basic Books.

Borosage, Robert L., and Eric Lotke. 2009. "A New New Deal?" *The Nation*, January 12, 2009, pp. 11, 12, 14.

Bosch, Gerhard, Ken Mayhew, and Jérôme Gautié. 2010. "Industrial Relations, Legal Regulations, and Wage Setting." In *Low-Wage Work in the Wealthy World*, edited by Jérôme Gautié and John Schmitt. New York: Russell Sage Foundation.

Boushey, Heather. 2009. "A Family-Leave Safety Act." *The American Prospect* 20(5): 27–29.

Bowles, Samuel, and Herb Gintis. 1982. "The Crisis of Liberal Democratic Capitalism: The Case of the United States." *Politics and Society* 11(1): 51–59.

Braverman, Harry. 1974. *Labor and Monopoly Capital: The Degradation of Work in the Twentieth Century*. New York: Monthly Review Press.

Breaugh, James A. 1985. "The Measurement of Work Autonomy." *Human Relations* 38(6): 551–70.

———. 1998. "The Development of a New Measure of Global Work Autonomy." *Educational and Psychological Measurement* 58(1): 119–28.

Breen, Richard. 1997. "Risk, Recommodification, and Stratification." *Sociology* 31(3): 473–89.

Bridges, William. 1994. *Job Shift: How to Prosper in a Workplace Without Jobs*. Reading, Mass.: Addison-Wesley.

Bronfenbrenner, Kate. 2009. "No Holds Barred: The Intensification of Employer Opposition to Organizing." Briefing Paper 235 (May 20). Washington, D.C.: Economic Policy Institute.

Buchinsky, Moshe, and Jennifer Hunt. 1999. "Wage Mobility in the United States." *Review of Economics and Statistics* 81(3): 351–68.

Burawoy, Michael. 1983. "Between the Labor Process and the State: The Changing Face of Factory Regimes Under Advanced Capitalism." *American Sociological Review* 48(5): 587–605.

———. 1985. *The Politics of Production*. London: New Left Books.

———. 2008. "The Public Turn: From Labor Process to Labor Movement." *Work and Occupations* 35(4): 371–87.

Burchell, Brendan, Diana Day, Maria Hudson, David Ladipo, Roy Mankelow, Jane P. Nolan, Hannah Reed, Ines C. Wichert, and Frank Wilkinson. 1999. *Job Insecurity and Work Intensification: Flexibility and the Changing Boundaries of Work*. York, U.K.: Joseph Roundtree Foundation.

Cameron, Kim. "Downsizing and the New Work Covenant." Unpublished paper, University of Michigan. Available at: http://webuser.bus.umich.edu/cameronk/downsizing%20-%20exchange%20paper.pdf (accessed Apri 2, 2011).

Caplow, Theodore. 1982. "Decades of Public Opinion: Comparing NORC and Middletown Data." *Public Opinion* 5(5): 30–31.

Cappelli, Peter. 1995. "Rethinking Employment." *British Journal of Industrial Relations* 33(4): 563–602.

———. 1999. *The New Deal at Work: Managing the Market-Driven Workforce*. Boston, Mass.: Harvard Business School Press.

———. 2008. *Talent on Demand*. Boston, Mass.: Harvard Business School Press.

Cappelli, Peter, Laurie Bassi, Harry Katz, David Knoke, Paul Osterman, and Michael Useem. 1997. *Change at Work*. New York: Oxford University Press.

Cappelli, Peter, and Monika Hamori. 2005. "The New Path to the Top." *Harvard Business Review* 83(1): 25–32.

Card, David. 2005. "Is the New Immigration Really So Bad?" *Economic Journal* 115(506): F300–F323.

Card, David, and John E. DiNardo. 2002. "Skill-Biased Technological Change and Rising Wage Inequality: Some Problems and Puzzles." *Journal of Labor Economics* 20(4): 733–83.

Casey, Bernard. 1991. "Survey Evidence on Trends in 'Non-Standard' Employment." In *Farewell to Flexibility?*, edited by Anna Pollert. Oxford: Blackwell.

Champlin, Dell. 1995. "Understanding Job Quality in an Era of Structural Change: What Can Economics Learn from Industrial Relations?" *Journal of Economic Issues* 29(3): 829–41.

Chatani, Kazutoshi. 2008. "From Corporate-Centred Security to Flexicurity in Japan." Employment Sector, Employment Working Paper 17. Geneva: International Labour Office.

Clark, Andrew E. 1997. "Job Satisfaction and Gender: Why Are Women So Happy at Work?" *Labour Economics* 4(4): 341–72.

———. 1998. *What Makes a Good Job? Evidence from OECD Countries*. OECD Publishing. Available at: http://ideas.repec.org/s/oec/elsaaa.html (accessed January 31, 2011).

Clark, Andrew E., Paul Frijters, and Mike Shields. 2008. "Relative Income, Happiness, and Utility: An Explanation for the Easterlin Paradox and Other Puzzles." *Journal of Economic Literature* 46(1): 95–144.

Clark, Andrew E., and Andrew J. Oswald. 1996. "Satisfaction and Comparison Income." *Journal of Public Economics* 61(3): 359–81.

Clawson, Dan. 2003. *The Next Upsurge: Labor and the New Social Movements*. Ithaca, N.Y.: Cornell University Press.

Clinton, William Jefferson. 1996. *State of the Union* [speech]. Transcript available at: http://clinton4.nara.gov/WH/New/other/sotu.html (accessed February 15, 2011).

Cobble, Dorothy Sue. 1991. *Dishing It Out: Waitresses and Their Unions in the Twentieth Century*. Urbana: University of Illinois Press.

Cohany, Sharon R., and Emy Sok. 2007. "Trends in Labor Force Participation of Married Mothers of Infants." *Monthly Labor Review* (February): 9–16.

Cohen, Joshua, and Charles Sabel. 2009. "Flexicurity." *Pathways* 2(Spring): 10–14.

Coleman, James S. 1990. *Foundations of Social Theory*. Cambridge, Mass.: Harvard University Press.

Commission of the European Communities. 2001. "Employment and Social Policies: A Framework for Investing in Quality." Commission of the European Communities COM (2001) 313 final. Brussels, Belgium.

Committee on Techniques for the Enhancement of Human Performance. 1999. *The Changing Nature of Work: Implications for Occupational Analysis*. Washington, D.C.: National Academy of Sciences Press.

Coontz, Stephanie. 2005. *Marriage, a History: From Obedience to Intimacy or How Love Conquered Marriage*. New York: Viking.

Davis, James A., Tom W. Smith and Peter V. Marsden (Principal Investigators). 2009. *General Social Surveys, 1972–2006* [cumulative file]. Available at: http://dx.doi.org/10.3886/ICPSR04697 (accessed February 15, 2011).

Dean, Amy B., and David B. Reynolds. 2009. *A New New Deal: How Regional Activism Will Reshape the American Labor Movement*. Ithaca, N.Y.: ILR Press.

De Witte, Hans. 1999. "Job Insecurity and Psychological Well-Being: Review of the Literature and Exploration of Some Unresolved Issues." *European Journal of Work and Organizational Psychology* 8(2): 155–77.

Dickey, Christopher, and Tracy McNicoll. 2008. "Why It's Time for a 'Green New Deal.' " *Newsweek*, 10 November: 49–50, 52–53.

Diebold, Francis X., David Neumark, and Daniel Polsky. 1996. "Is Job Stability Declining in the U.S. Economy? Comment." *Industrial and Labor Relations Review* 49(January): 348–52

———. 1997. "Job Stability in the United States." *Journal of Labor Economics* 15(2): 206–33.

DiNardo, John E., and Jörn-Steffan Pischke. 1997. "The Returns to Computer Use Revisited: Have Pencils Changed the Wage Structure Too?" *2010 Quarterly Journal of Economics* 112(1): 291–303.

DiPrete, Thomas A., Gregory M. Eirich, and Matthew Pittinsky. 2010. "Compensation, Benchmarking, Leapfrogs, and the Surge in Executive Pay." *American Journal of Sociology* 115(6): 1671–1712.

DiPrete, Thomas A., and K. Lynn Nonnemaker. 1997. "Structural Change, Labor Market Turbulence, and Labor Market Outcomes." *American Sociological Review* 62(3): 386–404.

Dobbin, Frank, and Terry Boychuk. 1999. "National Employment Systems and Job Autonomy: Why Job Autonomy Is High in the Nordic Countries and Low in the United States, Canada and Australia." *Organization Studies* 20(2): 257–91.

Dobbin, Frank, Lauren Edelman, John W. Meyer, W. Richard Scott, and Ann Swidler. 1988. "The Expansion of Due Process in Organizations." In *Institutional Patterns and Organizations: Culture and Environment*, edited by Lynn Zucker. Cambridge, Mass: Ballinger.

Doeringer, Peter B., Kathleen Christensen, Patricia M. Flynn, Douglas T. Hall, Harry C. Katz, Jeffrey H. Keefe, Christopher J. Ruhm, Andrew M. Sum, and Michael Useem. 1991. *Turbulence in the American Workplace.* New York: Oxford University Press.

Doeringer, Peter B., and Michael J. Piore. 1971. *Internal Labor Markets and Manpower Analysis.* Lexington, Mass.: D.C. Heath.

Dohm, Arlene, and Lynn Shniper. 2007. "Occupational Employment Projections to 2016." *Monthly Labor Review* (November): 86–125.

Dore, Ronald. 1997. "Jobs and Employment: Good Jobs, Bad Jobs, and No Jobs." *Industrial Relations Journal* 28(4): 262–68.

Drago, Robert. 1998. "New Systems of Work and New Workers." In *Contingent Work: American Employment Relations in Transition*, edited by Kathleen Barker and Kathleen Christensen. Ithaca, N.Y.: ILR Press.

Dunlop, John T. 1958. *Industrial Relations Systems.* New York: Holt.

Easterlin, Richard A. 1980. *Birth and Fortune: The Impacts of Numbers on Personal Welfare.* New York: Basic Books.

———. 1995. "Will Raising the Incomes of All Increase the Happiness of All?" *Journal of Economic Behavior and Organization* 27(1): 35–47.

Ebeling, Jon, Michael King, and Marshall Rogers. 1979. "Hierarchical Position in the Work Organization and Job Satisfaction: Findings in National Survey Data." *Human Relations* 32(5): 387–93.

Economic Council of Canada. 1990. *Good Jobs, Bad Jobs: Employment in the Service Economy.* Ottawa: Supply and Services Canada.

Edwards, Richard. 1979. *Contested Terrain: The Transformation of the Workplace in the Twentieth Century.* New York: Basic Books.

Ellwood, David T., Rebecca M. Blank, Joseph Blasi, Douglas Kruse, William A. Niskanen, and Karen Lynn-Dyson. 2000. *A Working Nation: Workers, Work, and Government in the New Economy.* New York: Russell Sage Foundation.

Engemann, Kristie M., and Michael T. Owyang. 2006. "Social Changes Lead Married Women into Labor Force." *The Regional Economist* (April): 10–11. Available at: http://research.stlouisfed.org/publications/regional/06/04/social_changes.pdf (accessed January 31, 2011).

Epstein, Cynthia Fuchs, and Arne L. Kalleberg, eds. 2004. *Fighting for Time: Shifting Boundaries of Work and Social Life.* New York: Russell Sage Foundation.

Families and Work Institute. 1997. "Study of the Changing Workforce: Executive Summary." Available at: http://familiesandwork.org/site/research/summary/main.html (accessed January 31, 2011).

———. 2002. "National Study of the Changing Workforce, 2002." Available at: http://www.familiesandwork.org/site/work/workforce/2002nscw.html (accessed February 15, 2011).

Farber, Henry S. 1997. "Job Creation in the United States: Good Jobs or Bad?" Working Paper 385. Industrial Relations Section, Princeton University.

———. 1998a. "Are Lifetime Jobs Disappearing? Job Duration in the United States, 1973–1993." In *Labor Statistics Measurement Issues*, edited by John Haltiwanger, Marilyn E. Manser, and Robert Topel. Chicago: University of Chicago Press.

———. 1998b. "Mobility and Stability: The Dynamics of Change in Labor Markets." Working Paper 400. Industrial Relations Section, Princeton University (June).

———. 2005. "What Do We Know About Job Loss in the United States? Evidence from the Displaced Workers Survey, 1984–2004." Working Paper 498. Industrial Relations Section, Princeton University.

———. 2008. "Short(er) Shrift: The Decline in Worker-Firm Attachment in the United States." In *Laid Off, Laid Low: Political and Economic Consequences of Employment Insecurity*, edited by Katherine S. Newman. New York: Columbia University Press.

Featherman, David L., and Robert M. Hauser. 1978. *Opportunity and Change.* New York: Academic Press.

Fenwick, Rudy, and Mark Tausig. 2001. "Scheduling Stress: Family and Health Outcomes of Shift Work and Schedule Control." *American Behavioral Scientist* 44(7): 1179–98.

Figart, Deborah M., and Lonnie Golden. 1998. "The Social Economics of Work Time: Introduction." *Review of Social Economy* 56(4): 411–24.

Fine, Janice. 2006. *Worker Centers: Organizing Communities at the Edge of the Dream.* Ithaca, N.Y.: ILR Press/Cornell University Press.

Firebaugh, Glenn. 1997. *Analyzing Repeated Surveys.* Thousand Oaks, Calif.: Sage.

Firebaugh, Glenn, and Brian Harley. 1995. "Trends in Job Satisfaction in the United States by Race, Gender, and Type of Education." *Research in the Sociology of Work* 5: 87–104.

Firebaugh, Glenn, and Laura Tach. 2011. "Income, Age, and Happiness in America." In *Social Trends in the United States, 1972–2006: Evidence from the General Social Survey*, edited by Peter V. Marsden. Princeton, N.J.: Princeton University Press.

Fischer, Claude S., and Michael Hout. 2006. *Century of Difference: How America Changed in the Last One Hundred Years.* New York: Russell Sage Foundation.

Fitzgerald, Joan. 2006a. "Getting Serious About Good Jobs." *The American Prospect.* 17(10): 33–37.

———. 2006b. *Moving Up in the New Economy: Career Ladders for U.S. Workers.* Ithaca, N.Y.: Cornell University Press.

Fix, Michael, and Jeffrey S. Passel. 1994. *Immigration and Immigrants: Setting the Record Straight.* Washington, D.C.: Urban Institute.

Fligstein, Neil, and Taek-Jin Shin. 2004. "The Shareholder-Value Society: A Review of the Changes in Working Conditions and Inequality in the U.S. 1976–2000." In *Social Inequality*, edited by Kathryn Neckerman. New York: Russell Sage Foundation.

Florida, Richard L. 2002. *The Rise of the Creative Class: And How It's Transforming Work, Leisure, Community and Everyday Life.* New York: Basic Books.

Fraser, Jill Andresky. 2001. *White-Collar Sweatshop: The Deterioration of Work and Its Rewards in Corporate America.* New York: Norton.

Freeman, Richard. 1997. *When Earnings Diverge*. NPA Report 284. Washington, D.C.: National Policy Association.

———. 2007a. *Do Workers Want Unions? More Than Ever*. EPI Issue Brief 182. Washington, D.C.: Economic Policy Institute.

———. 2007b. The Great Doubling: The Challenge of the new Global Labor Market." In *Ending Poverty in America: How to Restore the American Dream*, edited by John Edwards, Marion Crain, and Arne L. Kalleberg.

Freedman, Audrey. 1985. *The New Look in Wage Policy and Employee Relations*. Conference Board Report 865. New York: The Conference Board.

Frenkel, Stephen J., Marek Korczynski, Karen A. Shire, and May Tam. 1999. *On the Front Line: Organization of Work in the Information Economy*. Ithaca, N.Y.: ILR Press/Cornell University Press.

Frey, Bruno S., and Alois Stutzer. 2002. *Happiness and Economics: How the Economy and Institutions Affect Human Well-Being*. Princeton, N.J.: Princeton University Press.

Friedman, Joel, Isaac Shapiro, and Robert Greenstein. 2006. "Recent Tax and Income Trends Among High Income Tax Payers." Washington, D.C.: Center on Budget and Policy Priorities. Available at: http://www.cbpp.org/cms/index. cfm?fa=view&id=138 (accessed January 31, 2011).

Fullerton, Andrew S., and Michael Wallace. 2005. "Traversing the Flexible Turn: U.S. Workers' Perceptions of Job Security, 1977–2002." *Social Science Research* 36(1): 201–21.

Galbraith, John Kenneth. 1952. *American Capitalism: The Concept of Countervailing Power*. Boston: Houghton Mifflin.

———. 1967. *The New Industrial State*. Boston: Houghton Mifflin.

Gallie, Duncan, ed. 2007a. *Employment Regimes and the Quality of Work*. Oxford: Oxford University Press.

———. 2007b. "Production Regimes and the Quality of Employment in Europe." *Annual Review of Sociology* 33: 85–104.

Gallie, Duncan, Alan Felstead, and Francis Green. 2004. "Changing Patterns of Task Discretion in Britain." *Work, Employment, and Society* 18(2): 243–66.

Gautié, Jérôme, and John Schmitt, eds. 2010. *Low-Wage Work in the Wealthy World*. New York: Russell Sage Foundation.

Gautié, Jérôme, Niels Westergaard-Nielsen, and John Schmitt, with Ken Mayhew. 2010. "The Impact of Institutions on the Supply Side of the Low-Wage Labor Market." In *Low-Wage Work in the Wealthy World*, edited by Jérôme Gautié and John Schmitt. New York: Russell Sage Foundation.

Ghilarducci, Teresa. 2008. *When I'm Sixty-Four: The Plot Against Pensions and the Plan to Save Them*. Princeton, N.J.: Princeton University Press.

Giddens, Anthony. 1973. *The Class Structure of Advanced Societies*. New York: Harper and Row.

Ginzberg, Eli. 1979. *Good Jobs, Bad Jobs, No Jobs*. Cambridge, Mass.: Harvard University Press.

Gittleman, Maury B., and David R. Howell. 1995. "Changes in the Structure and Quality of Jobs in the United States: Effects by Race and Gender, 1973–1990." *Industrial and Labor Relations Review* 48(3): 420–40.

Gittleman, Maury B., and Mary Joyce. 1996. "Earnings Mobility and Long-Run Inequality: An Analysis Using Matched CPS Data." *Industrial Relations* 35(2): 180–96.

Golden, Lonnie. 2001. "Which Workers Get Flexible Work Schedules?" *American Behavioral Scientist* 44(7): 1157–78.

———. 2009. "Flexible Daily Work Schedules in U.S. Jobs: Formal Introductions Needed?" *Industrial Relations* 48(1): 27–54.

Golden, Lonnie, and Deborah M. Figart, eds. 2000. *Working Time: International Trends, Theory, and Policy Perspectives.* London: Routledge.

Goldin, Claudia, and Lawrence F. Katz. 2008. *The Race Between Education and Technology.* Cambridge, Mass.: Harvard University Press.

Goldin, Claudia, and Robert A. Margo. 1992. "The Great Compression: The Wage Structure in the U.S. at Mid-Century." *Quarterly Journal of Economics* 107(1): 1–34.

Goldthorpe, John H. 1980. *Social Mobility and Class Structure in Modern Britain.* New York: Oxford University Press.

———. 2000. *On Sociology: Numbers, Narratives, and the Integration of Research and Theory.* Oxford: Oxford University Press.

Gonos, George. 1997. "The Contest over 'Employer' Status in the Post-War United States: The Case of Temporary Help Firms." *Law and Society Review* 31(1): 81–110.

Goos, Maarten, and Alan Manning. 2007. "Lousy and Lovely Jobs: The Rising Polarization of Work in Britain." *The Review of Economics and Statistics* 89(1): 118–33.

Goos, Maarten, Alan Manning, and Anna Salomons. 2009. "The Polarization of the European Labor Market." *American Economic Review Papers and Proceedings* 99(2): 58–63.

Gordon, David M. 1996. *Fat and Mean: The Corporate Squeeze of Working Americans and the Myth of Managerial "Downsizing."* New York: The Free Press.

Gottschalk, Peter. 1997. "Inequality, Income Growth, and Mobility: The Basic Facts." *Journal of Economic Perspectives* 11(2): 21–40.

Gottschalk, Peter, and Robert Moffitt. 1999. "Changes in Job Instability and Insecurity Using Monthly Survey Data." *Journal of Labor Economics* 17(4): S91–S126.

Granovetter, Mark. 2005. *Getting a Job: A Study of Contacts and Careers.* 2nd ed. Chicago: University of Chicago Press.

Gray, John. 1998. *False Dawn.* New York: The New Press.

Green, Francis. 2006. *Demanding Work: The Paradox of Job Quality in the Affluent Economy.* Princeton, N.J.: Princeton University Press.

Green, Francis, and Steven McIntosh. 2001. "The Intensification of Work in Europe." *Labour Economics* 8(2): 291–308.

Greenhalgh, Leonard, and Zehava Rosenblatt. 1984. "Job Insecurity: Toward Conceptual Clarity." *The Academy of Management Review* 9(3): 438–48.

Gruenberg, Barry. 1980. "The Happy Worker: An Analysis of Educational and Occupational Differences in Determinants of Job Satisfaction." *American Journal of Sociology* 86(2): 247–71.

Grusky, David B., and Jesper B. Sørensen. 1998. "Can Class Analysis Be Salvaged?" *American Journal of Sociology* 103(5): 1187–234.

Hacker, Jacob S. 2006. *The Great Risk Shift: The Assault on American Jobs, Families, Health Care, and Retirement and How You Can Fight Back.* New York: Oxford University Press.

Hacker, Jacob S., and Paul Pierson. 2010. *Winner-Take-All Politics: How Washington Made the Rich Richer—and Turned Its Back on the Middle Class.* New York: Simon and Schuster.

Hackman, J. Richard, and Edward E. Lawler. 1971. "Employee Reactions to Job Characteristics." *Journal of Applied Psychology* 55(3): 259–86.

Hackman, J. Richard, and Greg R. Oldham. 1975. "Development of the Job Diagnostic Survey." *Journal of Applied Psychology* 60(2): 159–70.

Hamermesh, Daniel. 1999. "The Changing Distribution of Job Satisfaction." Working Paper w7332. Cambridge, Mass.: National Bureau of Economic Research.

Handy, Charles. 1990. *The Age of Unreason.* Boston: Harvard Business School Press.

Harrison, Ann E., and Margaret S. McMillan. 2006. "Dispelling Some Myths About Offshoring." *Academy of Management Perspectives* 20(4): 6–22.

Harrison, Bennett. 1972. *Education, Training, and the Urban Ghetto.* Baltimore, Md.: Johns Hopkins University Press.

———. 1994. *Lean and Mean: The Changing Landscape of Corporate Power in the Age of Flexibility.* New York: Basic Books.

Harrison, Bennett, and Barry Bluestone. 1988. *The Great U-Turn: Corporate Restructuring and the Polarizing of America.* New York: Basic Books.

Heckscher, Charles C. 1996. *The New Unionism: Employee Involvement in the Changing Corporation.* Ithaca, N.Y.: ILR Press.

Hesse-Biber, Sharlene, and Gregg Lee Carter. 2000. *Working Women in America: Split Dreams.* New York: Oxford University Press.

Heymann, Jody. 2000. *The Widening Gap: Why America's Working Families Are in Jeopardy and What Can Be Done About It.* New York: Basic Books.

Hirsch, Barry T., and David A. McPherson. 2010. *Union Membership and Coverage Database from the CPS.* Available at: http://www.unionstats.com (accessed February 3, 2011).

Hirsch, Paul M., and Michaela De Soucey. 2006. "Organizational Restructuring and Its Consequences: Rhetorical and Structural." *Annual Review of Sociology* 32: 171–89.

Hochschild, Arlie. 1997. *The Time Bind: When Work Becomes Home and Home Becomes Work.* New York: Metropolitan Books.

Hodge, Roger D. 2010. *The Mendacity of Hope: Barack Obama and the Betrayal of American Liberalism.* New York: HarperCollins.

Hodson, Randy. 1989. "Gender Differences in Job Satisfaction: Why Aren't Women Workers More Dissatisfied?" *Sociological Quarterly* 30(3): 385–99.

———. 2001. *Dignity at Work.* New York: Cambridge University Press.

Hoefer, Michael, Nancy Rytina, and Bryan C. Baker. 2009. "Estimates of the Unauthorized Immigrant Population Residing in the United States: January 2008." U.S. Department of Homeland Security, Office of Immigration Statistics, Population Estimates (February): 1–7.

Holzer, Harry J., Julia I. Lane, David B. Rosenblum, and Fredrik Andersson. 2011. *Where Are All the Good Jobs Going? What National and Local Job Quality and Dynamics Mean for U.S. Workers.* New York: Russell Sage Foundation.

Howell, David R., and Edward N. Wolff. 1991. "Trends in the Growth and Distribution of Skills in the U.S. Workplace, 1960–1985." *Industrial and Labor Relations Review* 44(3): 486–502.

Hunter, Larry W. 2000. "What Determines Job Quality in Nursing Homes?" *Industrial and Labor Relations Review* 53(3): 463–81.

Ilsøe, Anna. 2007. "The Danish Flexicurity Model—A Lesson for the U.S.?" Employment Relations Research Centre, Department of Sociology, University of Copenhagen.

International Labour Organization (ILO). 2004. *Economic Security for a Better World.* Geneva: International Labour Office.

Jacobs, Jerry A., and Kathleen Gerson. 2001. "Overworked Individuals or Overworked Families? Explaining Trends in Work, Leisure, and Family Time." *Work and Occupations* 28(1): 40–63.

———. 2004. *The Time Divide: Work, Family, and Gender Inequality.* Cambridge, Mass.: Harvard University Press.

Jacoby, Sanford M. 1985. *Employing Bureaucracy: Managers, Unions, and the Transformation of Work in the 20th Century.* New York: Columbia University Press.

———. 1999. "Are Career Jobs Headed for Extinction?" *California Management Review* 42(1): 123–45.

———. 2001. "Risk and the Labor Market: Societal Past as Economic Prologue." In *Sourcebook of Labor Markets: Evolving Structures and Processes,* edited by Ivar Berg and Arne L. Kalleberg. New York: Kluwer Academic/Plenum Publishers.

Jaeger, David A., and Ann Huff-Stevens. 1999. "Is Job Stability in the United States Falling? Reconciling Trends in the Current Population Survey and the Panel Study of Income Dynamics." *Journal of Labor Economics* 17(4): S1–S28.

Jahoda, Marie. 1982. *Employment and Unemployment: A Social-Psychological Analysis.* New York: Cambridge University Press.

Jasso, Guillermina. 1990. "Methods for the Theoretical and Empirical Analysis of Comparison Processes." In *Sociological Methodology 1980,* edited by Clifford C. Clogg. Cambridge, Mass.: Basil Blackwell.

Jencks, Christopher. 2004. "The Low-Wage Puzzle." *American Prospect* (January): 35–37.

Jencks, Christopher, Lauri Perman, and Lee Rainwater. 1988. "What Is a Good Job? A New Measure of Labor Market Success." *American Journal of Sociology* 93(6): 1322–57.

Juhn, Chinhui, Kevin M. Murphy, and Brooks Pierce. 1993. "Wage Inequality and the Rise in Returns to Skill." *Journal of Political Economy* 101(3): 410–42.

Kalleberg, Arne L. 1974. "A Causal Approach to the Measurement of Job Satisfaction." *Social Science Research* 3(4): 299–322.

———. 1977. "Work Values and Job Rewards: A Theory of Job Satisfaction." *American Sociological Review* 42(1): 124–43.

———. 2000. "Nonstandard Employment Relations: Part-time, Temporary, and Contract Work." *Annual Review of Sociology* 26: 341–65.

———. 2001. "Organizing Flexibility: The Flexible Firm in a New Century." *British Journal of Industrial Relations* 39(4): 479–504.

———. 2003. "Flexible Firms and Labor Market Segmentation: Effects of Workplace Restructuring on Jobs and Workers." *Work and Occupations* 30(May): 154–75.

———. 2007. *The Mismatched Worker*. New York: Norton.

———. 2009. "Precarious Work, Insecure Workers: Employment Relations in Transition." *American Sociological Review* 74(1): 1–22.

Kalleberg, Arne L., and Ivar Berg. 1987. *Work and Industry: Structures, Markets, and Processes*. New York: Plenum, Publishers.

Kalleberg, Arne L., David Knoke, and Peter V. Marsden. 1995. "Interorganizational Networks and the Changing Employment Contract." *Connections* 18(2): 32–49.

Kalleberg, Arne L., and Karyn A. Loscocco. 1983. "Aging, Values, and Job Rewards: Explaining Age Differences in Job Satisfaction." *American Sociological Review* 48(1): 78–90.

Kalleberg, Arne L., and Peter V. Marsden. 2005. "Externalizing Organizational Activities: Where and How U.S. Establishments Use Employment Intermediaries." *Socio-Economic Review* 3(3): 389–416.

———. 2010. "Changing Work Values in the United States, 1973–2006." Unpublished paper. University of North Carolina at Chapel Hill.

———. 2011. "Labor Force Insecurity and U.S. Work Attitudes, 1970s–2006." In *Social Trends in the United States, 1972–2006: Evidence from the General Social Survey*, edited by Peter V. Marsden. Princeton, N.J.: Princeton University Press.

Kalleberg, Arne L., Peter V. Marsden, Jeremy Reynolds, and David Knoke. 2006. "Beyond Profit? Sectoral Differences in High Performance Work Practices." *Work and Occupations* 33(3): 271–302.

Kalleberg, Arne L., Torstein Nesheim, and Karen M. Olsen. 2009. "Is Participation Good or Bad for Workers? Effects of Autonomy, Consultation, and Teamwork on Stress Among Workers in Norway." *Acta Sociologica* 52(2): 99–116.

Kalleberg, Arne L., Edith Rasell, Naomi Cassirer, Barbara F. Reskin, Ken Hudson, David Webster, Eileen Appelbaum, and Roberta M. Spalter-Roth. 1997. *Nonstandard Work, Substandard Jobs: Flexible Work Arrangements in the U.S.* Washington, D.C.: Economic Policy Institute.

Kalleberg, Arne L., Barbara F. Reskin, and Ken Hudson. 2000. "Bad Jobs in America: Standard and Nonstandard Employment Relations and Job Quality in the United States." *American Sociological Review* 65(2): 256–78.

Kalleberg, Arne L., and Aage B. Sørensen. 1979. "Sociology of Labor Markets." *Annual Review of Sociology* 5: 351–79.

Kalleberg, Arne L., and Stephen Vaisey. 2005. "Pathways to a Good Job: Perceived Work Quality Among the Machinists." *British Journal of Industrial Relations* 43(3): 431–54.

Kalleberg, Arne L., Michael Wallace, and Robert P. Althauser. 1981. "Economic Segmentation, Worker Power, and Income Inequality." *American Journal of Sociology* 87(3): 651–83.

Karasek, Robert A., and Tores Theorell. 1990. *Healthy Work: Stress, Productivity and the Reconstruction of Work Life*. New York: Basic Books.

Katz, Lawrence F., and David H. Autor. 1999. "Changes in the Wage Structure and Earnings Inequality." In *Handbook of Labor Economics*, edited by Orley Ashenfelter and David Card. Vol. 3A. Amsterdam: Elsevier Science.

Katz, Lawrence F., and Kevin M. Murphy. 1992. "Changes in Relative Wages, 1963–1987: Supply and Demand Factors." *The Quarterly Journal of Economics* 107(1): 35–78.

Keller, Rebecca. 2009. "How Shifting Occupational Composition Has Affected the Real Average Wage." *Monthly Labor Review* (June): 26–38.

Kerr, Clark, John T. Dunlop, Frederick H. Harbison, and Charles A. Myers. 1973. *Industrialism and Industrial Man*. London: Penguin Press.

Kim, Marlene. 2000. "Women Paid Low Wages: Who They Are and Where They Work." *Monthly Labor Review* (September): 26–30.

Kleiner, Morris. 2006. *Licensing Occupation: Ensuring Quality or Restricting Competition?* Kalamazoo, Mich.: W. E. Upjohn Institute for Employment Research.

Kochan, Thomas A. 2000. "Building a New Social Contract at Work: A Call for Action." *Proceedings of the 52nd Annual Meeting of the Industrial Relations Research Association:* 1–25.

———. 2005. *Restoring the American Dream: A Working Families' Agenda for America*. Cambridge, Mass.: MIT Press.

———. 2006. "The American Worker: Disposable or Indispensable?" *Work and Occupations* 33(4): 377–81.

Kochan, Thomas A., Harry C. Katz, and Robert B. McKersie. 1986. *The Transformation of American Industrial Relations*. New York: Basic Books.

Kohn, Melvin L., and Carmi Schooler. 1973. "Occupational Experience and Psychological Functioning: An Assessment of Reciprocal Effects." *American Sociological Review* 38(1): 97–118.

Koretz, Gene. 1996. "Job Stability—the True Story? It May Reflect Worker Insecurity." *Business Week*, 15 April: 30.

Krugman, Paul. 1997. *The Age of Diminished Expectations: U.S. Economic Policy in the 1990s*. Cambridge, Mass.: MIT Press.

Kruse, Douglas, and Joseph Blasi. 2000. "The New Employer-Employee Relationship," In *A Working Nation: Workers, Work, and Government in the New Economy*, edited by David T. Ellwood, Rebecca M. Blank, Joseph Blasi, Douglas Kruse, William A. Niskanen, and Karen Lynn-Dyson. New York: Russell Sage Foundation.

Kuhn, Peter, and Fernando Lozano. 2005. "The Expanding Workweek? Understanding Trends in Long Hours Among U.S. Men, 1979–2004." Cambridge, Mass.: National Bureau of Economic Research Working Paper 11895. Available at: http://www.nber.org/papers/w11895 (accessed January 31, 2011).

Kuttner, Robert. 1995. "Needed: A Two-Way Social Contract in the Workplace." *Business Week*, 10 July: 22.

———. 1996. *Everything for Sale*. New York: Knopf.

———. 2008. "Can the Democrats Think Big?" *The American Prospect*, March: 15–17.

Lareau, Annette. 2003. *Unequal Childhoods: Class, Race and Family Life*. Berkeley: University of California Press.

Layard, Richard. 2004. "Good Jobs and Bad Jobs." Center for Economic Performance occasional paper no. 19. London School of Economics and Political Science (April).

Leana, Carrie R., and Harry J. van Buren III. 1999. "Organizational Social Capital and Employment Practices." *Academy of Management Review* 24(3): 538–55.

Leicht, Kevin T. 2008. "Broken Down by Race and Gender? Sociological Explanations of New Sources of Earnings Inequality." *Annual Review of Sociology* 34: 237–55.

Leicht, Kevin T., and Scott T. Fitzgerald. 2007. *Postindustrial Peasants: The Illusion of Middle-Class Prosperity.* New York: Worth Publishers.

Lemieux, Thomas. 2006. "Increasing Residual Wage Inequality: Composition Effects, Noisy Data, or Rising Demand for Skill?" *American Economic Review* 96(3): 461–98.

———. 2008. "The Changing Nature of Wage Inequality." *Journal of Population Economics* 21(1): 21–48.

Lemiuex, Thomas, W. Bentley Macleod, and Daniel Parent. 2006. "Performance Pay and Wage Inequality." Unpublished paper. Vancouver, Canada: University of British Columbia.

Leonhardt, David. 2009. "The Big Fix." *New York Times Magazine,* 1 February: 22–29, 48, 50–51.

Levy, Frank, and Richard J. Murnane. 1992. "U.S. Earnings Levels and Earnings Inequality: A Review of Recent Trends and Proposed Explanations." *Journal of Economic Literature* 30(3): 1333–81.

———. 2004. *The New Division of Labor: How Computers Are Creating the Next Job Market.* Princeton, N.J., and New York: Princeton University Press and Russell Sage Foundation.

Levy, Frank, and Peter Temin. 2007. "Inequality and Institutions in 20th Century America." Working Paper 07-17. Department of Economics, Massachusetts Institute of Technology.

Lincoln, James R., and Arne L. Kalleberg. 1990. *Culture, Control, and Commitment: A Study of Work Organization and Work Attitudes in the United States and Japan.* New York: Cambridge University Press.

Lowe, Graham S. 2000. *The Quality of Work: A People-Centred Agenda.* Ontario, Canada: Oxford University Press.

Lowe, Graham S., and Grant Schellenberg. 2001. "What Is a Good Job? The Importance of Employment Relationships." Available at: http://www.cprn.org/doc.cfm?doc=50&1=en (accessed February 1, 2011).

Lukes, Steven. 1977. *Essays in Social Theory.* New York: Columbia University Press.

Mandel, Michael J. 1996. *The High Risk Society: Peril and Promise in the New Economy.* New York: Crown Business.

Mangum, Garth L., Donald Mayall, and Kristin Nelson. 1985. "The Temporary Help Industry: A Response to the Dual Internal Labor Market." *Industrial and Labor Relations Review* 38(4): 599–611.

Maslow, Abraham. 1954. *Motivation and Personality.* New York: Harper and Row.

Mason, Geoff, and Wiemer Salverda. 2010. "Low Pay, Working Conditions, and Living Standards." In *Low-Wage Work in the Wealthy World,* edited by Jérôme Gautié and John Schmitt. New York: Russell Sage Foundation.

Massey, Douglas S. 1995. "The New Immigration Ethnicity in the United States." *Population and Development Review* 19(3): 431–66.

———. 2007. *Categorically Unequal: The American Stratification System*. New York: Russell Sage Foundation.

Massey, Douglas S., and Nancy A. Denton. 1993. *American Apartheid: Segregation and the Making of the Underclass*. Cambridge, Mass.: Harvard University Press.

Massey, Douglas S., and Deborah S. Hirst. 1998. "From Escalator to Hourglass: Changes in the U.S. Occupational Wage Structure, 1949–1989." *Social Science Research* 27(1): 51–71.

McArdle, Megan. 2008. "No Country for Young Men." *The Atlantic* (January–February): 80–87.

McCall, Leslie. 2001. *Complex Inequality: Gender, Class, and Race in the New Economy*. New York: Routledge.

McCall, Leslie, and Lane Kenworthy. 2009. "Americans' Social Policy Preferences in the Era of Rising Inequality." *Perspectives on Politics* 7(3): 459–84.

McGovern, Patrick, Stephen Hill, Colin Mills, and Michael White. 2008. *Market, Class, and Employment*. Oxford: Oxford University Press.

McGovern, Patrick, Deborah Smeaton, and Stephen Hill. 2004. "Bad Jobs in Britain." *Work and Occupations* 31(2): 225–49.

McMurrer, Daniel P., and Isabel V. Sawhill. 1996a. "Economic Mobility in the United States." Opportunity in America series, companion piece to no. 3. The Urban Institute (October).

———. 1996b. "How Much Do Americans Move Up and Down the Economic Ladder?" Opportunity in America series, no. 3. The Urban Institute (November).

Meisenheimer, Joseph R. II, 1998. "The Services Industry in the "Good" Versus "Bad" Jobs Debate." *Monthly Labor Review* (February): 22–47.

Meyer, Marshall W. 2001. "What Happened to Middle Management?" In *Sourcebook of Labor Markets: Evolving Structures and Processes*, edited by Ivar Berg and Arne L. Kalleberg. New York: Kluwer Academic/Plenum Publishers.

Meyerson, Harold. 2006. "No Justice, No Growth." *The American Prospect* (November): 39–42.

———. 2010. "Work History." *The American Prospect* (June): 12–15.

Mincer, Jacob. 1974. *Schooling, Experience, and Earnings*. New York: Columbia University Press.

Mishel, Lawrence, Jared Bernstein, and Sylvia Allegretto. 2005. *The State of Working America, 2004/2005*. Ithaca, N.Y.: ILR Press.

———. 2007. *The State of Working America, 2006/2007*. Ithaca, N.Y.: ILR Press/Cornell University Press.

Mishel, Lawrence, Jared Bernstein, and Heather Boushey. 2003. *The State of Working America, 2002/2003*. Ithaca, N.Y.: ILR Press.

Mishel, Lawrence, Jared Bernstein, and Heidi Shierholz. 2009. *The State of Working America, 2008/2009*. Ithaca, N.Y.: ILR Press/Cornell University Press.

Morse, Dean. 1969. *The Peripheral Worker*. New York: Columbia University Press.

Mosisa, Abraham T. 2002. "The Role of Foreign-Born Workers in the U.S. Economy." *Monthly Labor Review* (May): 3–14.

Mouw, Ted. 2003. "Social Capital and Finding a Job: Do Contacts Matter?" *American Sociological Review* 68(6): 868–98.

Mouw, Ted, and Arne L. Kalleberg. 2010a. "Do Changes in Job Mobility Explain the Growth of Wage Inequality Among Men in the United States, 1977–2005?" *Social Forces* 88(5): 2053–77.

———. 2010b. "Occupations and the Structure of Wage Inequality in the United States, 1980s–2000s." *American Sociological Review* 75(3): 402–31.

Mouw, Ted, and Michael E. Sobel. 2001. "Culture Wars and Opinion Polarization: The Case of Abortion." *American Journal of Sociology* 106(4): 913–43.

Muffels, Ruud, and Ruud Luijkx. 2006. "Globalisation and Male Job Mobility in European Welfare States." In *Globalisation, Uncertainty, and Men's Careers*, edited by Hans-Peter Blossfeld, Melinda Mills, and Fabrizio Bernardi. Cheltenham, U.K.: Edward Elgar.

Nahapiet, Janine, and Sumantra Ghoshal. 1998. "Social Capital, Intellectual Capital, and the Organizational Advantage." *Academy of Management Review* 23(2): 242–66.

Nardone, Thomas J., Jonathan R. Veum, and Julie Yates. 1997. "Measuring Job Security." *Monthly Labor Review* 120(June): 26–33.

National Bureau of Economic Research. 2010. *U.S. Business Cycle Expansions and Contractions.* Available at: http://www.nber.org/cycles/cyclesmain.html (accessed February 3, 2011).

———. Various years. *Merged Outgoing Rotation Groups* (MORG) [database]. Available at: http://www.nber.org/morg/annual (accessed April 19, 2011).

National Study of a Changing Workforce. 1997. "Executive Summary." Families and Work Institute.

Neumark, David, ed. 2000. *On the Job: Is Long-Term Employment a Thing of the Past?* New York: Russell Sage Foundation.

New York Times. 1996. *The Downsizing of America.* New York: Times Books.

Oberlander, Jonathan, and Theodore R. Marmor. 2010. "The Health Bill Explained at Last." *The New York Review of Books* 57(13): 61–63.

Olmsted, Barney, and Suzanne Smith. 1989. *Creating a Flexible Workplace: How to Select and Manage Alternative Work Options.* New York: AMACOM, American Management Association.

Osterman, Paul. 1988. *Employment Futures: Reorganization, Dislocation, and Public Policy.* New York: Oxford.

———. 1999. *Securing Prosperity: The American Labor Market: How It Has Changed and What to Do About It.* Princeton, N.J.: Princeton University Press.

———. 2000. "Work Reorganization in an Age of Restructuring: Trends in Diffusion and Effects on Employee Welfare." *Industrial and Labor Relations Review* 53(2): 179–96.

———. 2008. "Improving Job Quality: Policies Aimed at the Demand Side of the Low-Wage Labor Market." In *A Future of Good Jobs? America's Challenge in the Global Economy*, edited by Timothy J. Bartik and Susan N. Houseman. Kalamazoo, Mich.: W. E. Upjohn Institute for Employment Research.

Osterman, Paul, Thomas A. Kochan, Richard M. Locke, and Michael J. Piore. 2001. *Working in America: A Blueprint for the New Labor Market.* Cambridge, Mass.: MIT Press.

Padavic, Irene, and Barbara F. Reskin. 2002. *Women and Men at Work.* Thousand Oaks, Calif.: Pine Forge Press.

Pager, Devah, and Lincoln Quillian. 2005. "Walking the Talk? What Employers Say Versus What They Do." *American Sociological Review* 70(3): 355–80.

Parkin, Frank. 1971. *Class Inequality and Political Order.* London: Paladin.

Peck, Don. 2010. "How a New Jobless Era Will Transform America." *The Atlantic* (March): 42–56.

Peck, Jamie. 1996. *Work-place: The Social Regulation of Labor Markets.* New York: Guilford Press.

Perlow, Leslie A. 1999. "The Time Famine: Toward a Sociology of Work Time." *Administrative Science Quarterly* 44(1): 57–81.

Pfeffer, Jeffrey, and James N. Baron. 1988. "Taking the Workers Back Out: Recent Trends in the Structuring of Employment." *Research in Organizational Behavior* 10: 257–303.

Piketty, Thomas, and Emmanuel Saez. 2006. "The Evolution of Top Incomes: A Historical and International Perspective." *American Economic Review* 96(2): 200–205.

Piore, Michael J. 1971. "The Dual Labor Market." In *Problems in Political Economy: An Urban Perspective,* edited by David M. Gordon. Lexington, Mass.: D. C. Heath.

———. 2009. "Second Thoughts: on Economics, Sociology, Neoliberalism, Polanyi's Double Movement and Intellectual Vacuums." *Socio-Economic Review* 7(1): 161–75.

Piore, Michael J., and Charles Sabel. 1984. *The Second Industrial Divide: Possibilities for Prosperity.* New York: Basic Books.

Polanyi, Karl. 1944. *The Great Transformation.* New York: Farrar and Rinehart.

Polivka, Anne E., and Thomas Nardone. 1989. "On the Definition of 'Contingent Work.' " *Monthly Labor Review* 112(December): 9–16.

Portes, Alejandro. 1998. "Social Capital: Its Origins and Applications in Modern Sociology." *Annual Review of Sociology* 24: 1–24.

Presser, Harriet B. 2003. *Working in a 24/7 Economy.* New York: Russell Sage Foundation.

Quigley, William P. 2003. *Ending Poverty as We Know It: Guaranteeing a Right to a Job at a Living Wage.* Philadelphia: Temple University Press.

Quinn, Robert, and Graham Staines. 2000. *Quality of Employment Survey, 1977:* Cross-Section [Computer file]. ICPSR07689-v1. Ann Arbor, Mich.: Inter-university Consortium for Political and Social Research, distributor, 2000. doi:10.3886/ICPSR07689.

Rajan, Raghuram G., and Julie Wulf. 2006. "The Flattening Firm: Evidence from Panel Data on the Changing Nature of Corporate Hierarchies." *Review of Economics and Statistics* 88(4): 759–73.

Reich, Robert B. 1992. *The Work of Nations: Preparing Ourselves for 21st-Century Capitalism.* New York: Vintage Books.

———. 2002. *I'll Be Short: Preconditions for a Decent Working Society.* Boston: Beacon Press.

———. 2010. *Aftershock: The Next Economy and America's Future.* New York: Knopf.

Robinson, John P., and Geoffrey Godbey. 1999. *Time for Life: The Surprising Ways Americans Use Their Time.* 2d ed. University Park: Pennsylvania State University Press.

Rosenberg, Samuel. 2008. "Long Work Hours for Some, Short Work Hours for Others: Working Time in the United States." In *A Future of Good Jobs? America's Challenge in the Global Economy,* edited by Timothy J. Bartik and Susan N. Houseman. Kalamazoo, Mich.: W. E. Upjohn Institute for Employment Research.

Rosenfeld, Jake. 2010. "Little Labor: How Union Decline Is Changing the American Landscape." *Pathways* 3(summer): 3–6.

Rosenthal, Neal H. 1989. "More Than Wages at Issue in Job Quality Debate." *Monthly Labor Review* 112(December): 4–8.

Royster, Deirdre. 2003. *Race and the Invisible Hand: How White Networks Exclude Black Men from Blue Collar Jobs.* Berkeley: University of California Press.

Rubin, Beth A. 1996. *Shifts in the Social Contract: Understanding Change in American Society.* Thousand Oaks, Calif.: Pine Forge Press, Sage.

Ruggles, Steven J., Trent Alexander, Katie Genadek, Ronald Goeken, Matthew B. Schroeder, and Matthew Sobek. 2010. *Integrated Public Use Microdata Series: Version 5.0* [Machine-readable database]. Minneapolis: University of Minnesota.

Salancik, Gerald R., and Jeffrey Pfeffer. 1977. "An Examination of Need Satisfaction Models of Job Attitudes." *Administrative Science Quarterly* 22(3): 427–56.

Samuelson, Robert J. 2006. "Anxiety amid the Prosperity." *Newsweek,* 20 February: 37.

———. 2009. "Our Sinking Welfare State." *Newsweek,* 29 June: 26.

Sassen, Saskia. 1998. *Globalization and Its Discontents.* New York: The New Press.

Saunders, Charles B., Hugh M. O'Neill, and Oscar W. Jensen. 1986. "Alienation in Corporate America: Fact or Fable?" *Journal of Business Ethics* 5(4): 285–89.

Schmidt, Stefanie R. 1999. "Long-Run Trends in Workers' Beliefs About Their Own Job Security: Evidence from the General Social Survey." *Journal of Labor Economics* 17(4): S127–S141.

———. 2000. "Job Security Beliefs in the General Social Survey: Evidence on Long-Run Trends and Comparability with Other Surveys." In *On the Job: Is Long-Term Employment a Thing of the Past?,* edited by David Neumark. New York: Russell Sage Foundation.

Schmidt, Stefanie R., and Shirley V. Svorny. 1998. "Recent Trends in Security and Stability." *Journal of Labor Research* 19(4): 647–68.

Schmitt, John. 2001. "Has Job Quality Deteriorated in the 1980s and 1990s?" In *Sourcebook of Labor Markets: Evolving Structures and Processes,* edited by Ivar Berg and Arne L. Kalleberg. New York: Kluwer Academic/Plenum Publishers.

———. 2007. "The Good, the Bad, and the Ugly: Job Quality in the United States over the Three Most Recent Business Cycles." Center for Economic and Policy Research (November).

Schor, Juliet. 1991. *The Overworked American: The Unexpected Decline of Leisure.* New York: Basic Books.

Schultze, Charles L. 1999. "Has Job Security Eroded for American Workers?" In *The New Relationship: Human Capital in the American Corporation,* edited by Margaret Blair and Thomas Kochan. Washington, D.C.: Brookings.

Schulze-Cleven, Tobias, and Henry Farrell. 2010. "Overcoming Institutional Drift: Toward Innovation in U.S. Labor Market Policy." Working paper no. 193. Berkeley Roundtable on the International Economy (BRIE), University of California, Berkeley.

Scott, Robert E., Thea Lee, and John Schmitt. 1997. "Trading Away Good Jobs: An Examination of Employment and Wages in the U.S., 1979–94." Briefing paper (October). Washington, D.C.: Economic Policy Institute.

Sennett, Richard. 1998. *The Corrosion of Character: The Personal Consequences of Work in the New Capitalism.* New York: Norton.

Sheppard, Harold L., and Neal Q. Herrick. 1972. *Where Have All the Robots Gone? Worker Dissatisfaction in the 1970s.* New York: The Free Press.

Shipler, David. 2004. *The Working Poor.* New York: Knopf.

Shuey, Kim M., and Angela M. O'Rand. 2004. "New Risks for Workers: Pensions, Labor Markets, and Gender." *Annual Review of Sociology* 30:453–77.

Silver, Beverly J. 2003. *Forces of Labor: Workers' Movements and Globalization Since 1870.* Cambridge: Cambridge University Press.

Slichter, Sumner, J. J. Healy, and E. R. Livernash. 1960. *The Impact of Collective Bargaining on Management.* Washington, D.C.: Brookings.

Smith, Robert Michael. 2003. *From Blackjacks to Briefcases: A History of Commercialized Strikebreaking and Unionbusting in the United States.* Athens: Ohio University Press.

Smith, Vicki. 2010. "Review Article: Enhancing Employability: Human, Cultural, and Social Capital in an Era of Turbulent Unpredictability." *Human Relations* 63(2): 279–303.

Sørensen, Aage B. 2000. "Toward a Sounder Basis for Class Analysis." *American Journal of Sociology* 105(6): 1523–58.

Sørensen, Aage B., and Arne L. Kalleberg. 1981. "An Outline for a Theory of the Matching of Persons to Jobs." In *Sociological Perspectives on Labor Markets,* edited by Ivar Berg. New York: Academic Press.

Soskice, David. 1999. "Divergent Production Regimes: Coordinated and Uncoordinated Market Economies in the 1980s and 1990s." In *Continuity and Change in Contemporary Capitalism,* edited by Herbert Kitschelt, Peter Lange, Gary Marks, and John D. Stephens. Cambridge: Cambridge University Press.

Special Task Force to the Secretary of Health, Education and Welfare. 1973. *Work in America.* Cambridge, Mass.: MIT Press.

Spector, P. E. 1986. "Perceived Control by Employees: A Meta-analysis of Studies Concerning Autonomy and Participation at Work." *Human Relations* 39(11): 1005–16.

Spenner, Kenneth I. 1990. "Skill: Meanings, Methods, and Measures." *Work and Occupations* 17(4): 399–421.

Spickard, David. 2007. "Jobs for Life." In *Ending Poverty in America: How to Restore the American Dream,* edited by John Edwards, Marion Crain, and Arne L. Kalleberg. New York: New Press.

Stainback, Kevin, and Donald Tomaskovic-Devey. 2009. "Intersections of Power and Privilege: Long-Term Trends in Managerial Representation." *American Sociological Review* 74(5): 800–20.

Streeck, Wolfgang, and Kathleen Thelen. 2005. "Introduction: Institutional Change in Advanced Political Economies." In *Beyond Continuity: Institutional Change in Advanced Political Economies,* edited by Wolfgang Streeck and Kathleen Thelen. Oxford: Oxford University Press.

Sullivan, Teresa A. 1978. *Marginal Workers, Marginal Jobs: The Underutilization of American Workers.* Austin: University of Texas Press.

Sullivan, Teresa A., Elizabeth Warren, and Jay Lawrence Westbrook. 2001. *The Fragile Middle Class: Americans in Debt.* New Haven, Conn.: Yale University Press.

Swinnerton, Kenneth A., and Howard Wial. 1996. "Is Job Stability Declining in the U.S. Economy? Reply to Diebold, Neumark, and Polsky." *Industrial and Labor Relations Review* 49(2): 352–55.

Szymanski, Albert. 1976. "Sexism and Racism as Functional Substitutes in the Labor Market." *Sociological Quarterly* 17(1): 65–73.

The Economist. 2009. "The Visible Hand." 30 May: 25–27.

Thomas, William Isaac, and Dorothy Swaine Thomas. 1928. *The Child in America: Behavior Problems and Programs.* New York: Knopf.

Tilly, Chris. 1997. "Arresting the Decline of Good Jobs in the USA?" *Industrial Relations Journal* 28(4): 269–74.

Tomaskovic-Devey, Donald. 1993. *Gender and Racial Inequality at Work: The Sources and Consequences of Job Segregation.* Ithaca, N.Y.: ILR Press.

Tomaskovic-Devey, Donald, Melvin Thomas, and Kecia Johnson. 2005. "Race and the Accumulation of Human Capital Across the Career: A Theoretical Model and Fixed-Effects Application." *American Journal of Sociology* 111(1): 58–89.

Tomaskovic-Devey, Donald, Catherine Zimmer, Kevin Stainback, Corre Robinson, Tiffany Taylor, and Tricia McTague. 2006. "Documenting Desegregation: Segregation in American Workplaces by Race, Ethnicity, and Sex, 1966–2003". *The American Sociological Review* 71(4): 565–88.

Toossi, Mitra. 2002. "A Century of Change: The U.S. Labor Force, 1950–2050." *Monthly Labor Review* 125(5): 15–28.

Treiman, Donald. 1977. *Occupational Prestige in Comparative Perspective.* New York: Academic Press.

Twenge, Jean M. 2006. *Generation Me: Why Today's Young Americans Are More Confident, Assertive, Entitled—and More Miserable Than Ever Before.* New York: Free Press.

Uchitelle, Louis. 2006. *The Disposable American: Layoffs and Their Consequences.* New York: Knopf.

U.S. Department of Labor. 1995, 1997, 1999, 2001, 2005. *Contingent and Alternative Employment Arrangements.* Washington: Bureau of Labor Statistics.

———. 2008. "Involuntary Part-time Work on the Rise." *Issues in Labor Statistics.* Bureau of Labor Statistics (December).

———. 2009. *Women in the Labor Force: A Databook.* Bureau of Labor Statistics report 1018 (September). Washington: Bureau of Labor Statistics.

———. 2011. Bureau of Labor Statistics Current Population Surveys, *Employment Status of the Civilian Noninstitutional Population, 1940 to Date.* Available at: http://www.bls.gov/cps/cpsaat1.pdf (accessed February 3, 2011).

Useem, Michael. 1996. *Investor Capitalism: How Money Managers Are Changing the Face of Corporate America.* New York: Basic Books.

Vallas, Steven Peter. 1999. "Rethinking Post-Fordism: The Meaning of Workplace Flexibility." *Sociological Theory* 17(1): 68–101.

Valletta, Robert G. 1999. "Declining Job Security." *Journal of Labor Economics* 17(4): S170–S197.

Viebrock, Elke, and Jochen Clasen. 2009. "Flexicurity and Welfare Reform: A Review." *Socio-Economic Review* 7(2): 305–31.

Waldinger, Roger, and Michael I. Lichter. 2003. *How the Other Half Works: Immigration and the Social Organization of Labor.* Berkeley: University of California Press.

Wallace, Michael, and David Brady. 2001. "The Next Long Swing: Spatialization, Technocratic Control, and the Restructuring of Work at the Turn of the Century." In *Sourcebook of Labor Markets: Evolving Structures and Processes,* edited by Ivar Berg and Arne L. Kalleberg. New York: Kluwer Academic/Plenum Publishers.

Warr, Peter. 1999. "Well-Being and the Workplace." In *Well-Being: The Foundations of Hedonic Psychology,* edited by Daniel Kahneman, Ed Diener, and Norbert Schwarz. New York: Russell Sage Foundation.

Weber, Max. 1947. *The Theory of Social and Economic Organization.* Translated by A. M. Henderson and Talcott Parsons. New York: Oxford University Press.

Webster, Edward, Rob Lambert, and Andries Bezuidenhout. 2008. *Grounding Globalization: Labour in the Age of Insecurity.* Oxford: Blackwell.

Weeden, Kim A. 2002. "Why Do Some Occupations Pay More Than Others? Social Closure and Earnings Inequality in the United States." *American Journal of Sociology* 108(1): 55–101.

Weeden, Kim A., Young-Mi Kim, Matthew Di Carlo, and David B. Grusky. 2007. "Social Class and Earnings Inequality." *American Behavioral Scientist* 50(5): 702–36.

Wessel, David. 2004. "The Future of Jobs: New Ones Arise, Wage Gap Widens." *Wall Street Journal,* April 2, 2004, pp. A1, A5.

Westergaard-Nielsen, Niels. 2008. *Low-Wage Work in Denmark.* New York: Russell Sage Foundation.

Western, Bruce, and Becky Pettit. 2002. "Beyond Crime and Punishment: Prisons and Inequality." *Contexts* 1(Fall): 37–43.

Whyte, William H. 1956. *The Organization Man.* New York: Simon and Schuster.

Wichert, Ines C., Jane P. Nolan, and Brendan J. Burchell. 2000. *Workers on the Edge: Job Insecurity, Psychological Well-Being, and Family Life.* Washington, D.C.: Economic Policy Institute.

Williams, Joan. 2000. *Unbending Gender: Why Work and Family Conflict and What to Do About It.* New York: Oxford University Press.

Williams, Robin M., Jr. 1968. "The Concept of Values." In *International Encyclopedia of the Social Sciences,* edited by David L. Sills. Vol. 16. New York: Free Press.

Willis, Rachel, Rachel Connelly, and Deborah DeGraaf. 2003. "The Future of Jobs in the Hosiery Industry." In *Low-Wage America: How Employers Are Reshaping Opportunity in the Workplace,* edited by Eileen Appelbaum, Annette Bernhardt, and Richard J. Murnane. New York: Russell Sage Foundation.

Wilson, William Julius. 1978. *The Declining Significance of Race: Blacks and Changing American Institutions.* Chicago: University of Chicago Press.

Wilthagen, Ton, and Frank Tros. 2004. "The Concept of 'Flexicurity': A New Approach to Regulating Employment and Labor Markets." *Transfer* 10(2): 166–86.

Wright, Erik Olin. 2000. "Working-Class Power, Capitalist-Class Interests, and Class Compromise." *American Journal of Sociology* 105(4): 957–1002.

———. 2008. "Three Logics of Job Creation in Capitalist Economies." Paper presented at the 103d Annual Meeting of the American Sociological Association. Boston (August 3).

Wright, Erik Olin, and Rachel E. Dwyer. 2003. "The Patterns of Job Expansions in the United States: A Comparison of the 1960s and 1990s." *Socio-Economic Review* 1(3): 289–325.

Wright, James D., and Richard F. Hamilton. 1978. "Work Satisfaction and Age: Some Evidence for the 'Job Change' Hypothesis." *Social Forces* 56(4): 1140–58.

Wyatt, Ian D., and Daniel E. Hecker. 2006. "Occupational Changes During the 20th Century." *Monthly Labor Review* 129(March): 35–57.

= Index =

Hudson, Ken, 128–29
Huff-Stevens, Ann, 97
human capital: and autonomy over work tasks, 136; policy issues, 205; racial-ethnic issues, 54–55; skill-biased technical change hypothesis, 111–13. *See also* education
human resource management, 32
Hunt, Jennifer, 120
Hunter, Larry W., 217*n*13

IBM model, 24
ILO (International Labour Organization). *See* International Labour Organization (ILO)
immigrants and immigration, 26, 49–52, 197, 204
Immigration and Nationality Act, 49
immigration law, 49, 197
incentives, economic, 198–99
inclusive labor market institutions, 17–18
income: and happiness, 170; and job satisfaction, 168; stagnation since 1970s, 36. *See also* wages and earnings
income averaging, 189
income inequality, 108–19, 122–23, 151
independent contractors, 75–77, 90–91, 202–3
individualism, 31, 33, 78, 84, 205–6
Industrial Areas Foundations (IAFs), 210
industrial relations system, 218*n*33
industrial union model, 24
inequality of income, 108–19, 122–23, 151
inequality of job quality. *See* polarization, in job quality
initiative. *See* autonomy, over work tasks
insecurity, job. *See* job insecurity
institutional investors, 28
institutional layering, 212–13

institutional transformations: macrostructural forces of, 21, 24–31; overview of, 12–13. *See also* employment systems
intensity of work, 154–58, 167
international cooperation, 214–15
International Labour Organization (ILO): employment relations, 88; job quality, 216*n*13; job security, 186, 189, 191; work hours, 150
intrinsic rewards: definition of, 7, 133, 144; and job satisfaction, 167; measurement challenges, 6, 132–33; trends, 144–46
involuntary job loss: data sources, 100; and job security perceptions, 102; measurement of, 95–96; policy issues, 188–89, 191–92, 212–13; trends, 95–98; and wage inequality, 122. *See also* unemployment rate
Italy: subcontracting approaches in, 37

Jaeger, David A., 97
Japan: CEO pay, 110; flexicurity system, 185; management approaches, 37; wage inequality, 112
Jencks, Christopher, 241*n*2
Jensen, Oscar, 175
JfL (Jobs for Life), 210–11
job autonomy. *See* autonomy, over work tasks
job creation policies, 192–93, 197–99, 200, 201, 209
job displacement, 38, 88, 95–98, 212–13
job insecurity: growth of, 15, 84, 85–88, 103–4, 180–81; and job satisfaction, 169; and labor force composition changes, 100–101; measurement of, 89, 99–100; perceptions of, 99–103; and real wage growth, 107
job ladders, 11, 23, 71, 94, 193
job loss. *See* involuntary job loss
job mobility, 93–94, 122–23

unemployment rate: and economic growth, 209; as economic stability measure, 208; and job insecurity perceptions, 99–100; and job quality, 15; and job satisfaction, 172–73; long-term unemployment, 98; as precarious work measure, 230n65; racial differences, 54, 204

unions and unionization: autonomy over work tasks, 137; decline of, 31–36, 108, 116–17, 154–55; and firm internal labor markets, 95; future role, 189–91, 202–3; international cooperation, 214–15; in manufacturing industry, 9–10; and occupational polarization, 70; postwar period (1945-1970s), 22–23; of public employees, 206–7; and real wage growth, 107; workers' desire to join, 190; work hours, 150; work intensity, 154–55. *See also* collective bargaining

United Kingdom. *See* Great Britain

Vaisey, Stephen, 241n2

Valletta, Robert G., 97, 98

values, cultural: individualism, 31, 33, 78, 84, 205–6

Vizcaino v. Microsoft, 248n6

wage insurance, 189

wages and earnings: definition of, 231n3; educational attainment impact, 42–43; gender gap, 107–8; good vs. bad jobs, 9, 10; immigrants' impact on native workers', 51–52; inequality, 108–19, 122–23, 151; measurement of, 5; minimum wage, 112, 117, 197; mobility, 120–23; racial gap, 108; service sector, 62–63; trends, 105–8; volatility, 121–22

Wagner Act (1935), 219n8

War on Poverty, 23

Warr, Peter, 240n1–2

Washington state: paid family leave, 210

Weber, Max, 134

welfare reform, 45, 207

white-collar workers: immigrants, 50; job displacement rates, 96; job insecurity, 86, 102; job satisfaction, 176; layoffs (1980s-1990s), 38; postwar growth, 22, 23; unionization, 33, 203; work intensification, 155–56

whites: educational attainment, 54; labor force participation rates, **44,** 52; occupational segregation, 53; social capital, 80; wages and earnings, 108

Wial, Howard, 92

Williams, Joan, 48

Wilson, William Julius, 54

Wisconsin Regional Training Partnership (WRTP), 211

Wolff, Edward, 222n65–66, 233n35

women: educational attainment, 41–42, 45; employer-provided health care coverage, 127, 128; intrinsic rewards from work, 237–38n29; job quality, 46–47; job satisfaction, 169; job tenure, 93; labor force participation rates, 43–47, 53; low-wage work, 234n43; managers, 65–66; professionals, 67; service sector employment, 30; wages and earnings, 106–8, **110;** work hours, 150–51, 152, **153**

work activities, control over: decision-making participation, 142–44; good vs. bad jobs, 9, 10; as job quality dimension, 5, 6–7; research considerations, 132–33; trends, 135–42. *See also* autonomy, over work tasks; intrinsic rewards; work schedule determination

work autonomy. *See* autonomy, over work tasks

worker centers, 203

worker power: decline of, 34–36; definition of, 31; importance of, 202; market power, 78, 160;